GOVERNING **INDIGENOUS** TERRITORIES

Juliet S. Erazo

GOVERNING INDIGENOUS TERRITORIES

ENACTING SOVEREIGNTY IN
THE ECUADORIAN AMAZON

Duke University Press   Durham and London   2013

© 2013 Duke University Press
All rights reserved
Printed in the United States of America
on acid-free paper ♾
Designed by Heather Hensley
Typeset in Garamond Premier Pro
by Tseng Information Systems, Inc.

Library of Congress Cataloging-in-Publication Data
Erazo, Juliet S., 1970–
Governing indigenous territories : enacting sovereignty in
the Ecuadorian Amazon / Juliet S. Erazo.
pages
Includes bibliographical references and index.
ISBN 978-0-8223-5440-6 (cloth : alk. paper) —
ISBN 978-0-8223-5454-3 (pbk. : alk. paper)
1. Pueblo Kichwa de Rukullakta. 2. Indians of South
America — Ecuador — Politics and government.
3. Indigenous peoples — Ecuador — Politics and
government. 4. Indians of South America — Amazon River
Region — Politics and government. 5. Indigenous peoples —
Amazon River Region — Politics and government.
6. Sovereignty. I. Title.
F3721.3.P74E73 2013
323.1198 — dc2   2013009714

For Eduardo, Alex, and Michelle

| CONTENTS |

CEDOC — Central Ecuatoriana de Organizaciones Clasistas (Ecuadorian Center for Class-Based Organizations)

COICA — Coordinadora de las Organizaciones Indígenas de la Cuenca Amazonica (Coordinator of Indigenous Organizations of the Amazon River Basin)

CONAIE — Confederación de Nacionalidades Indígenas del Ecuador (Confederation of Ecuadorian Indigenous Organizations)

CONAKINO — Confederación de la Nacionalidad Kichwa de Napo y Orellana (Confederation of the Kichwa Nationality of Napo and Orellana) (previous names: FEPOCAN, FOIN, and FONAKIN)

CONFENIAE — Confederación de Nacionalidades Indígenas de la Amazonía Ecuatoriana (Confederation of Indigenous Nationalities of the Ecuadorian Amazon)

EDF — Environmental Defense Fund

FEPOCAN — Federación Provincial de Organizaciones Campesinas de Napo (Provincial Federation of Napo Peasant Organizations) (later FOIN)

FOCIN — Federación de Organizaciones Campesinas e Indígenas de Napo (Federation of Peasant and Indigenous Organizations of Napo)

FOIN — Federación de Organizaciones Indígenas de Napo (Federation of Indigenous Organizations of Napo) (later FONAKIN)

FONAKIN	Federación de Organizaciones de la Nacionalidad Kichwa de Napo (Federation of Kichwa Nationality Organizations of Napo) (later CONAKINO)
GIZ	Deutsche Gesellschaft für Internationale Zusammenarbeit (German Agency for International Cooperation) (previous name: GTZ)
GTZ	Gesellschaft für Technische Zusammenarbeit (Agency for Technical Cooperation) (later GIZ)
IERAC	Instituto Ecuatoriano de Reforma Agraria y Colonización (Ecuadorian Institute of Agrarian Reform and Colonization)
IMU	Fundación Izu Mangallpa Urcu (Foundation Izu Mangallpa Urcu [Mountain of the Land of the Jaguar])
INCRAE	Instituto Nacional de Colonización de la Región Amazónica Ecuatoriana (National Institute of Colonization of the Ecuadorian Amazon Region)
NGO	Nongovernmental organization
PKR	Pueblo Kichwa de Rukullakta (Kichwa People of Rukullakta)
REDD+	Reducing Emissions from Deforestation and Degradation

| ACKNOWLEDGMENTS |

My first acknowledgments go, as always, to the people of Rukullakta, who have donated so much of their time, patience, and insights to assist me in this project. In particular, my heartfelt appreciation goes to Jaime Shiguango-Pauchi, Medardo Shiguango-Cerda, Wellington Yumbo, Beatriz Shiguango-Grefa, Nelson Chimbo, José Shiguango-Chimbo, Rosario Shiguango-Grefa, Carlos Alvarado, Jorge Aguinda, Angel Tunay, Yolanda Andy, and J. Leonidas Narváez, many of whom have not only been my key collaborators, but also my dear friends (and, in a few cases, my compadres).

This book began, many years ago, as a research chapter, which was written and rewritten several times as part of a graduate student writing seminar led by Fernando Coronil and Ann Stoler. It brings me great sorrow that Fernando passed away at such a young age and before he could see this book in print. His inspiration and spirit continue to bear fruit in my work and that of the many other students and colleagues he inspired. Thanks are also due to my other committee members, Steve Brechin, Ivette Perfecto, Kathleen Bergen, and especially Stuart Kirsch for guiding me through my first book-length project. My former fellow students Terry Woronov, Sandra Comstock, Crystal Fortwangler, Karen Hébert, Patty Mullally, Ed Murphy, Genese Sodikoff, Lourdes Gutierrez-Najera, Monica Patterson, Luis Fernandez, David Pedersen,

Jessa Leinaweaver, Jill Constantino, John Thiels, Ken MacLean, Peter Wilshusen, Matt Kotchen, Megan Callaghan, and Jeff Jurgens have also provided me with the intellectual and moral support to begin writing and continue on the path of scholarship. The then-nascent Anthropology and Environment Section of the American Anthropological Association—especially organizers Paige West, Pete Brosius, Melissa Johnson, and Nora Haenn—was another important source of inspiration as I pursued my unconventional, interdisciplinary doctoral program.

My analysis also benefited greatly from my time at the University of California, Berkeley, where I held a two-year postdoctoral fellowship. The environmental politics faculty there—including Donald Moore, Michael Watts, and especially Nancy Lee Peluso, as well as Jake Kosek, Amita Baviskar, Derick Fay, and Mark Carey, the other fellows—provided new lenses through which I could understand familiar material. Others I met through my colleagues at Berkeley, particularly Nancy Postero, Eduardo Kohn, and Elana Shever, provided useful feedback on early versions of some of the material here.

I also want to thank the incredibly supportive and dynamic members of my current department at Florida International University (FIU), especially Gail Hollander, Rod Neumann, Laura Ogden, and Rick Tardanico. Thanks to them and to Caroline Faria, Liliana Goldín, and Vrushali Patil for providing useful comments on my writing and analysis at various points over the past six years. Thanks also to Jeff Onsted for his help with bringing me up-to-date on using GIS software. I could not have asked for a better group of colleagues than the human geographers, cultural anthropologists, and sociologists who recently came together to form the new Department of Global and Sociocultural Studies at FIU.

Funding for the research and writing of this book has come from many sources, especially FIU's College of Arts and Sciences Summer Faculty Development Award, the S. V. Ciracy-Wantrup postdoctoral fellowship at the University of California, Berkeley, and dissertation write-up funding from Rackham Graduate School through a fellowship with the University of Michigan's Society of Fellows. Smaller but still significant funding was provided by a Morris and Anita Broad Fellowship, the Latin American and Caribbean Center, the Department of Global and Sociocultural Studies, and the Agroecology Program (all at FIU); and the School of Natural Resources and Environment, Department of Anthropology, Latin American and Caribbean Studies Program, and the Center for the Continuing Education of Women (all at the University of Michigan). Finally, thanks to a US Environmental Protection Agency Science to Achieve Results (STAR) grant and a James B. Reynolds Scholarship from Dartmouth College, I was able to spend fourteen months in Ecuador before even beginning the research described here.

The editors and staff at Duke University Press have been incredibly helpful in the publishing process, especially Gisela Fosado, who guided me through the process; and Christine Choi, the art editor, who helped prepare the many maps in this book for publication. My appreciation also goes to Ken Wissoker and Valerie Millholland, who saw promise in the project. I am extremely grateful to Marc Becker for serving as a (once anonymous) reviewer and for sharing his impressive expertise on Ecuadorian history. Last but not least, my deep appreciation goes to the other anonymous reviewer who challenged me to broaden my audience even further, and whose insightful advice improved this analysis beyond measure.

Finally, thanks must also go to the people who have stood by my side on a day-to-day basis since this project began over a dozen years ago. Michael Hathaway, my primary writing partner, has read so many versions of the chapters here that he probably deserves to be listed as second author. Given that his field site (Yunnan Province, China) is almost as far away from Ecuador as one can get without leaving the planet, any errors here remain fully my own. My family—including many Serenyis, Erazos, and Bartletts, but especially Eduardo, Alex, and Michelle Erazo—have been incredibly and consistently supportive. Thank you, Eduardo, for teaching me so much about Ecuador, and for taking our very energetic children to the park dozens, if not hundreds, of times so that I could enjoy quiet writing time. This book would not have been possible without you.

MAP 0.1 Location of Rukullakta.

It was late summer of 2001, during the second of seven research trips I have made to Rukullakta (pronounced Roo-koo-yáhk-tah), a legally defined territory in the Ecuadorian Amazon entirely inhabited and governed by Kichwa (also spelled Quichua) Indians. The previous year, I had completed a detailed history of Rukullakta, from its founding as a ranching cooperative in the early 1970s, through its current status as a self-governing, semiautonomous indigenous territory. During my second visit, I wrote an abridged version of this history and printed several dozen copies to distribute among Rukullakta's seventeen schools. The only thing left to decide was the title. I knew the title was important since it would frame the organization's history for young readers, and I anguished over several possibilities for weeks.

On numerous occasions, I tried to find out what Rukullakta's president, José Shiguango, thought of various options. My favorite was a slogan I had found in Rukullakta's archives, used before residents obtained legal title to their collective lands in 1977. In the years leading up to that date, 207 families came together, formed the cooperative, and began working together to raise cattle and create a government to manage their varied modernization projects. Their efforts convinced the state to do something unprecedented and almost unimaginable: grant them title to almost 42,000 hectares of their ancestral territory. This act was all the more important because the state had just encouraged a mass migration of poor settlers into their area, threatening indigenous people's access to the land where their families had lived for generations. The slogan I liked, scrawled in large letters on a number of pages in the archives, was "Sólo unidos venceremos!" (Only united will we overcome!). To me, it seemed to highlight the revolutionary beginnings of the organization.

It was clear that Shiguango did not want to use the slogan for a title, but I could not understand why, and he did not suggest an alternative. No doubt he found my impatience and frustration over the issue typical of his many interactions with foreigners and officials from Ecuador's government, who expect indigenous authorities to come to decisions quickly and decisively on behalf of their territory's population.

It took some time before I understood the reason for Shiguango's reluctance to use the slogan. "Only united will we overcome" came from the political Left. In the 1960s some men from the Rukullakta region traveled west to work on coastal plantations. They became participants in the rising union movement, and they learned the language and politics of union organizing. After returning to Rukullakta, they used some of the slogans they had heard on the coast to motivate their friends and neighbors during their campaign to form a cooperative. Variations of the "only united will we overcome" slogan have been repeated so many times in political speeches and protest marches around the world that I had never stopped to think about how it could be viewed negatively. When I finally paused to do so, I realized that Rukullakta's residents have not always been united. To assert that they must be united over the long term to maintain their access to land and to "overcome" those who strive to take it from them only highlighted the fact that they were still not fully in control of their lives or their territory. The slogan served as a reminder of their historical marginalization, as well as the exceptional obligations that modern nation-states often place on indigenous residents if they wish to maintain what was previously theirs.[1]

After much discussion, Rukullakta's elected leaders decided to use a title written in Kichwa rather than Spanish, in part due to the many indigenous language revitalization projects occurring both locally and nationally. Avoiding the obligation implied by "only united will we overcome," the leaders settled on a new title: *Ñukanchik Rukukuna Wankurishka Kawsay, 1970–2000* (roughly, "Our history of living together in a large group, 1970–

2000"). Although perhaps less romantic or revolutionary than the title I had suggested, their choice indicates a key aspect of sovereignty as experienced by the leaders and people of Rukullakta and beyond — the daily obligation to live and act together as a singular political entity within a bounded space.

When most people hear the terms "indigenous territory" or "indigenous sovereignty," they imagine that, compared to non-indigenous groups, indigenous peoples who live in their own territories are more culturally homogeneous, with shared values and priorities, making political unity straightforward or even natural. This was the type of thinking that inspired my own choice for the title. But Rukullakta's government did not come into being because its people wanted to follow indigenous leaders rather than nonindigenous ones. There was no history in this region of submitting to indigenous authorities over the long term, and most Kichwa are very leery of individuals who attempt to assume positions of authority. As is the case with indigenous Shuar who live to the south (and who are famous for forming the first indigenous federation in the Amazon), Amazonian Kichwa "continue to value liberty to an extent inconceivable in the United States, where almost every aspect of our lives is governed by law or some bureaucratic regulation" (Rubenstein 2002, 11). Convincing 207 heads of extended families to place their family's lands under the control of a cooperative government took years of campaigning and cajoling. During the campaign, one of its early leaders suffered a tragic accident and became bedridden. Many older members of Rukullakta told me that they had finally been convinced to become members of the cooperative when they visited their friend as he lay on his deathbed and used his last energies to advocate for the cooperative cause. Hearing stories such as this drives home the fact that living in a bounded indigenous territory with a centralized government has not always been easy for Rukullakta's residents. The enactment of sovereignty has always been, and continues to be, a political process, full of the negotiations and controversies over expectations and obligations that characterize most (if not all) political processes.

Today the governments of indigenous territories are engaged in negotiations with a number of more powerful entities as well as with the groups they represent. One reason for this is that the territories have been granted what Richard Stahler-Sholk refers to as "autonomy without resources" (2005, 37), as part of a larger set of neoliberal changes: states are decentralizing and delegating social responsibilities to local governments without providing sufficient financial resources to carry them out. Often unable to tax their residents, territorial leaders must seek funding by working with external entities, including state ministries, international nongovernmental organizations (NGOs), and multinational corporations. Such collaborations, however, often present difficult challenges. For example, should the leaders allow a petroleum company to build an oil well in the territory in exchange for a percentage of the profits, recognizing that an oil spill could contaminate the local soil and water? Or should a territory agree to receive payments from environmental organizations in exchange for conserving the local forest, a move that some people have interpreted as a ploy by outsiders to gain control of the lands indigenous people fought so hard to legally own? These hard questions are similar to those faced by governments worldwide, and the debates that surround them involve not only the sometimes conflicting values held by the territory's people, but also the dynamic relationships between the governments and residents of these spaces.

In this book, I argue that the enactment of sovereignty and the social relations that go with it are continually being negotiated, as leaders, their constituents, and a host of external entities — ranging from environmentalists to oil executives — seek to define the form that indigenous sovereignty will take. In tracing this process, I pay particular attention to varied efforts — those of residents, leaders, and outsiders — to determine the meanings and practices associated with what I call "territorial citizenship," the responsibilities and rights associated with living in an indigenous territory. In the context of a typically cash-starved territorial government, "sovereignty" is only an abstract concept without active citizens to produce it. Thus, in the context of new political openings for constructing a more meaningful sovereignty (associated with the growth of the indigenous rights movement as well as with neoliberal state decentralization), both territorial leaders and indigenous intellectuals have been hard at work in recent decades to define what an ideal "territorial citizen" should be. The ideas they propose about territorial citizenship are deeply tied to particular places but simultaneously transnational in that they are informed by the knowledge and perspectives gained through engagement with multiple outsiders.

I have spent the last twelve years studying the historical and contemporary struggles of Rukullakta, one of the longest-running "experiments" with territorial sovereignty in Ecuador, a country known as having the "most well-organized indigenous movement in the Americas" (Collins 2000,

41; see also Zibechi 2004).[2] Rukullakta's population has risen from about 2,000 people in the early 1970s to about 8,000 in 2011,[3] primarily through high birth rates but also through marriage with outsiders. Rivers that run through the territory eventually enter the Amazon, and its altitude ranges roughly from 500 to 1,200 meters. Because of its location on the foothills of the Andes and proximity to the Napo River, the area where Rukullakta is located is often referred to as the Upper Napo region.

Rukullakta's history, both as a cooperative and as a territory, has always been shaped by international and national changes. During the Cold War, the 1959 communist revolution in Cuba motivated many Latin American governments to address potential rural unrest before it threatened to overthrow them. International and national development experts saw the formation of cooperatives as a key strategy for reducing poverty and thereby stifling any nascent communist movements. A small group of activists in Rukullakta decided that if they wanted to gain legal title to a large area of land, they should take advantage of this political opening and form a ranching cooperative with as many members as possible. By the 1990s, the Cold War had ended and development organizations were becoming increasingly worried about environmental protection. In particular, they were concerned that the conversion of rainforests into farmland was a serious threat to biological diversity. There was also a growing sense among these organizations that indigenous people were particularly adept at conserving forests. International development funding priorities in the Amazon region therefore shifted away from encouraging small-scale farmers to produce cattle and market crops, and toward providing assistance for indigenous peoples to carry out environmental conservation and sustainable forms of development. Rukullakta's geographical location between the Andes Mountains and the Amazonian lowlands contributes to high levels of biological diversity, making it and the surrounding region a hot spot for conservation efforts. In 2000 Germany's bilateral aid organization, GTZ — for Gesellschaft für Technische Zusammenarbeit (Agency for Technical Cooperation), now called GIZ, for Deutsche Gesellschaft für Internationale Zusammenarbeit (German Agency for International Cooperation) — led an effort to obtain United Nations Biosphere Reserve status for much of the Upper Napo region, placing much of Rukullakta's territory under a high level of environmental protection. Partially in response to these global shifts, in 2006 Rukullakta's leaders changed their legal classification and name from "cooperative" to the "Pueblo Kichwa de Rukullakta" (or "The Kichwa People of Rukullakta").[4] With this change, they hoped to foreground their indigeneity, rather than their commitment to market-driven ranching and agriculture (implied by the term "cooperative"). No longer a cooperative with a president, Rukullakta is now seen by the local people as a "territory" with an elected *kuraka*. The latter term is sometimes translated as "chief," but that English word implies that the people in question were historically organized under a leader, which was not the case in this area. In fact, *curaga* is a term that was imposed by the Spanish during colonial times to create a hierarchy within the indigenous population, a hierarchy that made it easier for colonial authorities to control them. The indigenous intellectuals who promote using this term, however, are not romanticizing a colonial past. They are seeking autochthonous-sounding terms to signify and champion what are indeed very new social relations among indigenous people, and between indigenous governments and outsiders.

Rukullakta's shift in name, leadership terminology, and legal designation provide some sense of the global changes in development ideologies that its people have navigated as they have pursued sovereignty. Indeed, there has been a dramatic shift in what outsiders want Rukullakta's residents to do. No longer is the goal to cut down the forest, plant pasture, and raise cattle; instead, it is to conserve large areas of the territory for the protection of plants and wild animals.

Yet one of the key requirements associated with Rukullakta's sovereignty has remained remarkably unchanged. Time and time again, Rukullakta's leaders have been reminded that if they cannot control the actions of their people and guide them collectively toward the particular development priorities of the time, they could lose access to all sources of financial assistance, and possibly even to the lands where their ancestors have lived for centuries.

As may already be clear, I am interested in understanding the everyday practices of indigenous sovereignty. In this book I reveal how sovereignty is not merely and simply achieved by the acquisition of territorial rights but is attached to changing sets of expectations and obligations.[5] Outsiders expect, even oblige, territorial governments to act like modern states, making decisions about whether to allow particular development projects to take place within their territory. Those who fund development projects in indigenous territories expect local leaders to ensure that residents will participate wholeheartedly in their projects, following new rules and policies, providing their labor (often without pay), and showing enthusiasm for the project's goals. Residents also have high expectations of their leaders, wanting them to pursue development projects that will bring material improvements without requiring dramatic changes in the ways they work and live. Leaders, both as individuals and as representatives of the territorial government, expect residents to act as good territorial citizens. In particular, they want residents to attend assemblies, participate in decision making, contribute to the upkeep of the territory (such as clearing a soccer field or expanding a school), and volunteer for development projects, even though these initiatives might not bring significant income for years (if ever). Residents view these tasks as obligations that may or may not be warranted. Adding to the complexity of these expectations and obligations are the ever-shifting dynamics of opportunities and threats presented by diverse outsiders.

As has been the case with many anthropologists, my research project was not what I had originally imagined; instead, it was profoundly altered by the priorities of the people with whom I worked. Prior to beginning research in the Upper Napo region in 1999, I had already spent about fourteen months in Ecuador (ten in 1994–95 and four in 1997), and I had experienced little difficulty in finding people with whom to discuss my initial interest in ecotourism in indigenous communities. However, the territorial organization where I had originally planned to conduct dissertation fieldwork turned my project down, despite the fact that the president had approved it the year before. They felt that my desire to examine the interactions between environmental NGOs and their organization would be of little benefit to them and, if my conclusions were overly critical, could even jeopardize their access to sustainable development projects in the future. Indigenous people are increasingly aware of the potential dangers that can be posed by scholarly research and are more careful than in the past about whom they allow into their worlds (Warren and Jackson 2002, 3).

Through some mutual acquaintances, I met the leaders of another indigenous organization, the Rukullakta Cooperative, and learned that they were interested in having someone write a history of their organization, as many of the founding members had already passed away and the oral history project required more time than any of them had to spend on it. I wholeheartedly agree with Charles Hale's assertion that the most elemental methodological principle of activist anthropology is to "talk over research ideas with the people with whom you are primarily aligned, in hopes of producing knowledge that might be useful to them" (2006, 4). Thus, I was elated to find a collaborative research topic of local value and threw myself into the project.

After I had spent a few months conducting interviews, local leaders loaned me the cooperative's archives to study. The archives, referred to as the *Actas de la Cooperativa Agropecuaria San Pedro de Rucu-Llacta, Ltda.* (or *Actas*) throughout this book, are made up of thousands of pages of handwritten minutes of the meetings of both the administrative council and the larger assembly of members since 1970, recording those bodies' debates, disputes, and decisions. I also obtained and analyzed copies of aerial photographs taken by Texaco in 1973 and the Ecuadorian government in 1982 (both of which are currently housed in Ecuador's Military Geographical Institute) as well as satellite images from various dates, affording me a bird's-eye view of how debates over property lines and land use have shaped the landscape. Since that initial, ten-month period of fieldwork, I have returned six times to Rukullakta between 2001 and 2011, conducting additional interviews, visiting with friends, and continuing to trace the history of the organization.

The fact that Rukullakta's leaders wanted someone to document and publish the history of their organization is telling. The social movement that their parents formed in the late 1960s and early 1970s represented one of indigenous Ecuador's most successful efforts to secure legal ownership of a large area of land, and they are very proud of this history. Rukullakta's early leaders and founding members managed to convince the Ecuadorian government to give them title to 41,888.5 hectares of land. This translated into over 200 hectares per member at a time when most non-indigenous farmers moving into the Ecuadorian Amazon region from the highlands through state-backed colonization schemes were granted only 50 hectares. The success Rukullakta's members experienced contrasted starkly with that of many Kichwa families living in the region, who were left with insufficient land to sustain their previous ways of living.

Of all the indigenous peoples in the Americas, Amazonian Indians have a particular cachet: they are commonly seen as the most isolated from global forces, the most antithetical to Western civilization, and the most vulnerable to the devastation that can be caused by development projects. Yet, at least on most days, Rukullakta's leaders do not see themselves as barely hanging onto their territory, constantly at risk from colonists or transnational corporations that want to take it from them. They do not see themselves as "David battling Goliath," even though this is by far the most frequently invoked metaphor in both popular and scholarly accounts of indigenous peoples in the Amazon.[6] On the contrary, the leaders of Rukullakta more commonly see themselves as pathbreakers and visionaries, capable of forging the necessary alliances and identifying the appropriate paths toward creating a better life for their organization's members. This perception is also clear in statements made by other indigenous leaders dating back to the early days of the organization's history. Take, for example, the following quote from Rukullakta's archives, from a speech made by the president of the provincial indigenous rights organization (the Federación de Organizaciones Indígenas de Napo, or FOIN) to Rukullakta's members in 1976: "In Napo Province, there is one organization that is opening doors for work, for culture, economy, and social programs; I am speaking of your cooperative. It is the first organization that is advancing in the path of communal life in work, and in the economy" (*Actas*, July 17, 1976).[7] The quote not only highlights the way that indigenous leaders from both inside and outside Rukullakta have, during much of its history, thought of Rukullakta as a model for other indigenous organizations. It also points to the very high expectations of sovereignty that have guided the leaders' work over the past four decades.

The provincial indigenous rights leader quoted in Rukullakta's archives spoke about how the collective was making advancements in "communal work" and "the economy," demonstrating that indigenous leaders in this region have never seen their role as simply securing an area of land for their people so that they could live in isolation. They have also sought to improve their constituents' lives through a variety of projects, ranging from cooperative cattle ranching to ecotourism, and from public health campaigns to advancing adult literacy. From the beginning, leaders shared the long-term concerns associated with securing the "welfare of the [territory's] population, the improvement of its condition, [and] the increase of its wealth, longevity, health, etc." (Foucault 1991, 100). Yet such interests in improvement and welfare do not signal a simple conversion to a new universal or Western set of values. Instead, leaders have simultaneously sought to protect certain cultural practices and landscapes that they have identified as important to sustaining Amazonian Kichwa culture. Negotiating how to do both simultaneously, while navigating the territory's relationships with diverse and typically more powerful outsiders, has been and continues to be one of the biggest challenges leaders have faced as they pursue indigenous sovereignty.

Governing Indigenous Territories examines a paradox of modern indigenous lives. In recent decades, native peoples from Alaska to Cameroon have sought and gained legal title to significant areas of land, not as individuals or families but as large, collective organizations. On the one hand, obtaining these titles represents an enormous accomplishment: for centuries, indigenous peoples have been losing their access to land and natural resources, often with little or no compensation. On the other hand, obtaining collective title to land — or what is increasingly thought of as creating an indigenous territory — brings many changes for the people who live there. In particular, once a territory is legally established, other governments and organizations expect it to act as a singular and unified political entity, making decisions on behalf of its population and managing those who live within its borders. Without such a territorial government, it is difficult (if not impossible) for the population to continue to defend its interests in relation to the outside world. The territorial government must mediate between a host of outsiders and a not always united population, work to create consensus, and enact policies that will affect all residents. Thus, collective indigenous land titling, whose apparent purpose is to allow native peoples the freedom to escape from the everyday workings of bureaucracy and the state, paradoxically initiates new governmental structures within the territory and new dynamics of rule and discipline.

Many scholars and activists alike have regarded gaining territorial titles as virtually synonymous with achieving sovereignty, which they define as obtaining authority and control over territory from the states in which they are situated. This book demonstrates that sovereignty is more process than product. In particular, I show that sovereignty is necessarily an internally oriented process of subject making, one that requires new understandings of personhood and social obligation. Such changes take place not only between individuals, but also between them and a new entity known as the territorial government (a body that has a life of its own, even though the leadership may change every two years). These new relationships include differing sets of expectations, obligations, and forms of discipline. In many cases, territorial residents (especially in Latin America) have until recently lived on the margins of state control, and so these new, intimate forms of governance significantly alter people's lives.[1]

I use the term "sovereignty" rather than the term "autonomy," even though the latter is employed by indigenous activists in Latin America and most Latin Americanist scholars. I made this choice both to acknowledge my debt to scholars working in English-speaking settler states (particularly Australia, Canada, and the United States) and because the term "sovereignty" captures processes of rule better than "autonomy," which can imply isolation or independence from relationships of power. Although indigenous leaders have indeed pursued greater autonomy vis-à-vis the Ecuadorian government, they have not sought isolation. Instead, they have worked toward sovereignty in part by forming alliances with other governments, state agencies, and NGOs willing to fund development projects. For example, indigenous organizations desire greater control over the curricula taught in bilingual and intercultural schools, but they expect that the Ministry of Education will provide a level of funding for those schools comparable to that provided for other public schools in Ecuador, thus avoiding "autonomy without resources" (Stahler-Sholk 2005, 37). They also regularly seek funds from their provincial and municipal governments for infrastructure projects within their territories. Thus what they consider to be a struggle for autonomy is better understood as an effort to increase local control over the ways that education and other forms of development are practiced within indigenous territories, rather than as an effort to reject state-funded development. The same argument can be made about the agreements forged with various international entities attempting to shape indigenous landscapes and peoples through development projects. As Rudi Colloredo-Mansfeld has argued for Ecuador's highland Kichwa, "autonomy materializes more in strategic connections than in the zonal separation" (2009, 142–43; see also Cattelino 2008, 17; Warren 1998, 18). Indeed, in today's world, no governmental entity exists without extralocal ties and commitments.

There are two sets of insights concerning sovereignty on which I have built my analysis. The first set concerns the complex ways in which indigenous intellectuals and leaders are working toward defining and fostering difference, even as they increasingly engage in relationships that are shaped by global capital and transnational connections (Cattelino 2008; Escobar 2008; Rappaport 2005b; Tengan 2008). Jessica Cattelino, for example, believes that sovereignty is created through "collective assertions, everyday enactments, and lived experiences of political distinctiveness," although she emphasizes the relations of interdependence that exist between the Florida Seminoles and other sovereigns (2008, 17). Rukullakta's most active leaders have been motivated in part by a deep belief in, and a commitment to, what they see as the cultural distinctiveness of their people, even as they seek to improve their constituents' lives in ways that some may classify as modern or capitalist.

The second set of insights concerns ways in which indigenous sovereignty continues to be structured by colonial legacies and postcolonial inequities (see, for example, M. Becker 2011; Kauanui 2008; Povinelli 2006; and Simpson 2000). For example, Audra Simpson highlights the "forced cultural transformation of native culture through the bounding of people and bounding of space" (2000, 118). Although it can be easy for scholars to get caught up in the liberatory expectations of indigenous sovereignty movements as they spend months and even years speaking with activists, it is important to highlight that these movements have been and continue to be shaped by a history of colonialism and exclusion.

The expectations and obligations of sovereignty emerge out of these coexisting, mutually constitutive realities of indigenous lives. Indigenous sovereignty is not solely a social movement motivated in part by a search for alternative futures, nor is it simply the product of long-standing inequalities. Rather, it is the processes of negotiation and mediated practice that occur as these two realities confront one another. In Rukullakta, for example, leaders attempt to convince residents that they should feel obligated to the territorial government (and thus be willing to donate their labor and give up control over what they think of as their family's property), because the leaders believe that this is the best way to make the territorial government stronger. Stronger territorial governments are better able to withstand forces that threaten them and to negotiate favorable agreements with those who can contribute resources for development. Unfortunately, these obligations often come into conflict with residents' obligations to their families, which include connections to the particular areas of land their families had claimed prior to the formation of the collective organization. The enactment of indigenous sovereignty thus has involved a long history of negotiation and mediated practice, a history that continues into the present.

Governance and Regimes of Rule

Over the past three decades, there have been two major trends that have increased the number of legalized indigenous territories, as well as the number of roles filled by territorial governments. The first trend is the increasing international attention to the rights of indigenous peoples, best shown in the 1989 promulgation of the International Labour Organization's Convention on Indigenous and Tribal Peoples, which is the major binding international convention concerning indigenous peoples. Specifically, the convention "puts pressure on governments to recognize indigenous peoples' traditional lands and to grant indigenous peoples some form of administrative autonomy" (Offen 2003, 44). The convention inspired what Karl Offen calls a "territorial turn" in Latin America, a wave of titling of collective lands to rural indigenous and rural black communities in several countries, particularly Brazil, Colombia, Ecuador, and a number of countries in Central America (Escobar 2008, 319). It has also contributed to surging senses of ethnic pride among indigenous intellectuals. Some have become involved in advancing new political ideologies among their people by appropriating and politicizing pedagogy in bilingual schools, appointing activists rather than educational professionals as teachers (Rappaport 2005b, 124; see also Gustafson 2009, chapter 2). Similarly, in southern Mexico, intellectuals involved with the Zapatista movement are engaged in "the effort to continually transform society" through the construction of new social subjectivities and the promotion of radical democracy (Stahler-Sholk 2010, 269).

The second trend is that since the 1980s national governments worldwide have been increasingly pressured by international lending institutions to reduce the size of their state bureaucracies in order to reduce government spending. Especially in the poorest areas of the developing world, NGOs have taken over many of the public services that were previously considered the responsibility of states, and these organizations typically coordinate their activities with local governments and institutions rather than national ones. Territorial governments are among the local governments that serve as intermediaries for NGOs, helping to coordinate delivery of services and manage territorial residents' engagement in development projects.

In yet another example of territorial governments taking over the tasks normally associated with state and municipal governments, some community councils have resorted to punishing those believed to have committed crimes against community members, rather than relying on the police to do so (Colloredo-Mansfeld 2002; 2009; D. Gow and Rappaport 2002). Whether portrayed as practitioners of community justice or savage vigilantes, those who publicly pursue justice outside the state-sponsored system are asserting their desire to play a greater role in determining what can and cannot occur within their communities.

By looking at these diverse practices of community policing, development project mediation, educational activism, and pursuit of new ideologies through a single lens rather than treating them in piecemeal fashion, it is possible to see that many of the organizations typically understood as indigenous *rights* organizations, working to increase levels of autonomy in relation to the state, are simultaneously indigenous *governing* organizations, working to shape the members of their communities. In the case studied in this book (and I suspect in the others cited above as well) indigenous leaders are attempting to construct particular kinds of people through these various projects, people who will not only participate in long marches on the capital or make other short-term sacrifices to change national policy, but who will also relate to leaders and to one another in new ways.

In this book, I am indebted to Michel Foucault's writings on governmentality (1991) for my understanding of indigenous leaders' efforts to shape and empower their constituents, and to many scholars who have been inspired by him. Foucauldian scholars interpret government as the "'art' of acting on the actions of individuals, taken either singly or collectively, so as to shape, guide, correct and modify the ways in which they conduct themselves" (Burchell 1996, 19) — or, more succinctly, as "the conduct of conduct" (Dean 1996, 47). Most scholars using the lens of governmentality in the development literature mainly examine the practices of states, NGOs, or transnational institutions such as the World Bank (see, for example, Escobar 1995; Li 2007; West 2006).

Foucault, however, clearly envisioned government as a process that exists at multiple levels, even within the family. It is a moral exercise, since those who govern presume to know what constitutes virtuous and responsible conduct for individuals and collectives, and moral shaping occurs within many types of relationships (Dean 1999, 11). Thus, I seek to demonstrate the ways subalterns in general and indigenous peoples in particular (usually seen as only the objects of governmental action) can also be the agents of governmentality, rationalizing and disciplining their fellow group members while enlisting them in projects of their own rule.

Most scholars who apply the governmentality analytic to ethnographic and ethno-historical material portray new forms of discipline as inherently manipulative and self-serving (Starn 1999, 96–97). This may explain why they have been reluctant to examine governmentality and the associated formation of new subjectivities within indigenous social movements and territories.[2] Yet attempts to govern others and oneself are often made with good intentions. Barbara Cruikshank, for example, studies various social programs in the United States, such as the War on Poverty, that have ostensibly been designed to empower participants. She argues that "the will to empower others and oneself is neither a bad nor a good thing. It is political; the will to empower contains the twin possibilities of domination and freedom. . . . My goal, however, is not to indict the will to empower but to show that even the most democratic modes of government entail power relationships that are both voluntary and coercive" (1999, 2–3).

Like Cruikshank, I do not wish "to indict the will to empower." Indigenous leaders' actions have been critical in assuring their members' continued access to land and development funding. Rather, I am interested in the ways in which those in governing roles have worked to transform individual subjects (in this case, people who thought of themselves primarily as part of a kinship-based group, occupying family-owned land) into active citizens (in this case, of indigenous territories with collective titles and bureaucratic governments).

I am also interested in the ways members have shaped their leaders. As subsequent chapters will demonstrate, they have done this through demanding services that leaders might not otherwise perform, outspokenly criticizing leaders' activities, forging ties with external entities to increase their bargaining power in internal disputes, and actively ignoring the obligations leaders try to impose on them. By drawing attention to the multiple ways in which residents "conduct the conduct" of their leaders, and even to some extent the conduct of the various development organizations that seek to implement projects in Rukullakta's territory, I seek to describe something that goes beyond resistance to domination. Territorial governors are dependent on citizens to participate in various development endeavors (for example, to be present at meetings in which an international development organization wishes to elicit "public participation" to meet the requirements of its project, or to participate in a rally protesting the exploitation of resources such as petroleum). Citizens are able to communicate their disapproval of leaders or particular projects by not attending such events, thus forcing their leaders to seek different funding partners and pursue different plans. Thus citizens, by remaining in distant corners of the territory rather than gathering in Rukullakta's assembly hall, practice what I call government through distance, shaping the ways in which their leaders can shape them.[3] Most governmentality studies have been conducted in highly industrialized states and have examined governance at the national level. Thus, they have focused on the ways in which "centres of calculation" (Latour 1987, chapter 6) pursue their desires to influence distant persons, places, and processes. Understanding processes in Rukullakta provides insight into governmentality in the many other governing bodies that do not exercise the coercive power of highly industrialized states or wield the financial resources of multilateral development organizations.

One of the key strategies that indigenous leaders have used to promote their ideas of territorial citizenship is the construction of a number of different arenas for intervention. Leaders create and administer "governable spaces" (N. Rose 1999, 31–34). These "spaces" refer not only to physical sites (such as collectively run cattle pastures or schools) but also to realms for intervention (such as collective agriculture or bilingual and intercultural education). Although the spaces have varied over time, depending largely on available opportunities and the types of allies who have provided funding, there has been a relatively consistent emphasis by many Amazonian Kichwa leaders on promoting collectivist (as opposed to individualistic) economic, political, and social activity within these arenas.

Despite all the challenges they face, the people of Rukullakta have managed to maintain their collective title to the land, and their leaders in particular have maintained high expectations for the enactment of sovereignty. It is true that both techniques and the changing vision associated with leaders' governing have emerged through engagements with many social movements and groups (including the state, communists, missionaries, feminists, and environmentalists), but they have not been entirely determined by those groups. Although much of the funding for development projects has come from the state or international groups, the goals indigenous leaders pursued were not identical to those of the funders, and this shaped the meanings associated with involvement in the programs and the strategies that leaders employed to persuade their constituents to participate in particular ways. In other words, indigenous leaders have worked to produce a different type of person than other governing agents have, and it is important to understand these differences if we want to comprehend changes in indigenous lives, values, and ways of seeing the world.

Those filling leadership roles in Rukullakta have shared an interest in conserving the collective title, but they have differed in many of their other priorities and general perspectives on what will improve the welfare of residents. Territorial governance is dynamic, due to both the changing makeup of the government and shifting levels of legitimacy. Leaders are further differentiated by the fact that they have had access to very different levels of resources for encouraging compliance with their visions, and thus varying ability to "structure the field of other possible actions" (Foucault 1982, 791). Early leaders often overshot the boundaries of their legitimacy, working to shape members' behavior in dramatic ways, inspired in part by courses they had taken on cooperative formation. Subsequent leaders' efforts have been forged through relatively horizontal coordination with their constituents, within a larger context of marginality relative to the Ecuadorian state, the market, and international development trends. All of these factors have led to a very dynamic system of governance that has maintained some characteristics of a social movement, even as Ecuadorian indigenous organizations have become more institutionalized and have acquired more influence over state politics.[4]

Territorial Citizens

The word "citizen" typically refers to someone with a particular set of rights and responsibilities vis-à-vis a nation-state, and a special type of membership in that nation-state. This membership may be based on where one was born, one's ancestry, or other criteria, but once obtained, it is not easily revoked by the state. Recently, some Native North American scholars have begun to use the term to refer to the members of Native American tribes (see, for example, Lyons 2010; Teuton 2008) and to explore how thinking about tribal members as tribal citizens rather than just members shifts one's understanding of the relationship between those individuals and their tribal government.

The term is also useful for thinking about the residents of indigenous territories in other parts of the world. The initial 207 heads of households who signed up to be part of Rukullakta joined an organization, contributing the lands they claimed and a substantial amount of unpaid labor toward the creation of the cooperative. Subsequent generations have, in general, not made equivalent sacrifices, yet they assume that being born into the collective territory entitles them to certain rights — to use land within the collective title, select their leaders, and benefit from any development project or service being offered to other territorial residents. Leaders emphasize very different aspects of living in the territory, continually reminding residents that they have certain obligations and responsibilities, much as the leaders of nation-states do when speaking about the obligations of citizenship. However, as is the case with revoking national citizenship, actually expelling from Rukullakta's territory members who do not fulfill their obligations has been extremely difficult in practice.

In other words, what leaders are working toward is not simply sustaining a social movement in Rukullakta that is associated with defending the territory from external threats. Rather, they are attempting to construct territorial citizens, people who feel a sense of obligation toward the territorial government and are willing to act on that sense of obligation. Leaders believe that indigenous organizations that include such active, territorial citizens can more effectively confront threats to the integrity of their land holdings, negotiate relationships with outsiders, and manage land use within their territories. As part of their efforts, leaders employ "technologies of citizenship"

(Cruikshank 1993, 1999) — discourses, development projects, and other tactics that are aimed at making individuals politically active and capable of self-government. These technologies are often very well intentioned, yet they also constitute and regulate citizens (in this case, those of indigenous, collectively held territories). Negotiating the specific responsibilities and duties associated with territorial citizenship is one of the key sites of enacting sovereignty.

Governors of indigenous territories work to shape their members into territorial citizens, willing to accept new obligations toward the continuity of their territory and its government. Many firmly believe that they are empowering their members as part of this process. Simultaneously, members have worked to shape their leaders, as have a myriad of national and foreign entities. In the latter case, development organizations (including government agencies) have worked to shape leaders into promoters of modern agriculture, cooperativism, conservation, women's rights, and other causes that do not always — at least, at first — neatly connect with members' lives and ways of thinking about the world. Over time and through these diverse engagements, what leaders have asked of their citizens has changed somewhat, as have their strategies for promoting change, although often not as much as many outsiders would like. To understand changes in indigenous subjectivities and practices in the region, it is necessary to examine these multiple processes and engagements.

A concrete example from my fieldwork may clarify what I am describing here. One of the primary duties of Rukullakta's president (now known as the kuraka) is to sit in an office, Monday through Friday, nine to five, typically without pay (although periodically an NGO working in Rukullakta is able to budget a small stipend for a community liaison and will select the president to fill this role). During this time, the president attends many meetings with government and development project representatives and, between meetings, listens to the concerns and complaints of Rukullakta's citizens. On more than one occasion after a particularly long day of listening to such complaints, José Shiguango (president from 2000 to 2002) would look at me with an exasperated expression on his face and say: "They come here to talk about their rights, how they are not receiving what is due to them as members. I tell them that it is not only about rights, but also about responsibilities." He would then sometimes follow this statement with a specific, substantiating point, such as: "If they do not pay their annual quotas, how can I afford to make the necessary trips to seek more funding for agricultural credit?"

The view of citizenship espoused by Rukullakta's members — defined almost entirely in terms of the possession of rights — has much in common with that which is implicit in much political theory from the 1950s, 1960s, and 1970s. In the late 1980s and 1990s, political theorists began to argue that these notions of rights needed to be supplemented with the active exercise of citizenship responsibilities and virtues (Kymlicka and Norman 1994, 354–55), much as Shiguango argued with Rukullakta's members. However, scholarship in anthropology and on Latin American social movements has continued to focus almost exclusively on the rights aspect of citizenship. Many authors have emphasized how ethnic and racial minorities feel excluded from full citizenship in the nation-states where they live (see, for example, Pallares 2002; Postero 2007; Rosaldo 1994; Yashar 1998). When indigenous people increasingly staged powerful protests in their nations' capitals in the 1990s and 2000s, Nancy Postero and Leon Zamosc pointed to the "crucial issue of what kinds of rights indigenous people should be granted as citizens of democratic nation-states. . . . The promise of democratization is that the political, social, and economic marginalization that characterized indigenous relations with the state (and the elite classes that controlled it) would be replaced by a full and robust citizenship" (2004, 5). Other scholars have suggested the possibility of what has been called differentiated citizenship, in which indigenous people, by virtue of their special status in Western societies, would enjoy rights above and beyond those of non-indigenous citizens (Blackburn 2009; Young 1995). In short, the overwhelming emphasis has been not on what the state expects of citizens in terms of responsibilities, but on what citizens expect from their governments. It is perhaps not surprising, given this emphasis, that little has been written on what sorts of obligations indigenous territorial citizens in Latin America might have to their territorial governments.

Aihwa Ong's prolific writings on citizenship (1996, 1999, 2003, 2006), in contrast, highlight the fact that citizenship is not merely related to rights but is also a process of subject making. Like Ong, I am particularly interested in the "everyday processes whereby people . . . are made into subjects" (1996, 737), and, again like her, I view citizenship as dialectically determined by governors and governed. However, Ong views citizenship "in the context of the ways in which a set of common . . . values concerning family, health, social welfare, gender relations, and work and entrepreneurialism are elaborated in everyday lives" (2003, xvii). Citizenship for her, then, becomes a form of enculturation conducted not only by state agencies but also by civic groups, churches, refugee camps, health workers, and others.[5]

The implication of her analysis is that these diverse entities are all working toward an equivalent or largely overlapping form of enculturation, striving to imbue in citizens roughly the same values and behaviors as the state promotes. Specifically, she argues that "neoliberalism, with its celebration of freedom, progress, and individualism, has become a pervasive ideology that influences many domains of social life . . . setting the normative standards of good citizenship in practice" (1996, 739). She does not refute agency in these processes, but she addresses only that practiced by individuals, who "modify practices and agendas while nimbly deflecting control and interjecting critique" (2003, xvii). Ong is not alone in the way she understands governmentality. As Donald Moore has argued, "despite their considerable insights, [many] analyses of colonial and postcolonial governmentality have tended to emphasize an underlying 'grammar of modern power,' a coherent 'regime of intelligibility,' or a unified 'political rationality'" (2005, 8). Thus, scholars have tended to imagine governmentality as singular, rather than multiple, and as following a coherent and unified position.

Yet in my understanding of territorial citizenship, governmentality happens through multiple, overlapping centers that, although they share commonalities, articulate divergent projects of subject making (see also Moore 2005). In this book, I focus on a relatively local governing entity—the indigenous territorial government—that strives to construct citizens who feel responsibility toward the territory and who therefore practice certain duties as responsible, contributing citizens of that territory. Sometimes these projects overlap with the state's or development organizations' efforts to construct particular kinds of citizens, but sometimes becoming a better territorial citizen does not have any recognizable connection to becoming a better national citizen, and in fact it may involve challenging or ignoring some of the claims and aspirations of the state. By implication, it may be the case that other intermediary groups, including the churches and civic organizations described by Ong and the development NGOs described by Maria Elena García (2005) and Nancy Postero (2007), are working to create somewhat different types of citizens than what the state is working to produce, even though all three authors suggest that the NGOs are "doing the state's 'work'" (Postero 2007, 166).

Many indigenous leaders' ideas of appropriate duties and responsibilities are shaped by alliances with and the financial assistance provided by the Ecuadorian government, international development organizations, larger Ecuadorian indigenous federations, and transnational indigenous networks, and thus there is no denying that important aspects of their political projects can be similar. However, I argue that there are also important differences in the constitution of territorial citizens, in which indigenous leaders place the continuity of their territorial government above the priorities promoted by their various allies and funders. Thus, much like the states and the associated technologies of citizenship that are the focus of Ong's analysis, Rukullakta's government can be seen as constituting "a positive generative force that has responded eagerly and even creatively to the challenges of global capital" (1999, 21).

Unlike scholarship on Latin American indigenous organizations, Native North American intellectuals are not only increasingly using the term "citizen" to describe members of indigenous nations, but they are also starting to explicitly link citizenship to obligations. Part of this is a response to the growing recognition that US-imposed restrictions on minimal blood quantum, or percentage of Native American ancestry, is slowly but surely reducing the number of people who can claim Native American status according to US law. When a tribal member marries someone from outside the tribe, subsequent generations have lower and lower amounts of "native blood" and eventually cannot qualify to live on Indian reservations or obtain other government services that were promised to tribal members when their ancestors initially signed treaties with the US government. When tribal leaders echo the state's emphasis on blood quantum and exclude those individuals who do not meet the minimum requirement from tribal decision making, they are criticized by some native intellectuals for having internalized racist standards set by the colonizer (see, in particular, Kauanui 2008). Scott Richard Lyons (2010), condemning the rigid boundaries of blood quantum, proposes a type of naturalization process, in which those people who marry into a Native American tribe, or whose blood quantum falls below certain requirements, can fulfill certain other requirements (such as learning the native language) and thereby gain citizenship in that tribe. He thus sees citizenship as a way in which leaders can shape their citizens and "produce sovereign indigenous nations." He writes: "What are the proper criteria for indigenous citizenship? *Require what you want to produce.* If your heritage language is dying, then make fluency a requirement for citizenship. If your territory suffers from brain drain, make residency a requirement for citizenship. If you need capital, make commitment to the [indigenous] nation's laws a requirement for citizenship and level a progressive income tax" (2010, 186, italics in original). Here, the notion that Native American intellectuals and governing bodies should be actively shaping their people into a particular type of citizen is explicit.

Issues of blood quantum have not entered into the same sorts of state-sponsored political exclusions in Latin America. Until recently, most Latin American governments pursued ideologies of *mestizaje*, under which all national citizens were supposed to think of themselves as racially mixed, yet in practice indigenous people and dark-skinned mestizos experienced high levels of discrimination. Additionally, indigenous people in Latin America received title to their territories much more recently than most Native Americans in North America got titles to their reservation lands, so what to do about children of mixed marriages has not yet become a serious problem in Latin America. Although it is important to keep these historical differences in mind, Lyons's list of issues facing Native North American tribes (language loss, brain drain, and lack of capital) has much in common with the concerns of indigenous intellectuals in Latin America. It will be interesting to gauge the similarities and differences between notions of the ideal territorial citizen held in each region in the decades to come.

Importantly, Lyons also emphasizes that sometimes citizens rightly reject the obligations expected of them: "Civil disobedience is when the citizen tries to improve the nation by ridding it of some evil, and should be distinguished from resigning one's citizenship, or for that matter being a do-nothing sort of citizen" (2010, 173). Lyons's discussion of citizenship has much to offer scholars studying indigenous territories in Latin America, although his implication that indigenous sovereignty can be fully realized (when everyone speaks the language, there is sufficient capital, or everyone remains on the reservation) ignores the role that multiple, powerful actors play in constraining that realization. As Cattelino (2008) has argued, even billions of dollars in gambling revenue, a revitalized sense of cultural pride, and significant advances in wresting control of tribal administration from the US government have not created a situation in which Florida Seminoles no longer need to worry about threats to their territory or to their hard-won political gains; Seminole leaders still face powerful critics who think they earn too much money and exercise too much power. They must also continue to address many conflicts within the tribe as they govern it.

Territory as Both Place and Property

Building on important work that established the importance of place (Basso 1996; Feld and Basso 1996) and landscape (Schama 1995) to various cultures, scholars writing about territory in Latin America have highlighted how the collective titling of territories allows indigenous people to continue to live in landscapes that transmit historical memories, cultural knowledge, and moral lessons (see, for example, Escobar 2008; García-Hierro and Surrallés 2005; Rappaport 2005a; Santos-Granero 2005). According to this literature, indigenous people can have a strong "sense of place" (Feld and Basso 1996), forged through generations of dwelling in particular sites. Part of this sense of place can be understood as a type of intuition (Ingold 2000) or knowledge (Nadasdy 2004) that grows through long-term practice of skills that are specific to a particular environment. For example, over a lifetime of hunting in the same area, one can gain a keen sense of where animals are, which way they are moving, and how they will respond to a hunter's actions. Although some basic aspects of this knowledge can be taught, these scholars emphasize, much of it must be acquired through situated practice and experience.

Most scholars studying indigenous knowledge and perception have focused on hunting skills and knowledge of plants, both of which are vital to the acquisition of food and other necessary resources. However, environment-specific knowledge extends also to less-recognized skills such as moving through the landscape. This was never clearer to me than when I tried to navigate the deep mud that forms on rainforest paths that the residents of Rukullakta use to move cattle and mules between their homes and market centers. Each time I inadvertently left a rubber boot behind, plunging my already muddy foot two feet down into the mud in front of me, my guide would admonish me with the words "don't put your weight on your foot as you are walking." No matter how I tried, I could not figure out how to walk without putting any weight on my feet. Sometimes, my guide would try to make me feel better by telling me where other non-indigenous people had fallen along the way, which only made me realize that my own mishaps were being added to his sense of place and bank of stories to tell the next poor traveler. Sometimes, I would try to regain some of my pride by suggesting that he visit me during a Michigan winter, when I would try to teach him how to walk on the ice without falling. "Then," I would say, "you will know how I feel right now."

Residents of Rukullakta have a strong sense of place, and it is extremely important for them to live in the same place as their ancestors. This is revealed in the very name "Rukullakta," which means "old settlement." As Arturo Escobar, like many other scholars, has argued, "place continues to be an important source of culture and identity; despite the pervasive delocalization of social life, there is an embodiment and emplacement to human life that cannot be denied" (2008, 7). Strong attachment to place becomes clear in the many stories Rukullakta's residents tell about particular spots in the territory and the place names they select to commemorate events important to its defense. For example, Yawar Urku (Blood Mountain) refers to a mountain where a successful battle took place during the colonial period, when Spanish blood is said to have stained the mountain red. A strong commitment to place is also revealed in their long-standing desire to create a future for their children on this land. This motivates their interest in building a territorial economy that will allow their children to remain close to home when they reach adulthood, rather than having to move away to find a job.

For some scholars, a focus on place and local knowledge has served as a way of breaking with the "overdeterminations of a distinct 'global'" (Raffles 1999, 350), and I agree that ethnography can provide a lens into how each place is "a set of relations, an ongoing politics, a density, in which places are discursively and imaginatively materialized and enacted through the practices of variously positioned people and political economies" (Raffles 1999, 324). Yet many people have unfortunately used the concepts of place and traditional ecological knowledge to go to the opposite extreme of what Raffles suggests, describing what is made to seem like local autonomy by ignoring or downplaying the ways that transnational articulations and interactions shape places over time (Biersack 2006, 16). A related weakness of the recent focus on place and traditional ecological knowledge is the tendency to portray indigenous cultures as internally homogeneous or, alternatively, as losing their culture due to interactions with markets or outsiders.

In this book, I take a different approach by examining Rukullakta's residents' deeply felt, yet shifting, attachments to their territory through the lens of property. Addressing questions about who can do what and where within an indigenous territory is a key way of understanding the politics involved in enacting sovereignty. Research in political ecology spanning from foundational books (for example, Blaikie and Brookfield 1987; Neumann 2002; Peet and Watts 1996; Peluso 1994) through recent analyses (for example, Peluso and Lund 2011; White et al. 2012) have long revealed the mechanisms states, corporations, and international aid organizations use to gain control of property and resources previously used by indigenous and peasant groups. I aim to show how the normally distinct literatures on political ecology and place can inform one another through an analysis of property that is not limited to issues of ownership. Tracing the various ideas about property held by Rukullakta's residents provides incredible insight into their understandings of themselves as persons, as well as their relationships to one another, their leaders, and the land where they live. Residents have debated various questions associated with property regimes for their entire history of living together, in part because forming the collective territory involved dramatic changes from previous understandings of property, and in part because of the multiple, subsequent instances of outsiders (including development banks and conservationists) attempting to change property regimes in Rukullakta to fit their own agendas. Tracing debates about and the changing practices associated with property thus illuminates the enormous expectations that accompanied territorial titling, the deep attachments to place that confounded those expectations, the transnational relationships that have continued to shape those expectations and attachments over time, and the implications all of these have had on notions of territorial citizenship.

Some of the most interesting work in anthropology on property, and the deep connections between notions of property and both citizenship and personhood, has been produced by anthropologists working in the countries of the former Soviet bloc (see, for example, Alexander 2004; Dunn 2004; Humphrey and Verdery 2004; Verdery 2004). Residents of these countries went through dramatic changes and upheavals in their understandings of property and who they were as persons when their national economies transitioned from state-owned enterprises under socialism to privatized enterprises in the 1990s. Rukullakta's transition was quite different: indigenous leaders expected members to shift from understandings of property and personhood centered on extended kinship groups to a system in which land and people were governed by a territorial government. As in the former Soviet bloc countries, there were substantial challenges associated with these transitions. In both places, the challenges were heightened by the fact that participants simultaneously began a period of stronger engagement with capitalist markets and with Western-trained experts who had very different expectations about property and social obligations. (In the former Soviet bloc, a number of people from Western Europe and the United States became involved in the privatization process in the 1990s; in Rukullakta, residents became more involved in market-oriented cattle ranching schemes through development projects sponsored by the Ecuadorian government and multilateral banks in the 1970s.) These outside entities brought new practices and new understandings of how residents should relate to one another, the products they produced, and their employers. For Rukullakta's residents, a second wave of intensive engagement occurred in the 1990s and early 2000s, as environmentalists brought their own expectations and assumptions about social relations, contracts, and property into their negotiations with indigenous governments. Some of those expectations — that indigenous governments spoke for and controlled the land use practices of territorial residents, and that existing property regimes were conducive to initiating projects that required large areas of land — were surprisingly similar to those of the government officials who promoted cooperative cattle ranching in the 1970s. Yet, as will be shown in chapter 4, the sheer length of time that environmentalists have actively worked to shape indigenous understandings of the environment has produced more pronounced effects on indigenous subjectivities and relationships to nature than what occurred as a result of the relatively brief period that government agencies spent promoting cattle ranching in the 1970s.

Making Citizens, Making Leaders, Making Territories

As Rukullakta's leaders attempt to shape citizens and residents attempt to shape their leaders, both contribute to a more institutionalized territorial government, although it must remain dynamic to survive recurring external threats to the territory's integrity. A story from Rukullakta's recent history makes this clear. In 2011 the kuraka of the Kichwa People of Rukullakta signed a contract with Ivanhoe Petroleum to build an exploratory well within Rukullakta's territory after various residents had expressed an interest in having the company build a road to the well, a road that would also improve some residents' access to markets for their crops. The kuraka accepted a modest payment of US $1,000 from the company to act as its community liaison. When it became clear that a very vocal majority of residents was firmly opposed to the contract, he claimed that he did not sign it. Some say he even traveled to Quito to have a new national identification card issued with a different signature, so that he could claim that his signature on the contract had been forged. At a rapidly called assembly meeting subsequent to his actions, members rubbed hot peppers in his eyes (a punishment typically given to children) and deposed him.

A second-level leader, roughly equivalent to a minister of economic affairs, was asked to become the new kuraka. During an interview, he told me: "The people called on me to fill this role and I accepted. I had to quit my job to fill this unpaid position because they are looking to me to lead this organization. [Ministerial positions are much more part-time than the position of kuraka, and most ministers also have paying jobs outside the territorial government.] Our grandfathers and fathers left these lands, this organization in a good position. How can I disrespect them by failing in this duty?" (René Shiguango interview, June 15, 2011).

The new kuraka's sense of obligation is apparent, and he is not the only one to feel this way. After four decades, there are aspects of living in an indigenous territory that are now generally accepted, even though they were new as recently as the 1970s. There are many other aspects of people's behavior, however, that leaders have attempted to change unsuccessfully; members have resisted, either through vocal outcry or silent evasion. Territorial citizenship is a moving target, one that leaders pursue, members assess, and multiple outsiders attempt to grasp and shape to suit their own political agendas. Although observers of indigenous organizations typically emphasize the importance of tradition, Rukullakta's forty-year history illustrates that change may be as important as continuity in sustaining senses of shared ownership and identity. This book traces these processes over a span of four decades, as well as the changing subjectivities and understandings of personhood, property regimes, and nature that have accompanied them.

Outline of the Following Chapters

At the beginning of chapter 1, I provide a brief history of the region's interaction with missions and the colonial and federal government in the centuries preceding the formation of the Rukullakta Cooperative. Subsequently, the chapter turns to the early cooperative leaders' vision for indigenous empowerment during the turbulent 1960s, and the national and transnational encounters that shaped this vision. Many groups, including government agencies, encouraged indigenous people to form collective organizations so they could retain access to their land. This required electing leaders and designating some of the organization's land for communal use. Both requirements were sharp departures from earlier Kichwa understandings of social organization, personhood, and property. Yet a relatively small but vocal group of Kichwa saw the possibilities of forming collective organizations as empowering, rather than as simply an imposition by the state. Self-appointed local leaders guided numerous families through a vision of empowerment that deviated from the state's project but corresponded to it sufficiently to qualify their organization for special treatment.

In chapter 2, I examine the challenge that confronted leaders once the organization had been officially recognized: creating a community of members in a newly recognized territory that was amenable to indigenous governance. Sustaining collectivist energies and creating a long-term, economically collaborating entity with over two thousand residents were considerable goals, given members' strong preference for living autonomously. Leaders fought to maintain members' interest in their vision of empowerment by seeking development funding from a wide variety of sources. After just a few years, however, it became clear that the state-like vision of a large, economically collaborating group involved changes in social relations that were too dramatic for most residents. I conclude the chapter by arguing that despite the downfall of large-scale collectivism, important traces of this period and the early leaders' vision for empowerment continue in smaller-scale projects practiced by a large portion of the membership.

Although the first two chapters follow the history of Rukullakta in a chronological format, the final three chapters are organized thematically to allow me to draw attention to some of the key issues and processes that have characterized Rukullakta's enactment of sovereignty since the mid-1980s. In chapter 3, I analyze the complicated and contradictory ideas surrounding property that have plagued Rukullakta's government for decades. If early leaders had been successful in pursuing their vision for empowerment, the formation of the cooperative would have involved dramatic changes in the ways in which participants thought about property. Previous chapters emphasize the differences in priorities set by early movement leaders and those held by much of the membership, but this chapter reveals that it is wrong to assume that debates within the cooperative amount to disagreements between modernists and traditionalists. I identify three ideal types of property, each of which includes some aspects of older ways of understanding property and other aspects that are relatively new. Each of the three types is also tied to particular understandings of personhood, Kichwa identity, and citizen-leader relationships. Finally, each is connected to a distinct landscape, and I trace how these various landscapes have become more and less common at different points in the cooperative's history. My analysis of aerial photographs and satellite images from various points in Rukullakta's history reveals that rather than simply attempting to shorten distances to markets, members make their land use decisions based on deep-seated opinions about the value and meaning of territorial citizenship.

In chapter 4, I examine the rise of conservation-driven investments in the Upper Napo region since the mid-1980s. I trace how indigenous leaders in the cooperative and throughout the Ecuadorian Amazon have slowly shifted toward environmentalists' visions of conservation, even as they staunchly resisted what they saw as attempts to challenge their organizational autonomy. Not all indigenous organizations agree on the value of particular environmentalist projects or certain tenets of environmentalist thought. Differing opinions among leaders about particular programs emerge from the leaders' varying cultural values, understandings of property, and histories of engagement with outsiders, and these opinions contribute to distinct forms of environmental subject formation and different understandings of territorial citizenship.

I then turn to a key question in chapter 5. How is it possible that Rukullakta has remained strong despite the many challenges described in previous chapters? Through a close reading of Rukullakta's archives, it is possible to see how the territory's citizens have played an important role in shaping their leaders and legitimating their rule, in particular through appeals to the leaders for assistance in resolving local conflicts. I refer to such acts as everyday forms of indigenous territory formation, building on Gilbert Joseph and Daniel Nugent's concept of "everyday forms of state formation" (1994b). I then examine three additional forms, or "technologies. of citizenship" (Cruikshank 1993, 1999) pursued over the last decade, and reveal how all of them have been mutually constituted through the actions and imaginaries of leaders and citizens. This was particularly clear in the period between 2006 and 2009, when leaders worked to reinvent the cooperative to fit its new legal designation, the Kichwa People of Rukullakta. I conclude that reinvention is a key process in sustaining indigenous territorial organizations.

Living History as Fieldwork

Documenting and interpreting recent history is a process fraught with complications, as many, though not all, of the people involved in this history are still living. To make matters more complicated, the longer I spend engaged in understanding Rukullakta's history, the more I become a part of it. The following story highlights some of these dynamics.

I began my research in 1999–2000, as directed by the Rukullakta leadership of the time, by interviewing as many of the founding members of the organization as I could find. In the process of doing so, I discovered that there were a number of facts and interpretations on which people disagreed. For example, I was unable to determine who had been the first president of the cooperative, even though this was an issue of extreme importance to my informants. Many founding members of the organization identified Juan Shiguango as having filled that role. However, Carlos Alvarado — and a relatively small number of other people — told me that he himself had been the first president.

Several weeks later, I was granted access to the organization's meeting minutes (the *Actas*). In these archives, it stated clearly that Carlos Alvarado was the first president of the organization, and Juan Shiguango was the first vice president. Given my book-centric training, my tendency was to believe the written archive over the verbal accounts, but I also knew that Alvarado had written many of the minutes in the *Actas* in the early years. Thus, I thought, it was *conceivable* that Alvarado had lied in the meeting minutes, switching the roles that he and Shiguango filled. Another, less conspiratorial, possibility was that nearly all the people I was interviewing had joined the organization after Alvarado's presidency, since Shiguango was listed as the second president. A final — and perhaps the most likely — possibility was that Alvarado had been a self-selected president during the early organizational meetings of what they call the "Pre-Cooperative" in 1970–73, but by the time the state granted official recognition to the organization in 1974 and members had to select their president, Shiguango was the one they chose.

Prior to coming to this tenuous conclusion, however, I asked several people directly about the discrepancy. Older interviewees inevitably reacted with a disgusted snort or a dismissive and annoyed smirk about the possibility of Alvarado filling the role. Sometimes they would add, "Carlos Alvarado was just a young man at that time" (the implication being that at that time, it was only older men who were respected enough to become leaders). However, when I mentioned what the archives stated to the current cadre of leaders, all men in their late twenties or thirties, they embraced the new information. They complimented me for my keen investigative skills, since they had always been told that Shiguango was the first president. I appreciated their compliments, but I also felt uneasy. In the history I produced for them, I listed Alvarado as the first president, in part because he had been such a valuable informant to me, making me reluctant to imply that he was lying. I also did my best to respect the legacy of Juan Shiguango by including substantial coverage of the important organizational work he did prior to his untimely death. It was at moments such as these that I was forced to realize that the role of historian is not that of a detached, objective compiler of documents and oral accounts, but that of a shaper of collective memories and history itself.

In another twist, when I returned in 2001 to continue the research, Alvarado was no longer living in Rukullakta, having chosen to separate from his wife and move to the Galapagos. His wife and children approached the leadership, asking for financial assistance. The leaders decided to help the family in recognition of the key role Alvarado had played in obtaining the large land title that Rukullakta's residents enjoyed, especially during his time as the first president. I then realized that my seemingly harmless historical work as a student was having material as well as symbolic ramifications.

In subsequent years, I had my dissertation translated into Spanish and published by an Ecuadorian press (Erazo 2008). Each time I visit, I bring dozens of copies and receive almost as many requests for them. So far, no one has confronted me about my interpretations, even though I am sure they would not hesitate to do so if they felt the need (although admittedly, it is mostly younger people who take the time to read the book). More important, as Rukullakta becomes more and more a part of me, it has been my constant aim to produce a history that neither romanticizes nor unfairly condemns the activities of the organization and the larger indigenous movement to which it belongs.

The methods I have used have changed substantially over the last decade, both because my recent work and family obligations make extended trips difficult, and because of dramatic changes in Rukullakta. In 1999–2000, my primary task was to find and interview the founding members of the organization, most of whom were no longer actively involved in governance. Finding them often involved four-hour hikes through deep mud along cattle trails in the rainforest, only to find that the person I sought was away on a hunting trip, or running errands in Ecuador's capital. Even when I tried to take advantage of founding members' scheduled trips to the nearby mission town (which I learned about from their grown children who lived closer to me), the frequent Amazonian downpours often meant that the interviewee decided to stay at home and stay dry rather than make the scheduled visit. Fortunately, I was usually accompanied by a guide, and I lived just steps away from Rukullakta's central government offices. I was therefore able to engage in more relaxed conversations and participant observation between interviews. I was also able to spend evenings and rainy days attempting to decipher the handwriting in Rukullakta's *Actas* and reading other archives.

One of the recurring themes in my interviews was issues of property, and in 2000 I located two sets of aerial photographs of Rukullakta taken in 1973 and 1982, housed at Ecuador's Military Geographical Institute. Between my 2000 and 2001 fieldwork trips, I took courses in aerial photograph and satellite image interpretation as a way of visualizing the various processes and debates to which leaders and members had devoted so much energy — and to which the *Actas* gave so many pages. Interpreting aerial photographs and satellite images is an uncommon method of understanding debates over property. However, the images gave me insights into where new homes, agricultural fields, and pastures were established at different times, often against the will of leaders, allowing me to assess the relative strength of leaders to determine how the territory was being used at different points in time. I spent months trying to fit hand-drawn community maps of family-claimed property boundaries to the land cover maps I created with the aerial photographs and several satellite images from other points in time, in order to understand the connections between struggles over property regimes and changing land use. This process included two months of hiking through Rukullakta's territory with a global positioning system (GPS) and interviewing farmers on the past thirty years of land use, so that I could better assess the data provided by aerial photographs and satellite images.

A few years later, things began to change quite dramatically in Rukullakta. More and more people had periodic access to broadband Internet and owned cell phones — even people who still lived hours from the nearest road and had yet to obtain electricity in their homes.[6] I began to receive press releases, photos of important events, and professional-quality brochures as attachments to e-mails from leaders who have come to expect my periodic returns to Rukullakta as the organization's semi-official historian.

In 2008 a project organized by the Center for Environmental Studies in Latin America (subsequently called the Center for Conservation in Indigenous Lands in Western Amazonia) at the University of Texas at Austin invested the funds and hours necessary to map the community-held property boundaries I had struggled so long to understand based on hand-drawn community property maps. Today the government offices of Rukullakta are adorned with dozens of Geographic Information System maps that were created using the center's data, and leaders draft management plans that establish guidelines for land use decades into the future. Although in some ways it was disheartening to be outdone in terms of the production of geographical information, the availability of all these data has enabled me to understand some processes and relationships that I had not been able to see previously.

When I first began work in Rukullakta, I felt that my role was to observe and not interfere with what I perceived as a more fragile culture than my own. As time passed, it became increasingly clear to me that my assumptions could not have been further from the truth. Rukullakta's leaders actively seek allies, and I am only one of hundreds of foreigners who have played a role there. While I write books and articles, others offer money, utopian development projects, geographical analysis of land cover within Rukullakta's borders, technical assistance in projects Rukullakta's leaders have designed, and even documentary coverage of the leaders' efforts to control some of the effects of globalization in their territory.[7] Furthermore, Rukullakta's leaders have put my writings to their own uses. For example, the forty-page history and photos that I produced in 2000 traveled to Spain with a few leaders as they successfully attempted to obtain funding from a Basque foundation. Thus, I increasingly feel that it is my responsibility to contribute, at least in modest ways, to leaders' efforts to strengthen their organization rather than pretend I can sit on the sidelines. As my good friend Medardo Shiguango, head (as of 2012) of the Project on Geotourism for the Kichwa People of Rukullakta (the Pueblo Kichwa de Rukullakta, or PKR), likes to say to me, "*Doctora*, you are one of PKR's representatives in the United States. Your books will let people know about the work we are doing here."

CHAPTER ONE

HISTORY, EMPOWERMENT, AND RULE

The mid-twentieth century was a period of dramatic socioeconomic change for Kichwa and others in the Upper Napo region of Ecuador's Amazonian lowlands. Passage of the 1964 Agrarian Reform and Colonization Law encouraged people from the highlands and coast of Ecuador to settle in the less densely populated Amazonian region, putting indigenous lands there at risk. Indigenous residents of the lowlands — particularly those living near existing towns and planned roads — needed to act quickly to gain legal title to the lands they used or risk losing access forever. The cost of having topographers measure the extent of their property was often insurmountable for a family, particularly since many holdings were irregularly shaped and dispersed across the landscape, often several hours' walk from any road. The state colonization agency encouraged farmers to form collective organizations and to apply for group titles instead, a less expensive process. According to Ecuadorian law, forming a collective land-holding organization required electing leaders and designating some of the organization's land for communal use (Pallares 2002, 42–47). Both requirements were sharp departures from existing Kichwa understandings of social organization and property.

Yet some Upper Napo Kichwa saw the idea of forming a collective organization as potentially empowering, rather than as simply an imposition by the state. They envisioned a world in which Kichwa would be organized into large groups, extending far beyond their kinship networks and centered around leaders (themselves) who would motivate all members to work together to improve their lives. This chapter explores several of the cross-cultural engagements that contributed to these early leaders' expectations. It also examines the enormous departure that the leaders' vision represented from previous ways of living for their people. In particular, many Kichwa found long-term collaboration with unrelated people to be a new and frustrating obligation. Many also resisted the idea of ceding their family's land claims to a centrally managed organization. The tensions between people's existing obligations to their kin group and the loyalty that leaders expected them to feel toward a larger group of organizational members were significant, and they continue to this day.

In this chapter, I argue that although leaders from Rukullakta and other parts of the Upper Napo region pursued collective titles because they saw these as the best way to ensure that most of the land would remain in Kichwa hands, they simultaneously subjected their neighbors to new obligations, hierarchies, and understandings of personhood and property. The types of obligations, sacrifices, and sense of duty that leaders sought from their organization's members is closer to the way we understand citizenship than it is to the way we understand membership in an organization. Leaders justified this political project of creating what I call territorial citizens with the language of empowerment, telling prospective members that the best way to maintain access to land and to gain access to state welfare programs and funds for infrastructure projects (like bridges and community meeting halls) was to form a collective, land-holding organization. Although empowerment of others is often pursued with the noblest of intentions, it subjects intended beneficiaries to new relationships with those who are running the empowerment program (Cruikshank 1999, 2–3), and this was certainly the case in Rukullakta.

Some households in the Upper Napo region chose not to join the emerging, large organizations, deciding rather to seek land titles for small groups of people, usually connected by some degree of kinship. It soon became clear, however, that the state favored larger groups, particularly those who seemed dedicated to modernizing their agricultural practices. The state granted these groups more land per person and offered greater levels of assistance in completing paperwork, obtaining agricultural loans (local leaders hoped that profits from agricultural projects would help pay the costs associated with gaining legal title), and obtaining other state goods such as schools and health clinics. The state thus sent the message that access to state-granted rights—especially rights to property protection and access to state social welfare and infrastructural monies—was connected to the creation of intermediary organizations such as cooperatives. Having the rural populace grouped into relatively large organizations, represented by a small number of individuals and geographically connected to an administrative hub, facilitated state agencies' duties. It also increased the status of a few leaders in relation to the rest of the organization's members.

Many accounts of state attempts to gain control over indigenous lands emphasize the coercive nature of state policies and indigenous resistance to those policies. Rukullakta's experience was not a clear case of coercion. There were other viable solutions to the changing circumstances they faced: for example, some people chose not to join a collective organization, moving east to occupy lands that were not yet of interest to the colonists; others applied for land in smaller, kinship-connected groups. Yet, by granting titles to large areas of land only to those who formed or joined cooperatives, the state reshaped the actions of subjects. Rather than coercing people into forming cooperatives, the state's scheme "attempt[ed] to act on their actions, guiding them in [what they saw as] an improved direction" (Li 2005, 384). Local leaders, however, were critical actors in this process. They encouraged their friends and kin to pursue livelihood and other changes that did not exactly match the state's vision of modernization, but that corresponded to it sufficiently to qualify their organization for land titling and development programs, as will be shown below and in chapter 2. Understanding local leaders' roles and visions are critical components of understanding the differences between territorial citizenship and national citizenship.

I begin this chapter with a brief history of the Upper Napo region from the first Spanish incursions in the 1500s through the early twentieth century. Although far from comprehensive, this short historical account demonstrates two key points that some narratives obscure. First, the region's history of engagement with state bureaucracies and the market economy did not begin in the second half of the twentieth century (when the first roads to the region were constructed); in fact, it dates back several centuries. This engagement included periodic appeals to state agencies to reduce local forms of exploitation (such as the tributes that local political authorities demanded). Second, the region's history of engagement with colonial or state agents and markets has not been a slow, unidirectional march from isolation toward greater engagement. Rather, the region has oscillated between periods of greater engagement with the outside world and times of relative isolation, due in large part to shifting levels of desire from the outside for the region's resources.

I then describe in more detail the changes that occurred in the Upper Napo region during the twentieth century, especially as Kichwa families met with one another prior to the formation of the Rukullakta Cooperative. Leaders described to their neighbors and kin a particular vision for empowerment that would maintain access to territory but also involve important changes to livelihoods, property regimes, landscapes, and understandings of personhood. If they hoped to gain legal title to a large area of land, residents needed to demonstrate to state officials that they were modern Ecuadorian citizens, contributing to national modernization goals by actively engaging in an agricultural cooperative.

A Brief History of Colonization and State Formation in the Region

Many accounts of the Upper Napo region begin — as this chapter did — with the 1960s, describing the agrarian reform and construction of new roads that linked it to the national grid. This gives the impression that the local population existed apart from national processes prior to that time, which is false. Although Amazonian Indians in the region were able to maintain a high level of autonomy compared to their counterparts in the Andes, they also suffered intermittent but brutal exposure to new diseases and forced labor policies, dating back to the sixteenth century. In the following pages, I give a very brief description of the Upper Napo Kichwa's history of contact with missionaries, colonial and governmental officials, and other powerful outsiders (for a more in-depth discussion, see Muratorio 1991). Although these contacts caused much suffering, Kichwa also achieved important victories and learned how to use governmental channels to occasionally reduce the exploitation they faced.

In her discussion of the history of the Ecuadorian Amazon (or *Oriente*, as it is often called), Anne Christine Taylor (1994) divides the 360-year period between 1540 and 1900 into four general, and discontinuous, phases. The first was a relatively brief period (1540–80), during which the Spanish organized several expeditions in search of gold and cinnamon, entering through

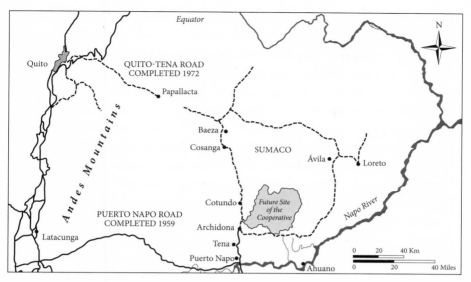

MAP 1.1 Quijos region, with Andean cities to the west. The map also indicates roads (solid lines) and significant paths (dashed lines) as of 1965. Adapted from Operational Navigation Chart M-25, published in 1967 by the Aeronautical Chart and Informational Center, US Air Force (based on data compiled in April 1965).

the Quijos region, east of Quito (see map 1.1). Contrary to their expectations, the Spanish found no gold and only very dispersed cinnamon trees (Oberem 1980, 67).

In 1559 the Spanish established Baeza, a town approximately halfway between Quito and what later became Archidona. From Baeza, the colonial administration worked to establish dominance over the various Indian groups living in the region through the system of *encomiendas*, or rewarding Spaniards with property for service to the crown. These land grants gave the beneficiaries (called *encomenderos*) access to Indian labor and tribute, which the Indians paid primarily with gold and cotton. Religious conversion of the Indians to Catholicism was undertaken concurrently, although it was less of a priority than the extraction of labor and tribute (Rogers 1995, 29, note 14). Indians worked in Spanish-owned fields, constructed houses for Spaniards, worked as domestic servants for them, panned gold, wove textiles, and carried both cargo and people (on chairs strapped to their backs) on frequent trips to and from Quito, crossing frozen Andean passes on foot in trips that lasted eight days or more, often without wearing shoes (Oberem 1980, 76–81; Muratorio 1991, 22–29).

To facilitate the extraction and administration of this labor, the Spanish forced members of the indigenous population to resettle in concentrated villages, called *reducciones*. These settlements fostered the spread of disease and limited the traditional mobility of indigenous people, severely reducing their access to fertile land and wild game and plants. There were periodic Indian uprisings against Spanish abuses throughout the second half of the sixteenth century, including one in 1560, in Cosanga, and two in 1562, in Cosanga and Baeza (see map 1.1). The Spanish were unable to stop these rebellions militarily, but they were able to pacify participants with gifts from Quito (Oberem 1980, 77). Subsequently, the Spanish moved south and east into new areas, establishing the town of Archidona in 1563. According to several of Rukullakta's residents, the exact location of Archidona changed a few times, and during at least one stretch of history, its location was within what is currently Rukullakta's territory. The missionaries collected tribute twice annually from the indigenous population, usually in the form of gold, cotton, and *pita* (a fiber obtained from the *Agave Americana* and other related species and used for making rope, cords, and paper) (Oberem 1980, 92–93).

In 1578 there was a regionwide, highly coordinated uprising led by indigenous shamans (including the now infamous Jumandy, who is further discussed in chapter 2), during which the Spanish and all their highland servants in the towns of Ávila and Archidona were killed. The rebellion was crushed in Baeza, and its surviving leaders were taken to Quito for trial and execution (Oberem 1980, 88–89). Within ten months, new *encomenderos* had arrived from the highlands, and the Indians were once again distributed among them for the extraction of labor and tribute. The local indigenous population decreased steadily as a result of disease, physical abuse, and flight from the region. Although population counts from colonial offices must be viewed with some skepticism, Blanca Muratorio estimates that the population in the Tena-Archidona region decreased by over 90 percent between 1559 and 1608 (1991, 41). Without a viable labor force, many *encomenderos* abandoned the region.

Through the process of abrupt colonization and subsequent abandonment of this part of the Amazon, the Spanish managed to convert an area that had included quite populated regions and been strongly connected through political, economic, social, and cultural ties to the Andes into a sparsely populated and isolated zone (Taylor 1994, 23–26; Uzendoski 2004).

The reduction in the indigenous population contributed to what is typically understood as an "ethnocidal simplification" of the Amazon's rich ethnic diversity (Muratorio 1991, 42; see also Hudelson 1981; Reeve 1985; Uzendoski 2004, 338). Kichwa became the mother tongue for many of the few indigenous people who survived in what are now the provinces of Napo, Orellana, and the western half of Pastaza.

The second of Taylor's phases (1640–1760) was characterized by the longer and less rapid development of a vast missionary front, spreading out from the few colonial posts that had survived from the previous period. The Archidona mission, established in 1660, provided the Jesuits with a base between Quito and an important mission in Maynas, in what is now Peru. White and mestizo settlement decreased between the seventeenth and eighteenth centuries, and the region remained poor and vulnerable to attack by non-Christianized indigenous groups. By 1725 Archidona and Ávila were considered Indian towns (*pueblos indios*), as nearly all the *encomenderos* had left the region.

The third phase (1770–1840) was characterized by the accentuated downfall of colonial establishments. Ecuadorian independence, gained in 1830, had little effect on the region. Rather, there was a continued decline in the non-indigenous population, dropping by two-thirds between 1768 and 1850. The indigenous population was able to recover some of its numbers and reclaim some of its previously controlled territory during this time (Oberem 1980; Taylor 1994).

Despite the low numbers of whites, exploitation continued in various forms in the period immediately after independence. Governors in the Ecuadorian Amazon earned relatively low salaries, which in Archidona they supplemented considerably with forced apportionments of goods to the Indians.[1] Moreover, officials in Archidona and other towns pressed Indians into service projects for the municipality, such as building and maintaining roads (Oberem 1980, 113). Administrative control was enforced through an imposed leadership structure known as *varayuj*, in which indigenous authorities called *varas* (staff holders) were selected from among powerful members in each extended patrilineal family. The *varas* were required to mobilize family members and friends to complete work projects, or face time in prison (Muratorio 1991, 80–81).

As in previous periods, the indigenous residents of the region took advantage of the relative inaccessibility of the forest, escaping into it when exploitation became too severe. Many maintained secondary homes and gardens in the forest and returned to the area near Archidona only after three or four months, when they needed manufactured goods such as matches, machetes, and salt. Kichwa also sought assistance from central state agencies when they deemed the policies of local officials and missionaries to be too harsh. For example, in a document dated June 13, 1846, the Indian authorities of Archidona and the area adjacent to the Napo River sent a complaint to the minister of the interior, reporting a long list of abuses and humiliations to which they were subjected by the local political chiefs. They demanded that the government take steps to put an end to these abuses, threatening to otherwise "abandon our villages and seek safe asylum in the remotest sites of our vast and mountainous province" (quoted in Muratorio 1991, 75). The central government took their complaints seriously, and after five months, the National Congress exempted Amazonian Indians from the "personal contribution," one of the tributes collected by the governor's office (Muratorio 1991, 75).

Taylor's fourth phase (1850–1900) was one of rapid increase in trade in various products from the region. The Jesuits increased their efforts to convert indigenous people (who still engaged in a fair amount of hunting and gathering) into a European-style peasantry. They required the Indians to work frequently on constructing public works (Muratorio 1991, 124), thus discouraging their trips to forest dwellings of three to four months that were common prior to this period. The Jesuits also introduced cattle ranching into indigenous productive practices. One mission chronicler, Lorenzo López San Vicente, justified these efforts in the following way: "[The mission is] preparing a solid basis for the formation of community property and providing an allurement for the Indians so that they might be reduced to village life" (quoted in Muratorio 1991, 81). During this period, the populations of the mission villages of Archidona and Tena remained moderate, consisting of about 1,000 people in the former and 500 in the latter (Jouanen 1977, 95).

A boom in the global rubber trade peaked in 1890, greatly influencing the Amazon and inspiring exploitation that far surpassed previous levels. In the Upper Napo region, rubber trees were relatively rare and of inferior quality, so the impact of the boom was smaller there than in other regions. Still, there was a slave trade associated with the boom, and an unknown number of people were forcefully relocated to areas of higher rubber concentration, including the Peruvian Amazon (Little 2001, 48–50; Muratorio 1991, 106–9).

In sum, during the two and a half centuries between 1660 and 1900, the Upper Napo Kichwa faced exploitation, disease, and many other difficulties, but most were able to spend part of their lives living in the forest, far from missionaries and state representatives. Due to difficulties in finding their way through the forest, whites were often unable to access the forest products they desired, including gold (panned from the rivers) and agave fiber. They could obtain these products only by allowing the indigenous people to take extended trips away from mission and government centers. Furthermore, some Kichwa used their trips between Archidona and Quito as porters to gain familiarity with government offices, and they were occasionally able to use this familiarity to lessen the exploitation they faced.

The Early Twentieth Century

The 1894 Special Law for the Oriente provided for the settlement of "vacant lands" (*terrenos baldíos*) in the Amazon region, but generally settlers were interested only in the lands surrounding towns.[2] As long as the Kichwa population could still find forested areas for hunting and clearing for their swidden gardens, there were no serious conflicts over land. The settlers took up cattle ranching or produced cash crops, the most important of which were cotton, coffee, rice, and sugar cane. Hacienda (large farm) owners gained access to Indians' labor by encouraging them to purchase items on credit — shotguns, cooking pots, cloth, and axes — at severely inflated prices, then forcing them to work to pay off their debts. Account books were regularly doctored by hacienda owners to maintain high levels of indebtedness and thereby ensure a constant labor supply (Muratorio 1991).

A new group of Catholic missionaries, the Josephines, established a presence in Archidona in 1922. According to Muratorio (1991, 164), they worked to integrate indigenous people into the national economy, in part by establishing boarding schools and providing training in mechanics, carpentry, and other crafts. Even with these intensified efforts, however, many Kichwa in the Upper Napo region engaged only intermittently with missionaries, traders, and civil authorities. In between these periods of engagement, they still spent significant portions of their time in the forest. To support this intermittent engagement, many families maintained two or more homes — one near Archidona and one in the forest — and moved back and forth between them. After some months of working for private ranchers, civil authorities, or the Josephine Mission, or even in the banana plantations on the Ecuadorian coast, most Kichwa would travel to their forest homes, where they would spend months at a time hunting, fishing, and growing food for personal consumption (Macdonald 1979, 1999).

An excellent sense of how much life changed during the twentieth century was provided by Manila Catalina Alvarado, who was born in 1910. In 2000, at the age of ninety, she spoke at length to me about her life and the changes in land use and social relations among Kichwa during her lifetime:

> When I was small, we lived in Nukunu [a region within the current Rukullakta boundaries]. My father died after traveling to Lago Agrio. My mother took us to Ahuano [on the Napo River — see map 1.1], where her parents had some land. We fished and grew manioc and plantain. There we had a lot of problems with disease, so we returned to Nukunu. A man asked for my hand in marriage there, and I went to Yawari [also within Rukullakta's current boundaries]. At that time, it was the custom to go where the husbands lived. I did not want to get married yet.

Here, Alvarado addresses issues of property, which was controlled through patrilineal groups. Because Alvarado's father had died, her mother felt the need to return to the region where her own father lived so that she could create gardens and feed her children. Problems with disease forced Alvarado's mother to subsequently return to her deceased husband's lands. Then an offer of marriage gave the family an opportunity to have greater claims to garden land in the region. Alvarado continued:

> We grew *chirimuya*, pineapples, beans, manioc, plantains, *machituna*, grapes, *wabas*, *apiu*, *pasu*, peanuts, and rice.[3] We didn't eat the rice; that was for selling to the *mishus* [white people]. We used the money to buy axes, clothes, blankets, machetes, and salt. My husband and sons traveled to the coast to work [on plantations] and brought us aluminum pots, which were sold there. Before that, we had to make the pots, and we cried when they would break! It was so much work to get the clay. I taught my daughters to do everything, to weave *shikras* [flexible net bags made out of natural fibers]. The men would make the baskets. We made fans out of feathers to fan the fire, beds out of *wadua* trunks.

As Alvarado's reflections indicate, by mid-century, Kichwa living near Archidona were increasingly engaged in the market economy. They earned wages through temporary work in plantations on the coast and sold rice for cash to purchase products that were difficult or impossible to make themselves. However, they also continued to value the ability to live on items that could be found in the forest. According to several informants, coastal plantation owners would send representatives to Archidona to seek workers in mid-century, promising high wages and other benefits. The Josephine missionaries encouraged young men to go, saying that they could earn money to either pay off their debts or to hold an impressive wedding ceremony.

Alvarado also described the work that she, her husband, and children conducted on a more regular basis:

> We left at 5 or 5:30 in the morning to work in the garden, until 11. We brought leaves, firewood, manioc, plantain. When it rained, we would not go. The husbands would cut down the trees for the gardens. Before, we made many gardens, and there was a lot to cut down — big trees. The men went to hunt, and the boys went with them. The small children helped in the gardens, and the big ones helped to cut down the trees. We put hot pepper in their eyes when they did not want to help, or hit them with *hortiga* [a branch that stings the skin]. We would go fishing with *barbasku* [a natural poison], but now there are no fish. We used to make large traps for fish. Now, we only grow manioc, plantain, and peach palm in the gardens; the earth does not give for anything else.
>
> Before, there was only one house in Yawari. The whole Shiguango family lived together. My father-in-law had four sons, and his brother had three [who all lived in the same house with their wives and children].

In these remarks, Alvarado reflects on how much the region close to Archidona had changed during the twentieth century. There was insufficient space in the area surrounding Archidona for families to properly fallow their gardens, reducing soil fertility ("the earth does not give"). This was in part because the population had grown significantly but also because families were spending more time in their homes located close to the mission rather than in their forest homes. In her final remarks, Alvarado continued to discuss the changes that had occurred during the twentieth century, in large part because of the efforts of the Josephine missionaries:

My parents were already Catholic. Those who did not want to be Catholics went further into the forest. They were the *aucas* [savages]. When my mother lived, the missionaries were travelers [only visiting the region every few months]. Later they came here to live. They would call us to pray, and we would go to Archidona to celebrate the mass, receive the word. The missionaries built schools, the priests and nuns taught. Women also could become catechists and would go house to house, even to the distant communities.

Alvarado highlights how the increased presence of missionaries started to affect the way Kichwa in the Upper Napo saw themselves and others. Those who chose not to live close to the mission were increasingly classified by those who did as "savages," indicating that the missionaries were partially successful in promoting their own value systems to those who lived nearby.

Land Reform

Agrarian reform began in the 1950s in response to the 1956 publication of the first national agricultural census, which revealed that Ecuador had one of the most imbalanced distributions of land in Latin America. In 1957 the Instituto Nacional de Colonización (the National Colonization Institute) was formed to support communities organized as agricultural cooperatives. Most cooperatives formed in subsequent years did not receive the support they needed and disbanded. The 1959 Cuban Revolution stimulated international concern for more active agrarian reform, as it was believed that inequality in land distribution in Latin America might fuel other Marxist movements (M. Becker 2008, 137). In 1961, led by the United States, the Organization of American States created the Alliance for Progress, a program that, among other things, sought to reduce material inequities in South America, increase per capita income, and promote democracy. In addition, leftist movements in Ecuador were muted by a conservative military coup in July 1963. The 1964 Agrarian Reform and Colonization Law thus favored capitalistic modes of production, attempting to abolish the *huasipungo* system that existed in highland Ecuador, under which large landowners gave agricultural workers a small plot of land in exchange for laboring on the hacienda and providing domestic service in the landowner's household. The 1964 reform also encouraged poor highlanders to colonize the less densely populated Amazonian lowland region. Furthermore, the reform outlawed land invasions and excluded from its benefits anyone who seized land violently or clandestinely (M. Becker 2008, 137–38).

At first glance, it might seem that these provisions were beneficial to lowland Kichwa, as they should have protected indigenous family territories from takeover. But Amazonian Kichwa did not hold legal title to their lands, and the ways in which they established claims to property were not recognized by non-Kichwa. The government continued its interest in the formation of cooperatives, which it believed would reduce the number of individual titles that would need to be issued, maximize the reach of both agricultural extension and loan programs, and increase the equity of land holdings. One pamphlet from the Center for Economic Conversion of Azuay, Cañar, and Morona Santiago (CREA), an agency that was promoting cooperativism in the southern Ecuadorian Amazon, makes the following appeal:

> *Campesino!* Your current situation is this: you live in complete neglect; you lack land and bread for your children; you cannot give them a good education; you do not have sources of work; you earn insignificant daily wages; you depend on *patrones* who exploit you; in sum, you lack all the necessary things to carry on a humane and dignified life. This is why you walk in poverty, frustrated and with nothing to do. CREA can offer you the necessary assistance to solve all the problems that today have you drowning in misery. Observe these photos of persons in the same situation as you, overwhelmed with necessities. But today their luck has changed, thanks to Cooperativism: they possess lands, sustenance, a home, a school, medicines, and credit. . . . You will not be alone or abandoned. Your new community will be a family where all will be thoroughly united. (Quoted in Salazar 1989, 110)

State-funded promotion of cooperatives was also happening in the Upper Napo region. Some indigenous families applied for individual titles to their land, although these titles were often quickly purchased by homesteaders from other parts of the country (Muratorio 1991).

Early Efforts to Organize

With the increased colonization of the region by people from the Ecuadorian highlands, some Kichwa became increasingly nervous about land availability, particularly those who had spent some time in banana plantations on the Ecuadorian coast. There, they had been exposed to the rhetoric of communist organizers who rallied against foreign ownership of Ecuadorian lands and in favor of peasant-owned cooperatives. These Kichwa saw a need to form collective organizations to inform their people about the potential consequences of selling so much land to non-indigenous colonists. Carlos Alvarado was one of these men. He wrote the following in a short, unpublished memoir about early organizing activities in the region:

> Back in 1965, if I am not mistaken, the truth is that I visited the zonal chief of IERAC [Instituto Ecuatoriano de Reforma Agraria y Colonización, the Ecuadorian Institute of Agrarian Reform and Colonization], Engineer Italo Moreno, to explain the land problems that were occurring daily in the zones of Rukullakta, Purutuyaku, Lusian, etc. [these are all areas that are currently within Rukullakta's borders]. The engineer very kindly granted me a document that said, "The zonal headquarters of IERAC extends this document to Mr. Carlos Alvarado, so that he will collaborate with the institute in controlling the purchase and sale of indigenous lands in the zone of Rukullakta, Purutuyaku, Lushian, and others, which are being conducted without the authorization of this headquarters, and which will be punished according to the law.
>
> From that time forward, I contacted the *compañeros* whom I knew the best and who lived closest to the above mentioned areas, in order to encourage them and stop the sale and marketing of their traditional homelands or properties. At first it seemed like [my ideas] were being accepted. . . . [but] when it comes to lands, there are always people in favor and people opposed. This is to say, the very *compañeros* and native brothers expressed the opinion that we are the owners of this land, we can sell it to whomever [we choose]; we want to exchange it for cattle. So those [colonists] who were interested took advantage, advertising that they had cattle for whatever negotiation or could settle any debt that our *compañeros* had. . . . Many friends left, heading to Lago Agrio, Orellana, and other places in the province. (Alvarado n.d., 1)

In this passage, it is notable that Alvarado approached a state agency for assistance in slowing the sales and that the official he spoke to seemed amenable to helping him. This was not a case of a state wanting to drive away indigenous people so that colonists could engage in more modern forms of agriculture. Instead, the state wanted to change indigenous people by integrating them more into the national economy (see also Whitten 1976, 268). It is also clear that at least some Kichwa did not interpret the increasing presence of colonists in the region as a problem, but rather saw it as an opportunity to get out of debt or to become more prosperous by selling their land for cattle. As Alvarado indicated in his memoir and also conveyed to me during a lengthy interview, he perceived the biggest hurdle in stopping the takeover of indigenous lands to be convincing fellow indigenous people that they should refuse to sell their land to others, and that they should join with other Kichwa to form organizations to apply for a collective title.

The Josephine Mission had also begun to worry about the displacement of the local population, which it had been working to shape for so many years. According to Venancio Alvarado (Carlos Alvarado's brother), in 1966 the missionaries encouraged about a dozen Kichwa men to form a regional chapter of CEDOC.[4] The mission's participation in the formation of this group was part of its attempts to further integrate Kichwa into the national economy, to protect their rights to land against takeover and purchase by colonists, and to extend its missionary influence (Perreault 2000, 140).

Early in 1968 Josephine missionaries selected two indigenous men to attend a leadership course sponsored by CEDOC in the highland city of Ambato. One of these men, Jorge Aguinda, attended the first half but then asked a friend to replace him for the second half.[5] That friend was Juan Shiguango, a carpenter, musician, and informal counselor, well respected by many of the Kichwa people in and around Archidona. For several years, Shiguango had been meeting with other aspiring indigenous leaders, in the hope of creating an organization to protect Kichwa land from the recent wave of colonization.

When Shiguango returned from the training course, he had "a different vision, a different ideology, a different energy for forming an organization."[6] His vision involved forming a cooperative, whose members would work together on agricultural projects to improve the lives of all. He spoke of how Shuar Indians (located in a more southern Amazonian province in Ecuador) had already formed a federation to pursue land claims, but that Kichwa should form a cooperative and thereby gain legal recognition of their claim to their lands.[7] He and other leaders began to speak more seriously to their friends and acquaintances about the potential benefits of forming a cooperative.

Thirty-two attendees of local courses offered by CEDOC joined Juan Shiguango and formed Prodefensa, an indigenous organization that was un-affiliated with the mission or any other organization and whose primary aim was to prevent the takeover of Kichwa lands by colonists. Venancio Alvarado, a member of this group, commented that its meetings "were very good, be-cause they fed our understanding, because we were not organized, no? That does not mean that we did not know—we had [extended] family groups that cooperated. What was lacking was to be legally formed, organized like a cooperative, with statutes and regulations" (interview, March 16, 2000). From the beginning, then, these organizations saw themselves not only as groups that could prevent outsiders from taking over indigenous lands, but also as creators of the "statutes and regulations" necessary to govern the ac-tivities of organizational members, thereby creating strong political entities that could continue to defend and pursue indigenous interests. The forma-tion of Prodefensa was also considered important to participants because, unlike the chapter of CEDOC, it was not associated with the Josephine Mis-sion. According to Venancio Alvarado, participants in the CEDOC group felt that the missionaries were primarily interested in using it to evangelize, not to empower the participants. But the participants wanted to focus on learn-ing about what sorts of organizations they would need to form, including what "statutes and regulations" they would need to adopt, to meet the state's requirements for obtaining secure title to land. They felt that missionaries' agenda of encouraging a more market-oriented, agriculturalist way of life was detracting from the primary goal of learning about state programs and using them to defend land claims. Prodefensa existed for only a few months, but several of its members went on to establish cooperatives and other peas-ant organizations. Of particular importance was the formation of the Fed-eración Provincial de Organizaciones Campesinas de Napo (the Provincial Federation of Napo Peasant Organizations, or FEPOCAN) by leaders from seven Kichwa regions, including Rukullakta, in June 1969. The group did not seek to acquire titles to land for its own use but saw itself as an educa-tional organization, spreading information and advice to Kichwa people on how to form organizations to gain legal titles to land (this is why its leaders were often simultaneously involved in organizations that were working to gain titles). It later grew into the largest indigenous rights organization in the province.[8] In August 1969 the newly elected president of FEPOCAN was sent by the International Solidarity Institute, part of the Konrad Adenauer Foundation of the German Christian Democrat Party (which supported farmer organizations and cooperatives throughout Latin America), to participate in a workshop on agricultural cooperatives and rural development (Perreault 2000, 143).

On December 14, 1970, some of the former members of Prodefensa convened the first mass meeting to form a cooperative in the Rukullakta region. Carlos Alvarado was an assistant catechist at the time, and he used his visits to widely dispersed Kichwa homes not only to encourage families to become more involved in the Catholic Church, but also to talk about the importance of getting organized. In the brief memoir he shared with me, he recounted the following:

> I traveled around continuously, announcing the possible concentration of people interested in becoming involved, and indicating [that we would meet in] Juan Shiguango's house, may he rest in peace. Furthermore, I indicated that one Saturday in Rukullakta, I would use the clear call of the conch shell, beginning in Rukullakta until the last corner of this sector. All the households would know what they should do. That's the way we did it one Saturday—you could even hear the drums from far away. I remember that [two] *compañeros* . . . arrived, blowing on a conch shell, and passed by my house—I was still sleeping. They told me that they had left at three in the morning, [coming] all the way from Nukunu. That day, we met with more than 150 *compañeros*, including men and women . . . [and] managed to get together the majority of our brothers and sisters. At that first meeting, we had no way to direct the session, because not one of us was prepared to lead that type of assembly. However, with the help of the *compañeros* . . . we led [the meeting] in order to motivate and explain the problems of the region, especially of land. All the participants understood the urgent necessity to organize an association. (Alvarado n.d., 1)

The difficulty of organizing a mass meeting becomes clear in the details that Alvarado gives. People lived far apart and had multiple residences. Early meetings were probably planned for the Christmas season because most families tended to spend holiday periods in the homes they had that were relatively close to Archidona (as opposed to their forest homes), so they could participate in mission-sponsored holiday rituals and festivities. Even so, many of these relatively close residences were a few hours' walk from the designated meeting spot. Alvarado was particularly interested in bringing together a group of people who held claims to connected areas of land to create a continuous area of land for the cooperative. Well-recognized methods of bringing people together, such as the blowing of a conch shell and the playing of drums, facilitated organizers' efforts. Still, Alvarado was clearly stunned at the first meeting's high turnout.

As this history shows, the idea of forming a cooperative emerged through an assemblage of the objectives, knowledges, and techniques of a diverse set of state agencies, international organizations, and local individuals. The Josephine Mission's participation in sending local people to cooperative formation classes was part of its attempt to protect its missionary influence and to further integrate Kichwa into capitalist markets. The German Christian Democrat Party and US Alliance for Progress were interested in promoting agricultural cooperatives and rural development to ensure peace and prevent communist revolutions. The Ecuadorian state was interested in modernizing its rural areas to reduce dependency on imports, increase popular support for the military junta, and reduce the inequities in land distribution after the country had been cited as one of the worst cases of inequity in Latin America. Last, but not least, some local indigenous people saw the opportunities being offered by the state as a path toward obtaining land security and, as will be further described below, improving the quality of life of those who participated in collective economic endeavors.

Constructing Community

Importantly, the legal category of cooperative that all of these actors were promoting required certain changes in indigenous lives. A significant portion of the land for which they sought title needed to be designated as collectively held land, and leaders needed to be elected to represent the larger group (Pallares 2002, 42–47).[9] For Upper Napo Kichwa, both the election of representative leaders and the concept of sharing title to land with dozens or even hundreds of other families were sharp departures from previous understandings of the household as a relatively autonomous political unit that actively claimed and defended access to particular territories.

Given these departures, it is not surprising that many Kichwa did not want to participate in the state's plans to give farmers' organizations title to lands. These Kichwa were happy to sell their partially cultivated lands near the new roads to highland migrants in exchange for cattle, which they then took to their second, more distant homes to raise and breed. Carlos Alvarado was one early leader who clearly saw the differences between the ways in which most Kichwa preferred to live and the plans promoted by the state and mission. He had attended public school all the way through high school (highly unusual for indigenous people at the time) and, as mentioned above, became an assistant catechist for the Josephine Mission. He thus knew the values of the various groups that were competing with Kichwa for land. The time he had spent working in coastal banana plantations and his exposure to communist organizers contributed to his seeing the cooperative model as a viable way to protect the land, but he knew that Upper Napo Kichwa were not accustomed to participating in large organizations and collaborating with people outside of their patrilineal kin group over the long term. He knew that the next step was to create an "us" that extended beyond people's kinship group to include multiple Kichwa families, so that a significant group of people and a significant area of land could be amassed in an application to the state to form a cooperative. This was not an easy task.

Benedict Anderson (1983), impressed by the power of the shared sense of community that exists among citizens of the same nation, traces the origins of nationalistic sentiment in Europe to the fifteenth century. Prior to that time, most people felt no attachment to their nation or to other people who lived in their nation beyond those with whom they interacted. They also had little notion of what was occurring beyond the immediate area around their village. With the invention of the printing press and the subsequent growth in printed materials available in vernacular languages (as opposed to Latin, which could be read by only a small percentage of the population), people began to feel a sense of what Anderson calls an "imagined community" with the hundreds of thousands who shared their language and national borders. Anderson uses the term "imagined" because individuals will never know most of the members of their group, yet they believe that they share something with the other members because of their shared nationality. Extending this idea, not only nations but any community beyond the size of groups interacting face to face may be considered imagined (Veber 2007, 81). Anderson uses the word "community" because people feel a sense of equality with others in the group, although differences in economic status may be profound. In the North American colonies that later became the United States, he argues, the printing press permitted the publication of perspectives that pitted Americans ("us") against the colonial British authorities ("them") and helped propel revolutionary fervor.

In the Upper Napo region, in contrast, most Kichwa were illiterate, and printed materials therefore had little importance in bringing people together.[10] It took years of inspirational speeches and door-to-door campaigning by the early leaders to build a sense of community among the members of multiple patrilineal descent groups that placed a strong value on family-centered autonomy and self-sufficiency. As noted above, Carlos Alvarado used his visits to people's houses as an assistant catechist to talk about the need to form a collective organization and apply for title to the land.

A different type of cultural production also built a sense of common history and common experience that is comparable to the effect that newspapers and other printed materials had in Europe and the North American colonies: traveling performance groups that specifically aimed to build pride in Kichwa culture and to ridicule the various groups that attempted to exploit Indians. In particular, there was a group called the Yumbus Chawamankus, made up of artists who went on to join the Rukullakta Cooperative (including Carlos Alvarado; see figure 1.1). It first performed in 1969 — the very year that FEPOCAN began and in the midst of Alvarado's efforts to build interest in forming a cooperative — and subsequently became very successful, performing across the country and even internationally.[11] The group performed songs and dances that celebrated the epic stories of indigenous heroes, including caricatures of non-indigenous people such as hacienda owners, soldiers, and authorities charged with collecting tribute or organizing public works projects (Bebbington et al. 1992). The performances also celebrated the everyday aspects of Kichwa culture, interspersing songs with scenes that depicted net fishing and manioc cultivation, as well as important ritual acts such as a man asking a woman's parents for her hand in marriage.

In the early twentieth century, public dancing was a shameful experience for many Kichwa in the region. Even today, many older people still remember how the missionaries would force them to dance at their wedding celebrations for the benefit of the missionaries and other local dignitaries, and how this was a very degrading experience for them. The Yumbus Chawamankus helped change the meaning associated with dancing and built a sense of pride in being Kichwa. One outsider's analysis of the role of the Yumbus Chawamankus in the region asserts that "the musical group . . . quickly converted itself into an irreplaceable part of the Congresses and Assemblies of the Napo [indigenous] organizations. In this way, a Kichwa identity consolidated itself in the north Amazonian valleys and on the banks of the Napo [River], from Misahuallí to Nueva Rocafuerte. In very little time, its pres-

FIGURE 1.1 The Yumbus Chawamankus perform during the inauguration of the Juan Shiguango Medical Dispensary, February 12, 1975. Carlos Alvarado is the performer in the center, facing the camera. Photographer unknown.

ence was recognized in the Amazonian region, and its music was quickly part of the meetings, festivities, and rituals, including those held by organizations representing other ethnic groups" (Bebbington et al. 1992, 83). The group's performances thus helped build a sense of "imagined community" across a wide area. They also added strength to the calls being made by Juan Shiguango, Carlos Alvarado, and others to form territorial organizations to prevent the takeover and purchase of indigenous lands by non-indigenous people.

As in the much larger groups described by Anderson, socioeconomic difference was an obstacle to building community. Although the differences that existed within the Kichwa community may seem minimal compared to those studied by Anderson, they were felt deeply at the local level. Some patrilineal groups claimed and defended large territories, while others felt they did not control enough land to meet even their basic nutritional needs. This perception of inequality becomes clear in one of Alvarado's speeches at the first organizational meeting of what later become the Saint Peter of Rukullakta Cooperative, also quoted below: "some have sufficient land and others have a parcel or small plot where they live, fighting among brothers" (*Actas*, December 14, 1970). Many other founding members of the organization described how shamans in particular, who were feared for their powers to make people and animals sick, were often able to gain control of large areas. Convincing these differentially situated families that they should bond together and combine their assets was neither simple nor straightforward.

The Josephine Mission unwittingly helped create a sense of common cause among some of those who went on to form the Rukullakta Cooperative. The mission began to expand its holdings during the same years that local leaders were promoting the formation of a cooperative, perhaps out of fear that the best pasture land would soon be claimed by colonists. In one instance, missionaries wanted to construct a road from Cotundo and claim all of the lands between Cotundo and Lupinu, some fifteen kilometers east of Cotundo (see map 1.1). These were the hunting and fishing grounds of many Kichwa families who went on to form Rukullakta, and the mission did not request permission from them or offer to purchase the land. As a group, fifteen affected heads-of-household approached the provincial IERAC office in Tena to complain about the mission's actions. Two representatives from the mission were also present. According to the analysis of one indigenous participant, because of the large number of Kichwa people who appeared, compared to the meager participation of missionaries, "we won!" (interview, March 25, 2000). IERAC directed the mission to stop the construction of the road. Through this experience, indigenous people were able to see that despite the rapid changes brought about by the agrarian reform, they could prevail by presenting a united front to state officials. Just as important, a sense of "us" grew among the families involved in the controversy with the missionaries, as well as among their neighbors and kin after hearing of the victory.

The first mass meeting of those who wanted to learn more about forming a cooperative is described in the Rukullakta archive (word capitalizations match the original):

> In the presence of Numerous participants, we discussed the land problems, where some have sufficient land and others have a parcel or small plot. . . . Upon realizing that all of this was small parcels, we proceeded to search for other ideas and new orientations. Then, one of the leaders said, let us form a Cooperative or a Pre-Cooperative, with the goal of searching for lands, where IERAC can intervene and grant them to all of the

Natives, especially us, since we are the owners of the land, but we have the right to make that known.

After a long debate, Mr. Carlos Pascual Alvarado Narváez and Juan V. Shiguango P. explained the ends of a cooperative, and how to organize a Union of Natives from this zone. (*Actas*, December 14, 1970)

In this passage, Alvarado and Shiguango's attempts to create a sense of community come through in a number of ways. Even though they admit that some Kichwa had "sufficient land," they quickly conclude that "all of this was small parcels," thereby creating a shared motive of needing to secure a large area of land. They also make the connection between being native and being the rightful owners of the land. Although the terms and slogans they used at early meetings — such as *compañeros* (companions) and "sólo unidos venceremos" (only united will we overcome), discussed in the preface — echo training courses on cooperative formation attended by early leaders as well as communist speeches those leaders might have heard while working on the Ecuadorian coast, there was no evidence that they felt a sense of solidarity with poor, non-Kichwa farmers, and the latter were not invited to join their organization. Rather, the leaders emphasized the importance of forming a "Union of Natives from this zone."

A Grand Vision for Empowerment

At the first meetings where the idea of a cooperative was presented, held in late 1970 and early 1971, some of the Kichwa men who had attended cooperative-formation courses put forth an alternative vision for the future, demonstrating how expectations of development accompanied the process of pursuing collective title. They spoke not only about applying for a collective title to defend the land from colonists, but also about a dramatic type of land reform, with more equitable distribution of land compared to what existed at the time. Additionally, they envisioned large areas of land set aside for collective, commercial endeavors such as cattle ranching. Although those members who contributed their labor to collectivist agricultural projects would be paid a wage for each day they worked, the profits from the endeavor would go to the organization for social programs, particularly educational ones.

Both ideas involved very different understandings of personhood than those held by many participants in these early meetings. The people who held claim to the largest areas of land were often those who had never felt the need to travel to the coast or otherwise work for wages. The property they claimed was intimately connected to their sense of who they were, as well as to whom they were connected through relationships of exchange. People who did not have access to sufficient areas of land could approach those who did with gifts (material goods or labor) and ask permission to use part of the latter's lands, beginning a relationship of mutual obligation that might be further strengthened through creating kinship ties (usually through the selection of godparents for one's children). Dividing up the land equally irrespective of family and social histories of obligation, as implied by the cooperative model, was very different from this other system. Rather than having land access be a reflection of one's personal power — the ability to cultivate connections to others and to respect the work one's ancestors had invested in claiming and maintaining the land — in the new conception, one would be entitled to a specific plot of land (equal in size to the plots of other members) simply because one was a member in the organization, and access to that plot would be granted and guaranteed by a central cooperative government. Exchange relations of labor and access to land, under this new conception, would no longer be continually renegotiated among multiple people involved in dense networks established over the course of many years, but would be calculated in terms of the number of days worked for a boss, the territorial government.[12]

Because of the enormous implications of the leaders' plan for Kichwa sociality and understandings of property, it required a considerable amount of promotion and some use of vague terminology to gain sufficient support. For example, during the third meeting, held on January 2, 1971, leaders and other attendees spoke more specifically about the "land problem":

> It is impossible to request individual delineation of land holdings, since the majority of people do not have enough land to live amply, because everything is in small parcels. The assembly, with all in agreement, decided to solicit IERAC for topographical equipment for a general delineation, and that this area would be called a *traditional land-holding*, as in for the education of the children. . . .
>
> The ends that a cooperative has include completing works for the social benefit. . . . One person alone cannot easily succeed, but if we work collectively we will have more work and more [agricultural] credit. There-

after, we will try to obtain bank loans to buy cattle and also to obtain collective land title, because in that way we will have fewer problems in paying for the [property] delineation. For those who do not have enough land, we will provide it in another place, but only if he is a member of this organization. (*Actas*, January 2, 1971; emphasis in original)

In this meeting, owners of larger areas of land were placated by the decision to call the collective land title a "traditional land-holding," contributing to their expectation that they would maintain claim to their lands once the cooperative was legally approved and the land title granted. However, that phrase was followed by "as in for the education of the children," which was not explained but carried some implication that the organization would have a say over how the land was used. Speeches given by meeting organizers strongly indicated that they did not expect that larger landholders would maintain their disproportionately large claims. The organizers repeatedly insisted that the priority must be "working for the social benefit" and promised additional lands to those who did not have enough, without actually specifying where these parcels would be located.

Seeing Like a State, but Not Exactly Like the Ecuadorian State

In a connected aspect of their broader improvement schemes, both the state and local leaders promoted the creation of multifunctioning community centers. The state expected to see community centers with school buildings, health clinics, and other public spaces to increase state influence in cooperative members' lives (through greater participation in formal schooling and public health campaigns, for example). Planned colonization schemes sponsored by the government in other areas of the Amazon during this time always included a service center around which colonists' homes were constructed (Uquillas 1984, 274).

Rukullakta's leaders believed that the creation of bigger and better public spaces would be an enticement to members to live and garden closer to one another, facilitating the organization of meetings and work activities. Juan Shiguango, the vice president, offered his land for the construction of the populated center. If the attendees at the January 2, 1971, meeting had agreed to this vision, it would have entailed constructing homes for the 180 extended families represented at that gathering in an area that at the time only included one home. It would have represented an enormous change in the way people lived, one that mirrored what the Catholic missionaries had been unsuccessfully promoting for centuries with their attempts to build *reducciones*.

Political scientists often postulate that the modern state has a fundamentally different way of understanding space, property, and land than the people who live in a particular area. For example, James Scott argues in *Seeing Like a State* (1998) that modernist state planners have a particular way of "seeing" that standardizes complex landscapes. Planners view land in the abstract, simplifying and generalizing both land use and land tenure regimes and thereby facilitating the pursuit of ideologically driven improvement schemes. In contrast, Scott argues, the people who live in areas targeted by state planners do not see their homelands abstractly; rather, they engage in complex, locally specific social practices associated with unique histories, community dynamics, and ecological settings. They have *mētis*, or contextualized, situated knowledge that has grown in particular locales over time and that is therefore uniquely appropriate to those places (273–80). Similarly, Henri Lefebvre (1991) contrasts the "spaces of representation," or the conceptualized, abstract spaces of social engineers and planners, to the "representational spaces" of users, which have their source in history and embody complex symbolisms.[13]

The early leaders of Rukullakta learned quickly to "see like states," but not all aspects of their vision matched those being promoted by the state or development groups that were involved in facilitating their organization's formation. They therefore became state-like without becoming simple extensions of the state. Unlike the missionaries and state officials who promoted nucleated settlements, the indigenous leaders had a profound understanding of the changes such a village would require. These leaders were completely willing to ignore centuries of widespread resistance to the village model as well as the predictable reluctance by large landowners to give up their holdings to be redistributed among all members. It could thus be argued that the leaders were engaging in even more of an abstraction of property and landscape realties than the state planners themselves, as the latter were largely ignorant of the way Kichwa participants were accustomed to living and using the land (Erazo 2011).

Although the attendees appeared to agree at first to move to Shiguango's property, protests by those who did not want to all settle in one place soon created a compromise position. Five day schools run by the Josephine Mission and built between 1963 and 1970 were already spread around the area just northeast of Archidona, and there seemed to be little incentive for the large number of interested families to live clustered together on Shiguango's land. Instead, it was decided to create regional subcenters surrounding the schools and to elect leaders from each subcenter, in a nested structure of representation (*Actas*, January 2, 1971). Those participants who claimed the lands near the schools agreed to have part of their lands used for the purpose of constructing community centers. Community histories written in the late 1990s still recognized the sacrifice made by these individuals, revealing that the close connection between particular kinship groups (as represented by their heads of household) and particular areas of land still remains strong in residents' understandings of the landscape. In terms of governance, representatives from each subcenter would meet with elected central leaders to discuss policies affecting the territory's population.

The resistance of attendees to living in a large, concentrated settlement was at least partially based on long-standing ideas about other people and the dangers of living too close to one another. Most Kichwa believed that diseases in people, animals, and plants were caused by the ill will or jealousy of others, particularly those who were not part of one's household. Thus, most felt it was best not to live too close to too many people for extended periods of time, since frequent contact could incite envy and malicious acts. Other problems associated with living in concentrated spaces included overused soils and reduced populations of wild game in the area surrounding the settlement. Thus, meeting participants replaced the rather drastic plan proposed by early leaders of having all households live on Shiguango's land with a plan that aligned more closely to their own landscape ideology. In particular, the new scheme followed their preference for having more space between households, or at least between hamlets.

The aerial photograph in figure 1.2 shows an early stage of what cooperative leaders called "urbanization" in one of the five subcenters in 1973. It includes a few homes (with their separate buildings for cooking behind them), a sports field, and a school. Figures 1.3 and 1.4 show the administrative hub of the cooperative (also called Rukullakta) nine years later, with a larger number of houses, pilot projects, public recreational areas, and administrative buildings. The 1982 landscape illustrates that the early leaders had succeeded in convincing numerous families both to construct homes in close proximity to one another, and to create public spaces that supported

FIGURE 1.2 Purutuyaku Subcenter, 1973. Black-and-white aerial photo, Instituto Geographico Militar, Quito.

the community-building aims of the cooperative. The small, equitably sized plots for households show that, at least within the small zones designated as community centers, leaders were successful in getting residents to think of land in terms of equal distribution, with individuals possessing a right to land associated with their citizenship in the cooperative and without the inequities that characterized previous land tenure regimes.

The leaders also hoped to turn all of the hunting and fishing territories located beyond the area occupied by the subcenters into collectively owned and managed land, calling it latifundio (large property) and planning to use earnings from it to fund social programs. In other cooperatives that were designed and tightly controlled by the state, a large portion of the land was also designated as communal property, and individual possession was restricted to ten hectares per colonist (Uquillas 1984, 274). The fact that Rukullakta's plan also included a large area for collective management must have been impressive to IERAC and undoubtedly contributed to the large title the agency granted Rukullakta. However, it was also part of the early leaders' deeply held social ideology, in which collective engagement in the economy would help empower Kichwa by enabling them to work collectively on many different projects.

FIGURE 1.3 Rukullakta Subcenter, administrative center of the cooperative, 1982. Infrared aerial photo, Instituto Geographico Militar, Quito.

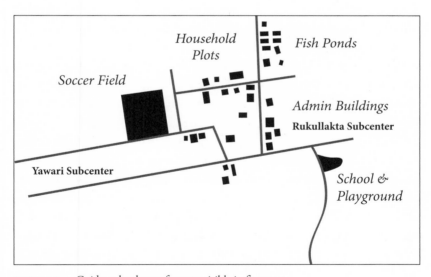

FIGURE 1.4 Guide to landscape features visible in figure 1.3.

Lectures given by leaders in the early meetings also show that they had quickly moved into the role of land use planners, imagining the vast holdings of meeting attendees as divided into zones based on such practical concerns as placing the civic center within reasonable proximity to the mission town, planned roads, and government offices; and the appropriateness of the eastern lands for a large cattle ranch in terms of topography and hydrology. Forming the organization, keeping track of over two hundred interested members, collecting contributions to help with the costs of applying for the land title, and creating a work regime for cattle ranching also involved leaders' taking on state-like responsibilities and ways of seeing. Leaders were not the only ones involved in this process; prospective members were also forced to imagine what life might be like if they adopted the changes in residence and work patterns that the leaders proposed.

Under the new scheme, members scheduled to work at the Lupinu ranch would live there temporarily and coordinate their work efforts with other members assigned to work there at the same time. As with other aspects of the vision, this would represent a dramatic shift from previous residence and work habits, which were based on the patrilineal household. However, this aspect of the grand plan also fit within the larger social and spatial ideology to which the leaders were committed. They made bringing people into more regular contact with one another a high priority, in the hope of increasing unity among them. The leaders were confident that the shared earnings of the new collective enterprise and the social programs sponsored by the cooperative would improve relations among members, rather than increase tensions among them.

In sum, the early leaders' social ideology included an emphasis on collectivist labor and living patterns as well as more equal distribution of work and benefits, inspired in part by communist discourses to which they had been exposed. It also included a commitment to some of the aspects of modernization promoted by the state, including both involvement in cattle ranching and other market-oriented activities, efforts to "urbanize" subcenters with public buildings and infrastructural conveniences, and promotion of state or mission-subsidized services such as school attendance and the use of Western medicine.

Yet leaders' ideology and associated landscapes were not simply products of communist and state influences. Instead, the leaders had their own notions of improvement, inspired by their own particular vision of empowerment. For example, part of the idea behind collective cattle ranching was that members could take turns caring for cattle, working on a very part-time basis in intensive spurts (approximately two weeks every three to four months). This would allow them to continue to engage in other activities such as extended trips to visit relatives, hunting trips, or short-term wage labor outside the cooperative. Leaders thus did not intend for members to engage in the daily, market-oriented activities that the state imagined for the beneficiaries of its modernization programs. In contrast, mestizo colonists on state-created cooperatives were expected to spend half of their daily working hours caring for collectively owned cattle (Hiraoka and Yamamoto 1980, 436). Kichwa in the Upper Napo region were already accustomed to alternating between periods of working for others, and periods in their forest homes, where they could hunt, fish, garden, and gather forest products. The leaders' notion of empowerment respected the long-defended right to spend these periods of time in the forest. However, they wanted the financial benefits that would normally accrue to the white hacienda owner, government official, or missionary to stay within the organization, funding social programs such as literacy classes and improved health care.

Some of the most profound changes entailed by the leaders' vision of empowerment, however, were not discussed openly at the early meetings about cooperative formation. First, by agreeing to this territorial organization and applying for a state-recognized, collective land title, members were locking themselves into a governance unit that went far beyond the limits of their own households. Even the *varas* system of forced labor, instituted first by the Jesuits and later by local government officials, operated through existing kinship structures and therefore respected existing social relationships and patterns of exchange. The cooperative structure being promoted by the early leaders, in contrast, involved long-term collaboration among various kinship groups and therefore did not allow the flexibility in negotiating social obligations to which Kichwa were accustomed. In this part of the Upper Napo region, it was common for several nuclear families from the same patriline to share residences and hunting territories, but the membership of households shifted over time. For example, Alonso Andi, a resident of Tena, describes living patterns during the first half of the twentieth century in the following way: "My father lived with all of his children in one house; we were a large household. In each corner of the house there was a *caitu* (bed) and in the center a large hearth. This is how we all lived together. . . . When the brothers and brothers-in-law [sharing a house] began to have children, they usually had fights, and then each one began to build his own house and they separated" (quoted in Muratorio 1991, 55). Andi's description shows how the memberships of family groups with claims to land were often inconsistent and flexible over time. Tensions would arise, causing some family members to move to another location, while new alliances would form through marriage or *compadrazgo* (ritual kinship). There was a loose affiliation with one's broader, patrilineal kinship group (including all descendants of a particular apical pair), known locally as a *muntún* (Whitten 1985, 91–92). Households would engage in exchanges with other households within their *muntún* and with people who were connected to them through marriage or *compadrazgo*. As with the constitution of the household, tensions could emerge within reciprocal exchange relationships and cause them to break down. Thus, the notion of a long-standing, bounded "community," even within a patrilineal descent line, did not describe the social obligations or living patterns as experienced by the people of this region as of the mid-twentieth century, prior to the institution of permanent land titles (MacDonald 1999, 12–15). Even recently, Michael Uzendoski has argued that the people in the Upper Napo community where he conducted research in the early 2000s "were not operating according to social principles of bounded groups; rather, they saw social life as fluid and relational, defined by pragmatic activities, concrete practices, and exchange" (2005, 12). Thus, forming a bounded group of people to live within a bounded territory in Rukullakta required developing a very new sense of loyalty and identity.

Second, as indicated above, the people attending the early meetings were left wondering if ceding their claims to land to the cooperative organization was something that was being done for the short term to please state officials, or whether they were permanently giving up the right to pass land from father to sons, and sons to grandsons. Beyond issues of heredity, if large landowners no longer had the ability to grant the right to use their land to people of their choosing, they were losing one of the most important ways in which they could build social ties. Leaders remained vague on the less attractive implications of becoming members of the new organization, needing to bring together people with claims to contiguous parcels of land.

Finally, the election of leaders — individuals whom one may not even know, much less trust, depending on the results of the election — who then had power to make decisions over land use and livelihoods was something with which Kichwa had little to no experience. Dividing up the year into two-week segments to ensure there were sufficient members traveling to the ranch and checking that work was evenly distributed required a substantial amount of planning and follow-up work on the part of the central leaders. It also entailed a separation between the monitors and the monitored, since leaders were in charge of keeping track of who was contributing sufficiently and who was not. In the past, powerful indigenous men within kinship groups were seen as intermediaries between their kin and the various groups that wanted to exploit their labor. Now, elected indigenous leaders — who might not be related or respected as an elder member of one's family — were no longer intermediaries between the group and the state, but rather those who demanded labor. If instituted as central leaders imagined, these changes would entail the creation of a new class of individuals within Kichwa society, individuals who were in a position to govern the territory's citizens.

Conclusion

Centuries of contact with missionaries, merchants, and colonial and government representatives provided Upper Napo Kichwa with experiences and knowledge that allowed at least some of them to successfully envision how to negotiate the dramatic changes in national policy in the 1960s and 1970s. One of these lessons was that state agencies could be allies in indigenous struggles, when approached in the right way. A second key lesson was the importance of access to forest lands for avoiding the worst forms of exploitation by outsiders. With this knowledge and with additional knowledge obtained through experiences working on the Ecuadorian coast, training provided by leftist organizations, and state agency outreach, some individuals were able to identify cooperative formation as a path toward gaining legal title to a significant area of land. Thus, contrary to beliefs held by many visitors to the area, the region's oldest indigenous organizations did not emerge simply in opposition to the state (although a change in state policy was a large part of the motivation), but rather through engaging with opportunities provided by the state.

Likewise, the communally held areas of land still managed by indigenous territorial organizations do not reflect age-old practices of sharing land — although that is indeed the case with other indigenous communities in other parts of the globe — but rather resulted from the particular way in which the state attempted to bring indigenous peoples under greater state control in the late 1960s and early 1970s. The state saw the formation of cooperatives as a path toward modernization of the Amazon region and as a way to increase the area's contributions to the national economy. A small group of men in the Upper Napo region were able to strategically identify these state and international visions of progress in the early 1970s and to present their organizations as well positioned to fulfill those visions. They were able to link a local vision of empowerment — in particular, the importance of maintaining Kichwa access to land — to national and international visions of landscape and social improvement, in which farmers lived in neat villages and cooperatively managed large pastures and livestock herds.

But identifying this potential solution to the loss of indigenous lands to settlers was only the first step in an extended process of creating the organization. Leaders had to overcome suspicions that they were just planning to steal members' monetary contributions and cattle earnings for their own profit, as well as tensions that existed among holders of neighboring properties. They did this through tireless campaigning and through the arts, particularly traveling performance groups that celebrated Kichwa culture and mocked the behavior of those who had historically exploited them. Once the leaders had started to establish a sense of "us" versus "them," they outlined a dramatic scheme for obtaining a large area of land. The scheme would involve changes in the social, political, and economic lives of the organization's members. Even at the beginning, members altered the vision to one that better suited the way they wanted to live. Some of the more profound implications of joining a collective, land-holding organization that included 207 households did not become clear, however, until the following years and decades. These included shifts in understanding of personhood, identity, subjectivity, property, the economy, and nature.

The next four chapters will look at each of the four interrelated issues of the territory's economy, property regimes, land use planning, and leader-citizen relationships in more detail. They will also trace the decades following the legalization of the cooperative and its land title to assess how members and leaders negotiated the unintended consequences and obligations associated with forming this new territorial organization.

CHAPTER TWO

COLLECTIVIST UTOPIAS AND "THE GRAVEYARD OF DEVELOPMENT PROJECTS"

An imposing statue greets visitors to the Napo provincial capital of Tena, about twelve kilometers south of Rukullakta. It portrays Jumandy, a muscular figure, spear in hand, poised for attack (figure 2.1). Jumandy is remembered as an indigenous hero who led a revolt against the Spanish in 1578, and he has become intimately connected in many people's minds with indigenous territory and sovereignty.

According to scholars, one of the most impressive aspects of Jumandy's rebellion was the scale of the organization involved. The rebellion included alliances among multiple linguistic groups living across a vast territory (Muratorio 1991, 40). Its initial leaders were the shamans Beto, from Archidona, and Guami, from Avila (see map 1.1). The shaman Imbate joined the effort, and the three sent for Jumandy and appointed him the general leader of the revolt. Beto's forces successfully sacked Archidona, Guami's did the same in Avila, and then they gathered together under Jumandy and set out for Baeza for the final assault. The Spanish were informed that they were coming, however, and crushed the resistance in Baeza (Uzendoski 2004).

In recent years, Jumandy has gained a more profound, mythic status. Students from the region write poems about

FIGURE 2.1 Statue of Jumandy in Tena, Ecuador. Photo courtesy of Michael Uzendoski.

him and often connect him to more recent uprisings. For example, one Kichwa anthropology student recently argued that Jumandy's spirit of struggle "persists in each native and is transmitted from generation to generation" (quoted in Uzendoski 2005, 150). In a recent documentary about Rukullakta titled *The Children of Jumandi*, then-kuraka Nelson Chimbo describes the hero's story in the following way: "Jumandi was one of the leaders, one of the kurakas, who was extremely mad because . . . well, he accepted up to a point the Spanish conquest. But what happened when he began to become aware of the abuses by the Spanish, abuses against our women, more than anything our young women . . . ? Jumandi rebelled. One day he said, 'No! Until now we have resisted, but we won't take any more!' He began to look for indigenous independence from the Spanish yoke" (Bennett and Diller 2009).

Jumandy's current importance is not only based on his resistance to Spanish oppression, however. He also has become a metaphor for the deep conviction held by some indigenous leaders that working together can bring empowerment. Those who train aspiring indigenous leaders in sites such as the Indigenous University of the Ecuadorian Amazon encourage them to strive to be like Jumandy, able to rally a large number of constituents to make very real personal sacrifices. They see a continuing need for indigenous people to collaborate on political and economic projects to improve their welfare. Part of the need for ongoing collaboration stems from what Richard Stahler-Sholk calls "autonomy without resources" (2010, 37). In other words, many social services that one might think fall within the purview of the Ecuadorian government, the Napo provincial government, or the Archidona municipal government are, due to neoliberal reforms, now left in the hands of Rukullakta's territorial government, which depends in turn on the voluntary labor of its citizens to get things done. If parents of Rukullakta's schoolchildren want plants near the school cut back so that their children will not be bitten by snakes hiding in the weeds, they must do it themselves. If they want repairs made or extensions built to schools with growing student populations, they may be able to obtain concrete blocks or zinc roofing sheets from a local politician or federal ministry, but they must do the actual building themselves. The same is true if they want two-feet-deep potholes in the territory's dirt roads filled in so that buses and taxis are willing to enter the territory. In contrast, those who live in the nearby town of Archidona are not required to donate their labor to maintain their roads or build their schools. Indigenous people living in territories and other very rural areas are expected to organize themselves to perform collective, voluntary labor on basic infrastructure projects in their communities, while other Ecuadorians generally are not. Rather than criticize this imbalance, many indigenous leaders have taken it as an opportunity to prove their own leadership skills. They hold Jumandy up as a role model — someone who was able to organize a large number of people to make sacrifices for the collective good.

As the previous chapter explained, historically most Amazonian Kichwa have tried to avoid subjecting themselves to political hierarchies beyond the extended family. These preferences are similar to those of other indigenous Amazonian groups (Brown 1993; Lauer 2006; Rubenstein 2007; Vickers 1989). In his survey of the Amazonian literature, Michael Brown found that "in the heat of millenarian enthusiasm, Amazonian peoples have sometimes experimented with the institutionalization of political hierarchy. . . . But under ordinary circumstances, an excessive taste for power in an Amazonian leader is likely to elicit ridicule, indifference, or evasive non-compliance from fellow tribesmen" (1993, 310). Yet the formation of the cooperative, engagement in collective cattle ranching, and subsequent joint efforts have been predicated on having reasonably strong and steady leadership. As this chapter will demonstrate, this has required a substantial amount of persuasion, and some leaders have been more successful than others at organizing their constituents.

Given that most members joined the cooperative organization in the early 1970s chiefly because that was an inexpensive way to gain legal title to land, it is perhaps not surprising that attendance at cooperative meetings and participation in collective work projects dwindled once the official title was close to being finalized. Leaders then fought to maintain members' interest in their vision of empowerment — which included working on cooperative, market-oriented projects under their management — by seeking development projects from a wide variety of sources. They hoped that by providing material incentives, they could hold off a return to the household focus and associated autonomy so valued by most of the members. For a few years, their strategy succeeded. They managed to obtain hundreds of thousands of dollars in development assistance (mostly loans, not grants), far more than other indigenous land-holding organizations in the region. In the mid-1970s, the state was eager to help peasant organizations that seemed dedicated to its modernizing mission, and Rukullakta's elected leaders convinced important officials that they shared the state's vision for progress.

Because cooperative leaders were able to position themselves as the ones who had "won" the projects for their members, they became intimately associated with those projects. They used their heightened legitimacy to create new "governable spaces" (Rose 1999, 31–34), or realms of governance, particularly in health and education. Strengthened cooperative leaders were, in turn, convenient for state officials, who hoped to increase agricultural production in the Amazonian region, further integrating it into the national economy. It was much easier for state agencies to collaborate with a few leaders than to work with each household individually.

Thus, in the very brief period from 1969 to 1975, cooperative leaders went from being marginalized residents of the forest, dreaming of ways to prevent the loss of their lands to colonists, to the managers of a 41,888.5-hectare area of land (roughly the size of Barbados), multiple large development projects, and state-funded public programs. Because many of the development projects were financed through loans, Rukullakta's residents were very quickly transformed from a loosely connected group of extended families with abutting claims to land into a collective economic entity with a large amount of debt to manage. Just as leaders took the job of building a sense of shared Kichwa identity very seriously in the early years (as described in chapter 1), they also began to take the job of managing the territory's collective economy very seriously, viewing themselves as uniquely poised to improve the welfare of their kin and neighbors. They imagined ways in which to divide the work among members, devised accounting systems for recording how many hours each person worked, provided reports to the state colonization agency, and negotiated transactions with the state development bank. The Ecuadorian state was a critical force in the way that this emerging, miniature state took shape, but local leaders managed to receive much of the credit (and criticism) for the dramatic changes occurring in landscapes and livelihoods.

Compare the trajectory of the territorial government to Fernando Coronil's analysis of the consolidation of state power in Venezuela:

> Throughout the nineteenth century the fragile Venezuelan state, chronically assaulted by regional *caudillos* [bosses], was unable to impose its control over the fragmented national territory. It was only when it was transformed into a mediator between the nation and the foreign oil companies in the early twentieth century that the state acquired the political capacity and financial resources that enabled it to appear as an independent agent, capable of imposing its dominion over society. (1997, 4)

Although operating on a much smaller scale, cooperative leaders similarly kept the territorial government viable by making it seem "magical," by "manufacturing dazzling development projects that engender[ed] collective fantasies of progress" (Coronil 1997, 5). As in Venezuela, state funding supported unprecedented infrastructural and agricultural projects in the mid-1970s. Leaders enjoyed heightened legitimacy when they could bring new community centers, bridges, and cattle to the cooperative's members. The political structure of Kichwa society, previously based on relatively small kinship groups organized around strong male elders, began to shift as a state-sanctioned organization that included thousands of individuals revolved around a few elected male leaders. As the territorial government became engaged in projects that required contributions of labor and collective debt, it gained a life of its own, and each resident had to negotiate his or her relationship to this political body.

During this period of heightened collective activity, the practice of the *minga* also began to change. *Mingas* historically were alternating reciprocal labor exchanges that occurred between families joined by marriage or *compadrazgo* (Uzendoski 2004, 340). For example, if a family wanted to build a new house, they would call on friends and members of their extended family to help them, rewarding them with food and drink and the promise of reciprocity in the future. *Mingas* thus served to reaffirm and strengthen social ties, or to weaken them when assistance was withheld or judged to be half-hearted. The meaning of *mingas* changed, however, with the formation of the cooperative, when participation in most *mingas* went from being a practice that reaffirmed one's desire to continue in a reciprocal relationship with family and friends to an obligation attached to one's membership in a communal land management organization. Today, the term most often refers to collective work days, when members are called to work together to improve a school or a road, for example. Imposing fines on those who did not comply became yet another task for Rukullakta's emerging bureaucracy.

Although it was the state that required performing *mingas* as one of the obligations of living in a cooperative, most members did not see *mingas* as an imposition from the state, especially since state agencies did not monitor compliance in any systematic way. Rather, members associated *mingas* with their own leaders. As long as members could see concrete improvements in their lives — a new school for their children, a new bridge or road that facilitated access to gardens and hunting grounds, or a new community hall for organizing social events, for example — they participated in large numbers. However, when funding for these projects dried up in the 1980s, and it became clear that those who had participated in caring for cattle owned by the cooperative would not be paid for their work, most members rejected the vision of collaborating on such a large scale and returned to the more familiar and intimate smaller collaborative groups. It became clear that the state-like vision of a large, economically collaborating group involved changes in social obligations that were too dramatic for most people. Furthermore, when funding from the state and international development organizations dwindled, members blamed their leaders, charging them with both incompetence and corruption, which made collaboration even more difficult.[1]

There have been important legacies of the 1970s age of collectivism. As has been the case for improvement schemes that colonial, NGO, and multi-lateral bank projects have pursued in other parts of the world, the market-oriented collaboration pursued in the cooperative's early years "left traces on livelihoods, landscapes, and ways of thinking" (Li 2007, 228). The first legacy has been in the set of expectations most indigenous people in the Upper Napo region have of their elected leaders, chiefly expectations that they will attract development projects. The second legacy concerns a prefer-ence for collaborating with smaller rather than larger groups, due to some of the negative experiences people had in the late 1970s. The final section of this chapter will document how collective, market-oriented endeavors in-volving smaller groups emerged and multiplied in subsequent decades, dem-onstrating that collectivism among non-kin was not completely rejected by those who lived through the early cooperative years.

"Pura Minga"

Founding members of the cooperative remember the early days as "pura minga" (nothing but collective work days), indicating that leaders made many, many requests for members to contribute their labor to organiza-tional activities. Leaders called on members to collectively clear trees from a three-meter-wide path around the lengthy border of the cooperative in preparation for filing their land claim. Opening the path around the lands in 1973 required three months of hard work. According to those who par-ticipated, the aspiring cooperative members were expected to carry enough food for themselves and the government topographers. They had to cross wide rivers with their supplies and use machetes and axes to clear trees and other vegetation from the boundary they were creating. Maria Inés Shi-guango, one of only three women considered to be among the 207 founding members of the cooperative (she was a widow and therefore considered head of her household), told me that it broke her heart to send her young sons out to help with the delineation, but that she had no choice because all families had to send representatives. She said her sons "could barely walk with all the food and equipment they had to carry, and they had to travel so far" (inter-view, June 23, 2000).

Then, after the delineation was complete, leaders continued to ask people to donate their labor toward projects that would impress state officials and therefore hopefully speed up the granting of the official land title, particularly clearing forest and planting pasture grass (*Paspalum fasciculatum*) for the collective cattle ranch. The accounting system demonstrates the early leaders' desire to document the activities of Rukullakta's members, as well as members' desires to be paid once earnings were realized. Each member's name and subcenter is documented for each period of work, with Xs for each full day and slashes for each half day. Not all members contributed equally (or even at all) to the ranching activities, and those who did expected to be compensated for the number of days they had worked once the cattle were sold, a few years later. Cooperative leaders took on the role of creating the documentation system, but they never attempted to estimate or budget how much they would have to earn from ranching to cover the cost of labor. Rather, they appealed to outside organizations for salary funds and complained that the "gringos"[2] did not want to pay the ranchers for hours worked (*Actas*, October 1974 and December 14, 1974). At the October 1974 meeting, José "Bartolo" Shiguango, then president of the cooperative proclaimed: "But since I have gold, I want to pay the workers, even if only for half, to compensate for their work." His promise is not mentioned again in subsequent entries, and several informants claimed that they were never paid.

Table 2.1 summarizes the data in the collective's record book and documents the amount of time that members invested both before any cattle arrived, and once they did, starting in March 1974. Fluctuations in both the number of people who journeyed to the collective pasture and the number of days that they stayed there indicate how difficult it was to implement this new work regime and to coordinate the activities of over 200 members. Between November 1, 1974 (when the cooperative was legally recognized), and May 1975, for example, five months passed with no one working on the fields, mending fences, or moving cattle to better areas of pasture. This period of inactivity in the cattle fields coincided with the months following President José "Bartolo" Shiguango's announcement that the organization would not be able to pay those who had worked on the ranch the amount promised in October 1974.

Beyond the issue of payment, there were additional problems with the expectation that all members should contribute equally. Members had different demands on their time (some worked in salaried positions, for example), different family structures (some families could send a teenage son to replace an adult), and different stakes in the success or failure of the entire coopera-

TABLE 2.1 WORK RECORDS FOR THE COLLECTIVE RANCHES

MONTH	NUMBER OF PEOPLE WHO WORKED	AVERAGE DAYS WORKED	TOTAL WORK DAYS
Sep 1972	31	8.45	262
Oct–Nov 1972	0	0	0
Dec 1972	67	7.58	508
Jan 1973	76	5.80	441
Feb–Mar 1973	0	0	0
Apr 1973	23	11.39	262
May–Sep 1973	0	0	0
Oct 1973	57	10.82	617
Nov 1973	67	9.01	603.5
Dec 1973	25	6.62	165.5
Jan 1974	55	8.37	460.5
Feb 1974	0	0	0
Mar 1974	17	8.00	136
Apr 1974	34	3.93	133.5
May 1974	8	3.38	27
Jun 1974	0	0	0
Jul 1974	9	3.00	27
Aug 1974	24	6.38	153
Sep 1974	0	0	0
Oct 1974	63	4.63	292
Nov 1974	16	9.13	146
Dec 1974–Apr 1975	0	0	0
May 1975	57	8.22	468.5
Jun 1975	72	10.34	744.5
Jul 1975	5	5.80	29
Aug 1975	41	10.94	448.5
Sep 1975	0	0	0
Oct 1975	20	13.30	266
Nov 1975	32	4.06	130
Dec 1975–Feb 1976	0	0	0
Mar 1976	7	6.86	48
Apr 1976	26	5.81	151
May–Jun 1976	0	0	0
Jul 1976	41	11.83	485

Compiled from the cooperative's "Cuaderno de Trabajos" (Work record book).
Note: The first cattle arrived in March 1974.

tive project. The idea of equal contributions also presumed that all two-week periods were equal despite variations during the year due to weather, the school calendar, and festivals.

After an initial period of appealing to the membership as a whole (as indicated by the mixture of subcenters listed in the work record book during the early months), the leadership moved to a new system in 1975. Elected presidents from each subcenter of the cooperative were expected to attend executive meetings, divide up responsibility for the collective ranch (with each subcenter responsible for a two-week or one-month period, depending on the number of residents), and then convince their relatives and neighbors to make the trip out to the ranch and work.

This system resembled the *varas* system that had been implemented by the Jesuits and municipal authorities in previous generations, using existing relationships of reciprocity as a conduit for making workers feel an obligation to participate. However, even with this seemingly more workable system, both subcenter presidents and members were inconsistent in their compliance.

There were also other signs of resistance to and disillusionment with leaders' collective labor projects and landscape vision during the early years. Thirty-two members of the Pre-Cooperative had temporarily donated one head of cattle each to begin the cooperative's ranching activities. These members, however, grew angry at the lack of coordination and withdrew their cattle between April and August of 1975. Secondly, the five subcenters began to split within just a few weeks after the legalization of the cooperative in November 1974, doubling from five to ten by mid-1975. In retrospect, members gave two reasons for these divisions: the long distances between the houses in the original subcenters made organizing work and meetings overly burdensome, and the elected representatives were insufficiently representing the interests of all their constituents.

Map 2.1 shows subcenter locations in the cooperative as of August 1977. The subcenters remained primarily within the southwestern area bounded by the Jondachi and Hollín Rivers, with only one (Istandi) in the area north of the Jondachi River. This indicates that tensions among subcenter residents (or between residents and their elected leaders) may have been the primary motivational force for subcenter division in most cases, rather than the inconveniences created by distance. For example, when members of Awkayaku (located between numbers 3 and 4 on the map) abandoned their origi-

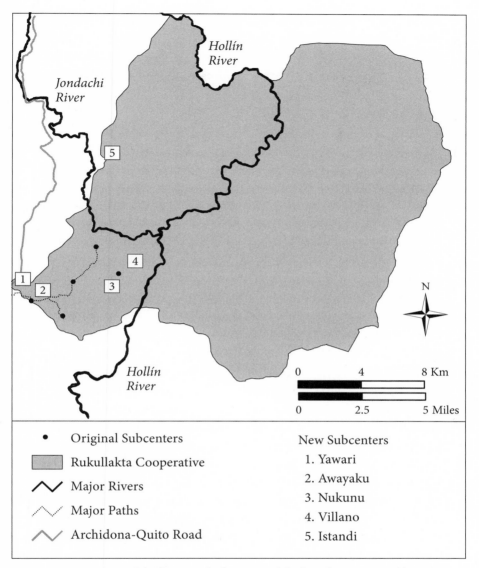

Hollín River

Jondachi River

5

Hollín River

N

| 0 | 4 | 8 Km |

| 0 | 2.5 | 5 Miles |

- Original Subcenters
  Rukullakta Cooperative
  Major Rivers
  Major Paths
  Archidona-Quito Road

New Subcenters
1. Yawari
2. Awayaku
3. Nukunu
4. Villano
5. Istandi

MAP 2.1 Locations of the five original subcenters and the five subcenters created between 1974 and 1975.

nal meeting place (the Awkayaku School) to form two separate subcenters (Nukunu and Villano), neither new subcenter was more than a kilometer from the original meeting site. This splitting reveals a departure from another important aspect of leaders' dramatic vision for change: members were not accustomed to being locked into collaborative relationships over the long term with a static group consisting of a large number of individuals. Just as kinship groups sharing a household would periodically divide in the past, subcenters began to divide as soon as the title legalization was complete.

These departures from the sweeping, modernist vision of the early leaders, occurring within the first few years of the cooperative's formation, reveal how even though leaders were state-like in their tendency to think about land and members abstractly, the organization they formed was not a state. It had no police or military to enforce the leaders' vision. The massive efforts made by members to achieving the vision leaders put forth in 1973 and 1974 quickly ebbed once the path along the cooperative's border was completed in 1973 and the organization achieved legal status in November 1974. By mid-1975, it became clear that leaders would need to do something more than give motivational speeches if they wanted members to continue to contribute to collective activities and feel obligations to the territorial government. This was despite the fact that the legal title to the collective territory was not final until December 15, 1977.

Funding Magic

Leaders recognized that access to state agencies' construction machinery and funds would greatly facilitate both their modernizing projects and their efforts to keep the organization viable, so they quickly sought ways to obtain them. An excellent opportunity arose in 1975, when the head of state under Ecuador's military dictatorship, General Guillermo Rodríguez-Lara, visited the Upper Napo region. The Yumbus Chawamankus performance group, led by the cooperative leader Carlos Alvarado, performed for the general. After the performance, Alvarado handed him a request for funds for infrastructure projects in the cooperative. In his brief history of the cooperative, Alvarado wrote: "The group prepared traditional Dances and presented them to the Chief of State and then handed him a request formulated by the Saint Peter [of Rukullakta] Cooperative, to the effect that this organization solicited and supported the creation of a Semi-directed Project. In that period, the luck of the organization was not lacking, and I think that just a few months passed before we learned that the . . . project was approved" (Alvarado n.d., 2; see also figure 1.1).

Alvarado's request was perfectly timed. The Ecuadorian state was funding a number of development projects for cooperatives in the Ecuadorian Amazon. In most cases, these projects were associated with colonization schemes, initially inspired by the state's desire to attract migrants from other parts of the country into the region, both to boost agricultural production there and to better secure national borders with Peru and Colombia. Planning for these projects began in the 1960s and the state colonization agency funded six projects in all. Most did not manage to attract the full number of colonists that the planners desired (Uquillas 1984, 261, 271). For example, the first project, Shushufindi, was initiated in 1972. It experienced great difficulties attracting settler families, despite both state investment in infrastructure and the fact that the area's soils were considered among the best in the Ecuadorian Amazon. Although planners envisioned settling eighty families in Shushufindi, only about thirty settled there (Uquillas 1984, 274–75). Rukullakta—with its eager leaders, membership of over two hundred families, and hundreds of hectares of recently created pasturelands—must have seemed like an ideal site to include in the program; it could greatly improve the program's perceived impact by increasing the number of families and cattle associated with it.

The project obtained by Rukullakta's leaders provided materials and technical assistance for schools, a small electrical plant, school gardens, roads, and hanging bridges over both the Hollín and the Jondachi Rivers, greatly facilitating access to the more distant areas of the cooperative. It also provided construction materials for two administrative buildings in Rukullakta, from where the project was managed; offered courses on accounting and leadership skills; and provided technical assistance on various cattle projects. Finally, state officials associated with the project helped cooperative leaders to sign agreements with the governor's office (*consejo provincial*) to obtain materials and machinery for various projects, with the Ecuadorian Institute for Social Services to get latrines for each house, and with the state-owned electric utility to have electrical lines installed in the Rukullakta Subcenter. As with the cattle projects, members provided the labor (although with no promise this time of future monetary compensation). In contrast to the cattle projects, they could see the fruits of their labor almost immediately, as a continuous stream of inauguration ceremonies marked the openings of new buildings, schools, and bridges. There was so much construction that subcenter presidents had a difficult time convincing people to give their time both to local subcenter projects and to taking care of the cattle, which compounded the difficulties leaders faced with organizing ranching responsibilities.

With the beginning of the semidirected project and its investments in concrete structures, roads, and other forms of what was called "urbanization," requests to form new subcenters and the division of existing ones halted completely for several years. Thus, it seems that these infrastructural projects provided a substantial boost to early leaders' efforts to keep the population within a limited number of subcenters. With fewer subcenters, central leaders could more easily attend subcenter-level meetings to request assistance in ranching or other collective activities and to remind members of what the leaders saw as the continuing value of the cooperative ideal.

Ironically, all of this activity occurred even before Rukullakta had gained legal title to any land. Given the cooperative leaders' effective wooing of the state and success in getting members to contribute their labor to multiple modernization projects, it is perhaps not surprising that the state was willing to give legal ownership of a much larger area of land to Rukullakta than what it awarded in most cases. According to several early leaders, at first, Pre-Cooperative members hoped to gain 10,000 hectares. However, once the leaders had completed their persuasive work, both convincing more and more people to add their hunting grounds to the group's holdings and convincing IERAC that they were worthy of a large piece of land, the total land titled amounted to 41,888.5 hectares (equivalent to 418.9 square kilometers, or 161.7 square miles). The title was finalized in December 1977, and represented a substantial achievement for the organization's 207 members and their families. Typically, IERAC was granting only 50 hectares per household for families that had migrated from the coast and highlands. Members of the Mondayaku Association (an indigenous association formed in 1975, just west of the cooperative) were granted the equivalent of 127 hectares per member, considered far above the norm for indigenous organizations (Perreault 2000, 89); Rukullakta members were granted even more — what amounted to 203 hectares per member. Rukullakta became the second largest cooperative, and the largest indigenous cooperative, in the country (interview, Gustavo Guerra, director, Desarollo y Autogestión [Development and Management of One's Own Affairs], January 20, 2000).

Beyond the expenditures of the semidirected project, the cooperative had its own funds to spend, gained as part of development projects and through members' small annual dues. The leaders' decisions about how to spend this money give insight into what their visions for empowerment and development were. For example, they opened a large store in 1973 that sold agricultural products and tools such as machetes and chainsaws, as well as nonperishable food, liquor, and cigarettes. Although the leadership voted at various times to invest money in inventory for the store, it never turned a profit. Some members purchased items on credit and were unable or unwilling to pay later; others simply took items from the store, saying that they had worked long hours for the good of the cooperative and deserved some compensation. Yet the store continued to operate, with some periods of closure, through the early 1980s. The leaders' continuing desire to invest in the store illustrates the importance they placed on having this symbol of organizational self-sufficiency and their strong belief that non-indigenous merchants had taken advantage of Kichwa for too long. Due to the regular influx of investment, the store remained impressive despite its financial troubles. A Shuar visitor to the area, Benito Bautista Nantipa, said that he remembers being extremely impressed when he visited Archidona in 1980 to find out that such a large store with such varied stock belonged to indigenous people (interview, May 11, 2000).

There were also several smaller, market-oriented projects during the mid- to late 1970s. The cooperative signed an agreement with Texaco in 1976 for the sale of plantains. In 1975 several members of the cooperative took out individual loans through the Fondo Ecuatoriano Populorum Progressio (Ecuadorian Populorum Progressio Fund), an NGO associated with the Catholic Church, to raise cattle and grow corn and rice, and leaders signed off as intermediaries in their loan agreements. With assistance from Peace Corps volunteers, a collectively managed fish farm was opened near Rukullakta in the late 1970s to produce tilapia, a quickly growing fish native to Africa. Several cooperative members established their own fish farm ponds based on the Peace Corps model. Another Peace Corps volunteer set up a biogas project (using methane from cattle for cooking); this particular project was not reproduced after his departure. Although the specific dates of each of these projects are not clear from the archives, all were in place by October 14, 1981, according to a work plan drafted that year ("Plan de Trabajos, San Pedro de Rucu-Llacta" 1981).

The most costly business investments that the cooperative's administration made included the following purchases: thirty horses to transport
ranchers to the Lupinu ranch, four outboard motors for a fishing initiative,
a refrigerator for the communal store, a billiard table for a communal pub,
a wood-chipping machine, and a Nissan pick-up truck (*Actas*, October 2,
1976; February 1, 1977; October 14, 1977; February 18, 1978; January 26,
1979; March 20, 1980). The latter was intended for the transport of both
leaders and members, and it was also used to transport students to school
for a small fare (*Actas*, March 23, 1979; August 3, 1979).

Members could not help but be astounded by all of the changes occurring around them. The cooperative seemed magical, capable of bringing
in previously unimaginable amounts of money and goods. Leaders' status
rose as the managers of these various projects. However, although members
loved the new gathering spaces and bridges, they did not always appreciate
the increased presence of state officials and other outsiders, who seemed to
be trying to control the actions of residents. According to one statement
in the *Actas*, "people who are not members of the cooperative visit almost
every day" (*Actas*, July 24, 1976). Complaints about the visitors started ap-
pearing in 1976, such as the following discussion, which occurred at an assembly meeting for all members: "Regarding the last point, questions were
asked about the Semi-directed Project [the multifaceted, state-funded development project described above]. Some felt almost squashed (*aplasta-
dos*) because having the IERAC officials was like having a boss (*patrón*) inside the cooperative. To this point the *compañero* [President] José Francisco
Shiguango explained that the Semi-directed [Project] is assistance from the
State" (*Actas*, March 6, 1976). Here, the president of the cooperative quickly
dismisses the expressed concern. The role of state agents is simultaneously
minimized; the presence of IERAC officials is simply to offer "assistance" to
a project that cooperative leaders were managing. The minutes do not document further dissent, indicating that the president's words were enough to
prevent a protracted discussion about the issue.

Social Movement Leaders Become Governors

Leaders expanded their reach by becoming increasingly involved in other
aspects of people's lives, particularly health and education. They formed
a chapter of the peasants' health insurance program (*seguro campesino*). It
began with 215 family heads as members, almost the same number (and

the same individuals) as had formed the cooperative. The first leaders of the chapter overlapped substantially with the first two administrations of the cooperative—José Francisco Shiguango was president of both, Carlos Alvarado was secretary of both, and Venancio Alvarado was a representative to the former and accounts manager of the latter.

The insurance program provided reduced-cost hospital care and prescription medicine to members, who formed local chapters and paid monthly dues. The local chapter in Rukullakta was officially inaugurated on February 12, 1975. In November of the same year, members completed building a medical dispensary, the construction of which was funded by both cooperative leaders and the Ecuadorian Institute of Social Security (Instituto Ecuatoriano de Seguridad Social). The cooperative leadership decided to name both the dispensary and the local chapter after the recently deceased leader Juan Shiguango. The leaders hoped that every time the cooperative's members got a vaccination or received subsidized health care, they would remember whose tireless efforts to organize had brought them these benefits and examine their own accomplishments in light of his.[3]

Soon thereafter, health promoters (*promotores de salud*) from the cooperative began attending capacity-building courses held by the Institute of Social Security, where they learned about Western medicinal and sanitation practices and were urged to encourage their neighbors to, among other things, boil their water, eat fruits and vegetables, and see a licensed doctor when they were sick. More important to the indigenous leaders than particular teachings, however, was the opportunity to demonstrate a concrete benefit of organizational participation, including the free training courses, vaccination programs, and subsidized medicines.

A speech given by Camilo Bolivar Tapuy, president of FEPOCAN, the Napo provincial indigenous rights organization, also reveals that Rukullakta was seen as an example that should be followed, particularly in terms of its level of organization:

> The *Seguro Campesino* is advantageous for this Commune—we have to take advantage of help provided by the central government, which is being given to organized groups. You members have to meet the obligations set by the statutes of the Commune, [specifically] a monthly payment of twenty *sucres* by each member. Let's not see our *compañeros* continuing to drink liquor, because with this we are losing our work, our

sacrifice, our sweat. In Napo Province, there is one organization that is opening doors for work, for culture, economy, and social programs; I am speaking of your cooperative. It is the first organization that is advancing in the path of communal life in work, and in the economy. (*Actas*, July 17, 1976)

The vision Tapuy promoted corresponded closely to that of elected cooperative leaders during the early years of the semi-directed project. Members were expected not only to participate eagerly in collective work projects and cooperative meetings, but also to financially support the ongoing functioning of the cooperative, FEPOCAN, and the peasant's health insurance program. If members wanted to benefit from training opportunities being offered by the state or loans mediated by the cooperative, they needed to demonstrate an ideological commitment to communal life and work (which could be demonstrated through sober participation in that life and work). The tone of Tapuy's speech also indicates that not all members were completely convinced of the rewards afforded by "communal life in work, and in the economy." Rather, leaders needed to regularly remind them of these benefits.

Like Tapuy, Jorge Aguinda, Rukullakta's fifth president, frequently gave speeches about his own notions of well-being, during his 1976–78 term. For example, he advised the following:

Children should become accustomed to consuming, little by little, from [the age of] one month on, juices and other products high in vitamins and proteins and other minerals so that they develop normally and do not have development problems in the future; so that they do not get sick, we should prevent disease rather than cure it, receive vaccinations rather than sorcery. Of course, it is worthwhile to take medicinal drinks, community medicine that is within our reach, which is to say, plant medicines. [But] now it is good that we have health promoters who are collaborators in all of the communities; you can come easily for a consultation and obtain medicines without going to the town pharmacy. (*Actas*, April 29, 1977)

In this speech, Aguinda is showing his allegiance to a philosophy of physical well-being taught in mission schools (which he, unlike most cooperative members, attended as a child). According to this perspective, poor health is caused by malnutrition, viruses, and bacterial infections, rather than the ill-will of and sorcery practiced by others.[4] He is using his respected position as president to encourage listeners to privilege the philosophy behind Western medicine over understandings of well-being associated with sorcery. Aguinda also worked to reduce alcoholic consumption, seeing it as a hindrance to economic progress. On July 24, 1976, he made the following speech: "One day in a meeting, [liquor sales] were prohibited. It was approved by the leaders that all types of liquor should disappear. After a few days all were in compliance. For the past few months, however, individually owned stores have been selling liquor without the authorization of the Cooperative. In the first place, they have made the Cooperative look bad, because drunks yell and sit around drinking [rather than working]. People who are not members of the Cooperative visit almost every day. . . . I put this on the table for your consideration" (*Actas*, July 24, 1976). His speech was apparently convincing (Aguinda is widely recognized as a powerful person and orator). The other elected leaders responded affirmatively:

At that moment several *compañero* leaders commented, saying that for a while they had been realizing that it is not a good thing to sell liquor. First off, when people are drunk they want to hit people, even those who aren't drunk. Furthermore, the same *compañeros* fight each other. Before, when there was not anyone selling booze, work was done better. Even the leaders at this table drink; when someone needs them, they find them drunk. For these reasons and to avoid all of these problems, it was agreed by both the Administrative Council and the Vigilance Council that there should be no more sales of alcohol [within the cooperative's borders]. (*Actas*, July 24, 1976)

These speeches and the numerous policies passed in the 1970s make it clear that Rukullakta's leaders thought of themselves as governors of a territory, able to set policies regarding economic activities that took place there and even to govern what people did during their free time by eliminating the liquor stores. Leaders also emphasized the importance of elementary schools and adult literacy programs. Through these programs, leaders hoped that cooperative members and their children would learn skills critical to engaging with non-Kichwa merchants and government officials, particularly the abilities to speak, read, and write in Spanish. Along with his speeches about nutrition and vaccination programs, Aguinda often made speeches about the value of sending children to school. For example, at one point during his presidency he said: "There needs to be more importance placed on the education of the children. The parents of school-aged children should send them to school so that they learn there, with time, how to be a responsible leader, educator, [and] collaborator" (*Actas*, April 29, 1977). Here, Aguinda is emphasizing education not so the young could go on to work in Ecuadorian cities, but so they could continue to defend and promote the interests of other Kichwa people at home. The path toward being able to do this, he indicated, was through participation in mission- or state-sponsored education.

Cooperative leaders also worked to have the Ministry of Education assign additional teachers to the area so that members could create new schools closer to where they lived, making it easier for parents to send their children to school.[5] The construction of schools closer to where families were living during at least part of the year had a dramatic influence on the number of children attending school (Erazo 2003). According to several interviewees, many parents were afraid to send their young children to Archidona to study. They worried that the missionaries would kidnap their children, or that adolescents who had learned Spanish would be forced to work for the mission or join the military. Once there were schools closer to people's homes and parents could see that their organizational leaders obtained local positions of prestige in part due to their schooling, parents felt more secure about having their children participate in formal education.

Due to the efforts of cooperative leaders and the willingness of members to contribute both building materials and the necessary labor, three new schools were added between 1975 and 1976 to the five that already existed (see figure 2.2). Carlos Alvarado, then serving as elected secretary to the cooperative, served as volunteer teacher in one of them until the Napo Office of the Ministry of Education agreed to pay a teacher to work there. If people could not move to the areas surrounding the original five schools, those schools could come to them.

In sum, leaders began to take the job of governing very seriously, becoming increasingly involved in trying to shape how cooperative residents treated their bodies and raised their children. The Ecuadorian state was a critical actor in determining which aspects of cooperative members' lives were being shaped, since it provided the funding for vaccination campaigns and schoolteachers, but it was not an overly visible one from the local perspective. Leaders managed to claim much of the credit for the dramatic

FIGURE 2.2 Awkayaku School and surrounding area, September 1973. Black-and-white aerial photo, Instituto Geográfico Militar, Quito.

changes occurring in landscapes and livelihoods. Members further associated these projects with leaders when they realized that not all organized groups in the region were as successful at obtaining state resources as their organization was. As in Coronil's (1997) portrayal of how Venezuelan leaders consolidated state rule by controlling foreign petroleum dollars, early leaders' apparent control over state money and resources enabled them to transform the lives of members and their own roles as leaders while they expanded the range of their rule.

Hard Times for Collectivism

Even with continuing funding from the state for the purchase of construction materials, it was difficult to maintain for more than a few years members' amazement at the modernization they saw. By early 1977, members had tired of going to centrally organized *mingas* (collective work days) and cooperative assembly meetings, a sentiment that grew stronger after the collective land title was finalized at the end of that year. Once the title was settled, there no longer seemed to be an immediate need to demonstrate collective spirit and cooperativism. For example, for over half a year in 1977, the leaders attempted to organize just one project — the construction of a meeting house in Archidona, which would also provide a temporary place for members to sleep when they were conducting official business there. In the end, the leaders decided to hire paid laborers to build the house because they could not get enough members to contribute their labor without pay.

Although cooperative leaders never saw voluntary activities as a full-time pursuit, they did have substantial expectations. According to the archives, they hoped that members would devote ninety days each year to collective activities, including both *mingas* and meetings (*Actas*, September 8, 1978). At the time the leaders came up with this figure, fewer than half of the members were even attending the semi-annual assembly meetings (*Actas*, June 28, 1978; February 20, 1979). By mid-1978, subcenter presidents were complaining regularly about how their members were not participating in collective labor responsibilities: "The *compañeros* members do not want to work on the *haciendas* that the subcenter Rukullakta has, and they are totally lost and they also do not want to attend the sessions. He [one subcenter president] said that for the last time he is going to have a session on Saturday to see what the members tell us" (*Actas*, November 3, 1978). As shown by this quote, once the land title was finalized in December 1977 and it was clear that no one was going to be paid for caring for the cattle, it became extremely difficult for leaders to motivate members to participate in collective activities.

The State Withdraws Support

Things became even worse in December 1978, when the infrastructure projects associated with the semi-directed project came to an abrupt halt through the restructuring of state institutions. According to Carlos Alvarado, "after 3 years of sacrifice and labor we had to say good-bye after there was a decree from the Military Government, creating the Instituto Nacional de Colonización de la Región Amazónica Ecuatoriana [National Institute of Colonization of the Ecuadorian Amazon Region, or INCRAE] ... [which assumed] control of the ... Project" (Alvarado n.d., 4). Cooperative leaders resisted the change, sending official letters requesting that IERAC remain in charge, but they watched in despair as the two trucks and the tractor that had been assisting them in their projects, particularly with road construction and subcenter urbanization, were driven back to Quito.

The new government employee who took over the project in early 1979 was never popular with cooperative members, who accused him of being lazy and staying locked up in his house with the social promoter for women's activities. During the three years in which this representative worked in the cooperative, he introduced only one new infrastructural project (an assembly hall that had not been completed as of 2012) and one new agricultural project, involving twenty water buffaloes, which arrived in July 1982. Members still remember the latter experience with both humor and frustration, as the animals were very difficult to control. Since there were so few animals, members decided to care for them near Purutu, a relatively densely populated residential area. The water buffaloes escaped from their pastures, destroyed gardens, and ate everything in their path, including some agrochemicals left out by a high-school student for use in an agronomy experiment. After only a few months, leaders decided to sell the animals and pay off the loan rather than suffer additional losses.

After the representative had spent three years "only sleeping," cooperative residents, primarily women, formed an ongoing picket line around his home until he agreed to leave and never return. Even though the INCRAE representative did not seem to be doing anyone any particular harm by being there (with the exception of the damage caused by the water buffaloes), the cooperative members preferred to publicly terminate the project, rather than have a situation in which someone was earning a salary from the state under the false pretense of assisting them with their activities.

Money Matters

The first payments for the cooperative's cattle loans came due in 1979, and leaders had an extremely difficult time meeting them. What happened to all of the projected earnings? The irregular care the collective's cattle received was only part of the picture, compounded by a general lack of familiarity with how to care for the animals. Starting in 1976, the cattle received on loan were from an improved variety bred in Panama, in the sense that they grew more quickly than those that had arrived on previous loans. However, the new animals required vaccines and supplements to grow properly. Although the *Actas* record various training courses held for leaders, particularly in accounting and management, there is little mention of training in ranching or in the identification of common bovine ailments. Ranchers' lack of familiarity with recommended vaccines and available treatments led to increased incidence of premature death and stillborn calves. Several founding members still talk about how the post-1976 cattle varieties did not "respect" (stay behind) the barbed wire fences the members made, often escaping into the surrounding jungle and turning into wild animals that could be stopped only with guns. Pasture grasses were also vulnerable to disease and blight (*Actas*, May 5, 1978).

It is unclear whether ranching could have produced profits even if Rukullakta's members had been more familiar with the industry. Nearby Archidona had a slaughterhouse and farmers' market, and it appears that sufficient local demand for beef existed. Another cattle project in neighboring Mondayacu also failed after a brief period of success, despite its greater proximity to a major road (Bebbington et al. 1992, 91–93). Although Shuar ranchers operating to the south of Rukullakta enjoyed substantial profits in the 1960s and 1970s prior to widespread problems with overused soils (Bebbington et al. 1992, 87; Salazar 1989, 603), mestizos and whites engaged in state-directed ranching projects to the north did not (Hiraoka and Yamamoto 1980, 436; Uquillas 1984, 276). Thus, Rukullakta members were not alone in their difficulties.

What can be discerned from the archives and from retrospective analyses by members is that, by deciding to take care of cattle east of the Hollín River, leaders subjected the animals to greater risk of snakebites and falls during transport and greatly limited their access to veterinary care. There is also evidence that some of the cattle never even made it to the cooperative, instead remaining with the intermediaries involved in loan transactions. The *Actas* record the following case: "The bank asked for a small favor — if we could give the bank one calf as a gift. This request was approved, and in this session was authorized" (*Actas*, February 18, 1978). In this passage, it is clear that bank employees were taking advantage of indigenous leaders' perception that the bank was doing them a favor by giving them the cattle loan and thus deserved reciprocal favors from them.

Many of the financial troubles also stemmed from the optimistic visions and decisions that leaders made during the early years. As mentioned above, they incurred large expenses in working toward their comprehensive vision by buying a truck and inventory for the store. They also spent money on increasing the land holdings of the cooperative. The collective land title the cooperative received was pockmarked by a few areas of private holdings owned by non-Kichwa colonists, purchased from Kichwa families before the social movement to form the cooperative had taken shape. As part of their efforts to consolidate the cooperative territory, leaders used members' annual dues (and possibly money from selling cattle) to purchase this land.[6] The *Actas* mention four land purchases (February 7, 1976; March 18, 1976;

February 25, 1978; January 12, 1979), one of which was of 340 hectares. A survey conducted in 2009 recorded Rukullakta's holdings as consisting of 44,836 hectares, up from the 41,888.5 hectares in the cooperative's original land title (Bennett and Sierra n.d.)

Furthermore, some members and subcenter leaders sold collectively owned cattle on their own when they needed access to money (*Actas*, October 25, 1975; June 5, 1976; October 6, 1978; November 3, 1978). This was not unlike the situation with the communal store, from which some members took items without paying, saying that they deserved compensation for the many hours of unpaid labor they had given to the cooperative. The practice of selling cattle without authorization began early, shortly after the first loans were made:

> The *compañero* President [of the cooperative] explained regarding the sale of cattle, that many times they have been sold without the permission of the subcenter president. To sell, it is always necessary to ask permission from the president of the subcenter to not have problems in the sale. Furthermore, there are other *compañeros* who have sold them alone [for their own profit], and this type of sale is like a robbery. Persons who sell alone in this way will be sanctioned by us with the authorities. . . . Furthermore, the President said, many animals have been sold young and skinny, for extremely low prices; it is better to fatten these animals and not lose them so cheaply. (*Actas*, October 25, 1975)

Three years after this 1975 warning, a few members were still selling cattle for their own profit, and they were singled out by name at council meetings. The *Actas* include this "report by the President of Kupa: He said that the [collective] work is going well. The cattle are well. There are 35 alive and 6 dead. . . . He then informed us that some *compañeros* are selling the cattle without informing you [the cooperative president], especially the *compañero* E . . . S . . . sold a cow and has spent the money badly (*el dinero ha malgastado*)" (*Actas*, October 6, 1978). As word spread of the few cases of flagrant infractions, so did cynicism concerning collective work and investment. A few leaders also took advantage of their positions to rob the organization, as was the case with the subcenter president of Lushianta. He was unable to attend one administrative council meeting and designated someone to go in his place. The latter took the opportunity to advise the rest of the administrative council of what had been occurring in the subcenter: "For the

Lushianta sector, acting representative V . . . N . . . informed [us] that we are not doing the [collective] work well because of the failures of the [sub-center] president, who is selling animals without the authorization of the members. It appears that the money is being used to pay for the car that [the president] has. As president, he has spent 43,000 *sucres* [almost US $2,000 at that time], having sold the subcenter's cattle — 6 cows and 8 calves" (*Actas*, July 22, 1978). Procedures for dealing with failures to pay debts to the co-operative or "illegally" selling cattle were not well established and were diffi-cult to enforce. Enforcement involved a new conception of personhood (in which the culprit was viewed in isolation from his or her many connections with other members of the cooperative) and a new conception of culpability (in which the infraction was viewed as temporally isolated, detached from longer histories of reciprocity and exchange). It also involved a new concep-tion of property, in which those who had helped raise the cattle held only an indirect claim to those animals because it was mediated through the central leadership (see Dunn 2004, 128). All of these changes were rejected by some members of Rukullakta when they blatantly broke the rules that leaders at-tempted to establish.

Compounding these difficulties was the fact that the cooperative had no jails or police power and had to rely on peer pressure and persuasion by those who remained committed to the idea of a new society associated with market-oriented collectivism. As one former president explained to me, sending a cooperative member to the jails run by the white establish-ment to try to get the member to pay his or her debts, as white employers did in the early and mid-twentieth century, was distasteful. It implied that the cooperative was incapable of governing its own members. Furthermore, sending a member to the jail in Archidona would only increase the finan-cial burdens experienced by the families of the accused individuals, as they would have to pay fines to the Archidona police as well as pay off the debts to the territorial government.

Smaller expenses included food for assembly meetings (including, peri-odically, the slaughtering of one of the cows bought with the loans) (*Actas*, February 7, 1976; May 15, 1976; June 24, 1986); providing assistance to mem-bers who were sick or who had lost their home in a fire (*Actas*, March 9, 1979); and donations to schools, literacy programs, and even the Red Cross. At one point, money lent to the cooperative for the cultivation of rice was diverted to cover the annual fee for the peasants' health insurance program, so that all cooperative members could continue to benefit from it (*Actas*, May 17, 1975). The cooperative also made individual loans to members and even to other communities located outside the territory, neither of which made consistent repayments. In 1978 the Administrative Board formed a credit committee to address the serious financial difficulties people caused when they received loans from the territorial government and failed to pay them back. However, this committee rarely met.

As long as funds existed to replace the store's inventory and to make new loans to those who requested them, repayment infractions could be downplayed by cooperative leaders, and the rhetoric of successful collaborative modernity could continue. Although leaders worried that the money would run out, the various attempts they made to come to an organizational solution (such as forming credit committees, searching for additional funds, and putting social pressure on those who owed them money or sold cattle without permission) failed to completely solve the problem.

The accumulation of several investments that did not produce income for the cooperative created a situation in which there were no more funds for leaders to distribute. Thus, those who requested loans after there was no more money to lend resented not only particular leaders, but also the territorial government itself as an unfair institution. Furthermore, the necessity of making payments on loans even when there were no funds for the payments led some elected leaders to ask their constituents for something (money or cattle to sell) with little hope of being able to reciprocate later (although expressions of their intention to obtain new credit often follow the requests for money). When members grew tired of contributing, cattle from newer loans were sold to make payments on older loans, compounding the debt problem in the longer term.

Cooperative leaders pressured subcenter presidents, who then had to pressure their subcenter members to pay the difference between what was earned from selling the remaining cattle and the balance owed. Each time the cooperative defaulted on a payment, penalties and interest added to the total debt. For many members, who had little experience in calculating interest or even dealing in large cash transactions, it seemed clear that they were being cheated by their leaders.

A Financial Cushion

Cooperative leaders were able to obtain a fairly sizable development project from the Inter-American Foundation in late 1980, but the funding seemed to disappear almost as quickly as it arrived. Funds were provided for the purchase of a vehicle (US $25,200, or 630,000 *sucres*) and cattle (US $60,800), the identification of buyers and marketing (US $20,000), education and capacity building (US $6,600), and materials (US $8,240) (*Actas*, July 16, 1980). Despite these rather large sums, leaders did not use them in such a way as to promote collectivism, as they had done in the mid-1970s. The *Actas* indicate that the funds were used primarily to make the final payments on the collective's Tena Development Bank loan and to pursue a few other small projects, such as buying some of the last privately held parcels within the cooperative's borders. As a consequence, attendance at cooperative assemblies remained low, and subcenters continued to divide. Five new subcenters formed and were recognized by the cooperative between 1981 and 1988, moving even further from the early leaders' vision of members living and working together.

Outside consultants, headed by the British geographer Anthony Bebbington, were later contracted by the Inter-American Foundation to write a follow-up report. According to their analysis, which attempts to emphasize the positive results of what at first glance were a series of "failed development projects," the loan to the Rukullakta Cooperative was used in the following way:

> The cattle holdings were amplified from 342 heads to 437 with the acquisition of 95 BHRAMAN [*sic*] cattle, for which adaptation to tropical environments was known from previous technical experiences. The cattle were redistributed by the Organization to 12 associated communities, later amplified to 16 with the new [sub]centers that were created during the course of executing the project. In total, 165 heads were acquired, but due to the lack of stable management and adequate care, they diminished remarkably. An estimated 10 percent were lost due to snakebites and problems associated with the irregularity of the terrain in the fattening fields. The Cooperative later sold the animals because of these problems; in any case, the communities of Ishtandi, Villano, and Tiacuno maintained a few animals, which with time have been converted into points of breeding for improved varieties for the whole of the orga-

nization. The earnings from sales were invested in the acquisition of land, to construct an organizational locale, as well as transportation equipment and maintenance of a communal store. It was [also] possible to pay off a debt acquired by the National Development Bank. (Bebbington et al. 1992, 94–95)

The relatively lax vigilance of the Inter-American Foundation (the project lasted nine years) allowed leaders to redirect funds in a manner that better suited their more immediate priorities.

National and International Shifts

In 1979 Ecuador held democratic elections, ending the military dictatorship that had privileged the Amazon in its modernizing vision. Shortly thereafter, a generalized debt crisis in Latin America, spurred partially by monetary policies in the United States and England, abruptly ended a period of high governmental borrowing and greatly reduced the funds available for modernization projects and other public spending (Sheahan 1987, 120–24). Economic adjustment policies began in Ecuador in 1982, and four years later they became what the sociologist Leon Zamosc called "draconian," as "government measures sought to eliminate stimulus programs, abolish protection and subsidies, reduce price controls, promote exports, open up the economy to the international market, reduce public spending, devalue the currency, and foster increases in interest rates" (Zamosc 1994, 51). Whether or not cooperative members were well informed about the changes occurring in Quito and internationally, the political and economic shifts had profound effects on the organization's access to development funds. The central Ecuadorian government no longer provided multifaceted, multiyear development programs such as the one it had granted to the Rukullakta Cooperative between 1975 and late 1979.

With a lack of centrally managed infrastructural and service projects, participation in cooperative-level meetings and activities seemed pointless to the majority of residents by the mid-1980s. Furthermore, people's optimism regarding their own abilities to earn returns on investments clearly outpaced their optimism regarding the cooperative government's ability to earn profits through collective work projects. On April 25, 1984, a special assembly meeting was called to address the debt issue, and the *Actas* record the following resolution: "Although it is somewhat dangerous to mortgage the cooperative's land title, the members expressed that they wanted to first pay off a certain amount [of the previous debt]. Then, in a voice vote held in the assembly hall, the majority asserted in loud voices that YES WE WANT A NEW CREDIT [loan] FROM THE TENA DEVELOPMENT BANK [capitalization in original]. For each member 10 to 15 head [of cattle]" (*Actas*, April 25, 1984). The members specified that they wanted a certain number of cattle per person, rather than per subcenter, showing that they were primarily interested in taking care of the cattle and the loans on an individual basis. They were even willing to risk the collective land title to obtain these loans. After all of the frustrations surrounding loan payments, members no longer trusted one another enough to engage in larger, collective loans. The frustrations they faced in taking care of the Panama breed cattle were not enough to scare them away from future cattle ranching. Past experiences with collective debt were, however, enough to scare them away from future *collective* cattle ranching.

Subcenter Organization

From the preceding history, it could be argued that Rukullakta is another case of a failed development scheme. Both the state and local leaders wanted to see Upper Napo Kichwa engaging in large-scale, collectivist, market-oriented projects, but these projects required dramatic changes in people's understandings of personhood, property, and the proper relationship between leaders and constituents, as well as a level of voluntary compliance that was difficult to maintain across such a large group of people, especially over the long term. Indeed, when I first visited Rukullakta in 1999, employees from small development organizations working in the region called Rukullakta the "graveyard of development projects." Even cooperative leaders struggled with feelings of defeat, as demonstrated by a speech given by the president who ended his term on January 9, 1988, after completing his three years in office:

> The leaders who were elected in the General Assembly on February 9, 1985, as the Administrative Council and the Vigilance Council have not collaborated at any moment, failing to meet our entrusted duties and obligations, such as in this Assembly. This is why the *compañeros* subcenter presidents have completed the functions rather than the Administrative Council and Vigilance Council. Principally, the President and

Accounts Manager have [instead of initiating new projects] faced all of the problems, such as [negotiating payments with] the Tena Development Bank; the issue of lands owned by nonmembers; [and] members' issues. . . . In the administration, it has not been possible to do anything major since the members have not fulfilled their obligations to pay annual dues, which has made it difficult to mobilize and seek funds for the organization. (*Actas*, January 9, 1988)

With no more state or international funding to provide materials or financing, the central leaders' role as project managers was over for the time being. Members practiced what I call government through distance, purposely refusing to attend cooperative assembly meetings and rejecting the obligations that leaders attempted to impose on them to pay their share of the collective debt. Leaders were unable to imagine ways to rekindle residents' commitment to the cooperative during this period and therefore focused on managing its relationship with outside organizations and individuals.

However, the quote from the president also reveals something else — the growing importance of subcenter leaders. Indeed, after the Tena Semi-Directed Project effectively ended in 1978, collective work projects continued to be organized and completed at the subcenter level. Subcenter presidents increasingly went directly to elected officials and government agencies in search of financial or other types of assistance, rather than waiting for cooperative leaders to find a large source of funds to replace the previous projects. In community histories that small groups from each subcenter wrote during workshops organized by the NGO Desarollo y Autogestión between 1998 and 1999, it is possible to see the diversity of these projects:

Subcenter Lushianta: "In 1979, the members gathered funds to purchase a lot from a colonist who still lived in Lushianta, Jaime Huaco." (Desarollo y Autogestión 1998–99, Lushianta section)

Subcenter Nukunu: "In 1983, members constructed communal ponds for fish cultivation. In 1992, they constructed the road and bridges." (Desarollo y Autogestión 1998–99, Nukunu section)

Subcenter Purutuyaku: "There were several students who had already finished [elementary] school, and they [the members] decided to request that the Hispanic Office [of the Ministry of Education] put in a high school. In 1980, they succeeded in getting a junior high school [grades 7–9]." (Desarollo y Autogestión 1998–99, Purutuyaku section)

Subcenter Tampayaku: "In 1979 they constructed a meeting hall, 6 by 9 meters and two floors high, with the first floor made of cement [rather than the more quickly deteriorating wood planks]. In 1984, the community obtained a system for piping water [to the population center] through an agreement with the Municipality of Archidona. . . . In 1991, a second meeting hall was built through an agreement with INCRAE and the Municipality." (Desarollo y Autogestión 1998–99, Tampayaku section)

When outlining the history of their subcenters to me, members consistently described these projects as "achievements of the organization" (*logros de la organización*). Completing them typically involved extended petitioning of the local offices of state agencies or local politicians for building materials and convincing subcenter members to put in several days of work without pay. Subcenter presidents in particular spoke about what they accomplished during their presidency with a substantial amount of pride.

These subcenter histories demonstrate that members had found some value in pursuing collective work projects and what they call "organized living" (*la vida organizada*), but they preferred to collaborate with smaller groups of people, and less frequently than the collective's early leaders had envisioned. Members preferred to think of themselves as having the majority of their citizenship obligations negotiated with their subcenter leaders, not the cooperative government. Although subcenters usually included multiple patrilineal groups, they were still much closer in size to the older, household-based collaborating groups than the cooperative was, which included over 4,000 residents by the late 1980s. Furthermore, although tensions could be high or grow between families within a subcenter, the ability of people to break away and either join another, existing subcenter or form a new sub-center gave them more flexibility than what was afforded by the bounded geographical limits of the cooperative. Additionally, people's suspicions of subcenter leaders tended to be less than those of central leaders since the scale of the subcenters' projects was much smaller, with donations typically taking the form of building materials rather than cash. Spatial proximity allowed members to feel that they could monitor the activities of their leaders and ensure that they were not benefiting privately from projects designed for the community. Almost all of the projects described were ones that involved infrastructural improvements, with clear and immediate benefits to those who participated in constructing them—unlike the cattle project, with its long and highly uncertain path to profits. Finally, although not easy, organizing labor was simpler at the subcenter level than at the cooperative level due to the reduced distance both between houses of the various participants and between homes and the location of the actual work.

The cooperative model as pursued by the state in the Ecuadorian Amazon included the expectation that residents would continue to work together indefinitely to produce products for market. Cooperative leaders, by virtue of holding their offices, were in charge of pursuing this goal. This put them at odds with most members, who preferred to collaborate at much smaller scales. This dynamic was clearest when some members split off from their subcenters and attempted to form new ones. Despite the collectivist spirit demonstrated by the members of the new community as they worked together to build a new school, new meeting hall, and other infrastructure, cooperative-level leaders have remained reluctant to allow subcenters to divide. They have always fought against the tendency to form new subcenters, preferring members to work out problems in existing ones. Despite this resistance, five new subcenters were formed between 1981 and 1988, which coincided with the period during which central leaders had the least legitimacy among members.

Leaders are not the only ones who appreciate collectivist spirits that extend beyond the initial phase of subcenter formation. Infrastructure, including buildings; communal fields used for sports, school recess, and some community festivals; and access roads and paths require periodic maintenance, and the cooperative's residents often commented on the strength of the collective spirit of a particular subcenter by referring to its ability to complete and maintain such projects. It is common to hear statements such as "subcenter X was very *organizado* [organized, meaning that people worked well together]. They built the school, the assembly hall, and a bridge and were always meeting to plan new projects. Now, they never meet and everything is falling into disrepair. Their president never shows up for [cooperative-level] council meetings, either." There is also a certain amount of competition between subcenters, and successfully completed projects in one subcenter have sometimes inspired others to initiate similar ones.

These comments and the ability of many subcenters (now called "communities") to grow quite large without splitting demonstrates that the age of collectivism has had lingering effects on members' ideas about the right way to live and work. These effects are also visible in multiple, small collectivist ventures that are regularly imagined and enacted by the residents of Rukullakta. On multiple occasions, people have come together to invest their personal savings in goods to sell at a small, cooperatively run store in their subcenter, in which store members share operating tasks, earnings, and losses. As NGOs have made microloans available in recent years to both individuals and groups, women's associations have applied for the loans, purchased chicks, and shared the tasks of caring for them, slaughtering them, and finding buyers for them. Individuals also engage in these business ventures, but there is a sense that collective engagement in economic projects is preferable. On the numerous occasions when I have asked people why they are engaging in a collective economic endeavor, they typically answer that it is better for all to benefit equally, otherwise problems can arise from jealousy (Erazo 2010).

"Problems" in this explanation refers to acts of sorcery, as it is widely believed that jealousy and ill will bring illness to envied individuals, or to their children or animals. I will examine the issue of sorcery further in chapter 5, but for now it is worth noting how collective economic activity is newly positioned as a manner of reducing sorcery's negative effects. In the past, people attempted to reduce the occurrence of sorcery spatially, moving to their forest homes for extended periods of time or building homes in a new area to get away from people who might want to harm them. Today, it is more common to hear about how people engage with their neighbors in collaborative activities as a way of reducing jealousy. Although spatial avoidance strategies still occur (including the division of subcenters), many people now believe that some types of social tension can be reduced through increased engagement rather than evasion.

Conclusion

The difficulties cooperative leaders and members experienced in the 1970s cattle projects highlight the fact that large-scale, long-term collectivist economic endeavors involved government-resident and leader-constituent relationships that were foreign to most of Rukullakta's residents at that time. Once it seemed certain that the collective would receive an official title to the land, cooperative leaders struggled to maintain collectivist spirits. They kept the organization viable for a few years by making the organization seem magical, as state dollars funded unprecedented infrastructural and agricultural projects in the mid-1970s. Leaders enjoyed heightened legitimacy when they could bring new community centers, bridges, and cattle to cooperative members. One of the lasting effects of this time is the strong association many members have between "strong leadership" and "ability to attract development projects." Leaders are judged by fellow leaders, constituents, and external allies by their ability to motivate constituents to participate in collective activities and to attract development resources from outsiders. Leaders who can inspire many people to attend meetings with state or NGO representatives and to donate their labor for development projects are more likely to impress those representatives and attract additional projects. Thus, "organized living" has come to represent an ideal state of sustained development, in which leaders are able to attract development projects, motivate local participation in those projects, and thereby attract even more development projects. These new understandings of leadership were predicated on the creation of a territorial economy, in which the economic prospects of Rukullakta's residents became increasingly entwined during the 1970s and early 1980s.

Yet when the funds and associated magic subsided, it became clear that the shift toward a collective economy was not as dramatic as it originally appeared. Disillusioned members began to practice government through distance to convey their dissatisfaction with the leadership, staying away from the cooperative's administrative offices and assembly meetings. The long-term impact of the age of collectivism is better understood as one of lingering effects and changed attitudes toward the value of working collectively to achieve certain ends. Although members no longer invest their energies in major, loan-backed projects managed from the center, they do take out smaller loans for market-oriented, collectivist projects that include ten to twenty participants. They also collaborate on community improvement projects, calling *mingas* (collective work days) to clear community soccer fields, maintain or expand school buildings, or place new logs on muddy paths that lead to major roads. Thus, in the 1980s and 1990s, subcenter organizations took over many of the roles previously pursued by cooperative-level leaders. In doing so, participants demonstrated their preferences for an intermediate-size collaborative work group — smaller than that envisioned by central leaders, but larger than the patrilineal kin groups within which they were more accustomed to collaborating prior to the 1970s.

Still, the dream of uniting large numbers of indigenous people to make meaningful improvements to indigenous lives through shared sacrifice remains a strong one. Even as aspiring leaders may set their sights (at least initially) on smaller groups to lead, Jumandy continues to grow in mythic status, inspiring some of these leaders to have very high expectations for indigenous economic and political collaboration.

CHAPTER THREE

THE PROPERTY DEBATE

On my way to my cement-block house in the summer of 2001, I frequently passed the administrative offices of the Rukullakta Cooperative. One day, a large piece of butcher's paper announced a gathering for a representative from each of the 700-plus households. According to the sign, the meeting was *extraordinaria*, meaning that it was not one of the semiannual meetings required by the cooperative's charter but was being called to discuss more immediate issues. One of the three problems listed on the itinerary was the "land problem" (*problema de tierras*). The land problem has plagued leaders and residents alike since the mid-1980s, and it stems from three underlying realities. First, Rukullakta's territory is bounded, and even though its government has in the past purchased a few thousand hectares to eliminate gaps within their legalized holdings, they no longer have the funds to purchase additional land. Second, due to high levels of population growth in Ecuador's northern Amazonian region over the past four decades (resulting from in-migration as well as high birth rates), it is no longer possible for Rukullakta's residents simply to abandon the territory and move to lands that are not being actively claimed by anybody else, as it was in the 1970s. Now, if they want to move out of Rukullakta to farm elsewhere, they must first purchase land, an expense beyond the means of most residents. Third, once nearly all the cattle were sold off to make loan payments in the late 1970s and early 1980s, the Rukullakta Cooperative was a cooperative in name only. What was left was a bounded area of land with a growing group of residents, all of whom felt they had some claim to the land within the collective title, even those who had been too young to play a role in the formation of the cooperative. In other words, Rukullakta was a bounded territory with a defined group of citizens but no agreed-upon vision for its future.

Because of these three realities, there have been, and continue to be, heated debates about how land can be claimed and used within Rukullakta's boundaries, which are fundamentally debates over property regimes. These debates have implications for the roles of leaders and the rights of citizens, including who can claim what parts of the territory, and who, if anyone, has the authority to set rules and policies regarding land use.

In taking stances within these debates, citizens often look back to the time prior to formation of the Rukullakta Cooperative. Kichwa family groups living in the region claimed hunting, fishing, and gardening territories as their own and defended their claims to that property, ensuring the availability of sufficient space to accommodate the shifting cultivation, hunting, and fishing that they practiced. If an owner did not actively defend his land, someone else would eventually claim it, which sometimes led to a dispute. When this occurred, boundaries were set through a process of negotiation (and sometimes intimidation) between family groups or through consultation with powerful shamans (Macdonald 1979, 44–47). Shamans often claimed the largest areas of land, as their neighbors feared that the shamans would use their ability to cause illness if challenged (see chapter 5 for more on shamans).

The formation of a collectively owned territory with a central government raised new questions over who could do what and where, questions that needed to be resolved for people to know what sorts of agricultural activities they could pursue. Would those who contributed large land claims to the cooperative-formation movement maintain their claims to those lands once the cooperative title had been issued? Or would much of the collective title be managed as public lands, under the purview of the territorial government? Would those who claimed little or no land prior to the formation of the cooperative (but who had contributed their labor to delimiting the territory and raising the cooperative's cattle) be given a plot of land to call their own? If so, where would it be?

As can be inferred from these questions, debates about property are strongly attached to different perspectives on the rights of citizens and what will improve their welfare, as well as the proper role of the territorial government. The challenges associated with resolving such questions can be compared in a general way to dramatic transformations in property regimes that have been experienced in other parts of the world, even though the specifics of each situation vary. In particular, anthropologists working in countries in the former Soviet bloc have made fascinating connections between the changes in social relations and understandings of the self that accompanied the 1990s transitions in that region from state-managed, socialist enterprises to privatization. For example, Catherine Alexander (2004) discusses the varying understandings of the state that emerged in her conversations with residents of Kazakhstan following substantial privatization of state-owned companies. The variability she describes parallels the understandings of their territorial government among Rukullakta's residents:

> In the first place, what did "the state" *mean*? Some informants spoke of the state *as* the people: that which is state-owned is therefore owned by the people — a Hegelian-Marxist conception. At the same time, another key model of the relationship between the people and state posited the state as representative *of* the people, managing and owning assets on their behalf — essentially a paternalistic model. The third idea of this relationship saw the state as other, which encompassed a range of constructions. There was the state as enemy of the people, something to be negotiated around. At the other end of the continuum, the state was nothing and nobody, for its complete diffusion into all realms of life meant that it effectively disappeared; being everywhere it was also nowhere. (2004, 253–54)

In Rukullakta there were also three general understandings of the territorial government, each of which was linked to particular understandings of property, citizenship, and personhood. Some in the cooperative, whom I call the collectivists, envisioned a strong territorial government that was representative of the people, managing and owning assets on their behalf. They envisioned citizens engaging in large-scale, collectivist agricultural projects on collectively held lands, managed by elected leaders, with only small areas set aside for family-owned, subsistence-oriented gardens. Under this construction, citizenship entailed a strong commitment to the territorial government and the notion that enterprises managed by the territorial government would provide benefits for all citizens.

A second group, whom I refer to as the conservatives, assumed that the pre-cooperative land claims, which varied greatly in size from family to family, would be reinstated once the collective title had been obtained (and there was less of a need to pretend to the state that major changes had taken place). For them, the role of the territorial government was closer to that of a liberal nation-state, legitimating and protecting claims to private property. Although I label them "conservatives" to highlight their emphasis on historical land claims and identity, their desire to fix ownership boundaries permanently within Rukullakta's territory is one that has been informed by state-supported notions of private property. This is very different from the system that existed prior to the formation of the cooperative, under which land claimers needed to defend their territory continuously from incursion and takeover by other Kichwa.

The third group, whom I refer to as the egalitarianists, hoped that the land would be divided equally among all citizens to be used as each person desired, recognizing the sacrifices that all founding members had made to make the legal title a reality. Under this construction, the role of the territorial government was initially a strong, paternalistic one, as it enforced its ability to decide who could claim what land, taking parcels from the land-wealthy and distributing them to the land-poor. Once redistribution was accomplished, however, the role that egalitarianists envisioned for the territorial government was closer to what conservatives envisioned: defending property boundaries within the territory, but otherwise not interfering much in how people used those lands. Under the egalitarianist construction, both government and land-poor citizens had substantial obligations to one another initially, but these waned once the land distribution was complete.

Although previous chapters emphasized the differences in priorities between Rukullakta's early leaders and much of the cooperative's membership, this chapter reveals that it is wrong to assume that debates within Rukullakta over property, personhood, and leader-citizen relationships amount to disagreements between modernist leaders and tradition-bound residents. All three positions — collectivist, conservative, and egalitarian — combine aspects of older ways of doing things with some of the notions that the state promoted in the 1960s and 1970s (and, to some extent, that missionaries had promoted even before then). The earliest leaders were strongly collectivist, but later administrations included individuals who were more conservative or egalitarian. I say "more" because although I define these three positions as mutually exclusive, nobody actually took an extreme position—both collectivist-leaning and the conservative-leaning individuals understood that every founding member deserved and needed some land to call his or her own. Likewise, those who advocated egalitarian division of the land recognized that older, valid claims to land did not simply disappear with the receipt of the official title, and that having some commonly managed spaces was desirable (for schools, for example). Despite these concessions, battles raged over how much should be commonly versus privately managed, how much of their claims pre-cooperative owners should be able to maintain, and which areas should be distributed to those who did not have sufficient (or any) land. Advocates of all three positions attempted to justify their particular vision as key to both ensuring the continuity of Kichwa culture and improving residents' standard of living.

Much recent work on property regimes among indigenous peoples living in collective territories has focused on eliciting the norms that people hold regarding their collectively held lands (see, for example, C. Becker and León 2000; Bennett and Sierra n.d.; Bremner and Lu 2006; Lu 2001). Scholars' attention to norms, rules, and sanctions tends to be related to a desire to identify indigenous organizations that hold and enforce environmental conservation goals within their territories. As Jason Bremner and Flora Lu argue, "focusing on identifying the goals of indigenous common property institutions can identify opportunities for alliances . . . between indigenous groups and external organizations with complementary goals. Focusing on the effectiveness of internal management rules and norms will help determine whether indigenous institutions have the capabilities necessary to meet their goals" (2006, 517). In other words, these analyses are often motivated by a desire to determine whether indigenous people can be trusted to manage their lands in an environmentally sustainable way (as assessed by nonindigenous scholars from other parts of the world).

What these accounts do not emphasize in the judgments they make about indigenous property regimes is the enormous transition that was involved between the property regimes that existed prior to the issuing of a collective title and those that outsiders have expected to accompany such a title. Nor do these accounts address the roles that diverse outsiders have played in shifting the terms of these internal property debates over the past four decades. In this chapter, I emphasize how property regimes and their implications for governance and citizenship have as much to do with persuasion as they do with norms (see also C. Rose 1994). Citizens of Rukullakta have shaped the landscape as part of their efforts to persuade others of their property perspectives, and the following pages highlight many of the landscape-shaping acts and the ways in which these acts are intended to persuade others. Furthermore, many individuals and organizations from outside Rukullakta — including Ecuadorian government officials and development organizations of various stripes — have attempted to persuade Rukullakta's residents to change their understandings and practices associated with property regimes. Because of these various acts of persuasion (accompanied at times with significant resources), interviewing local people about norms associated with property would elicit very different responses, depending on when in history they were interviewed and, indeed, with whom the interviewer spoke. This does not mean that Rukullakta's citizens are incapable of collaborating with conservationists or managing their territory sustainably (as chapter 4 will further reveal), but it does mean that judging their capacity to practice conservation through analysis of supposedly static property norms is simply misguided.

Finally, the shifting struggles among property collectivists, conservatives, and egalitarianists have been inscribed on the landscape. Different notions of appropriate property divisions are associated with distinct patterns of clearing land for grazing and agriculture. Briefly stated, the collectivist dreams of early cooperative leaders included a spatial concentration of land use activities. This meant heavy clearing of some regions for population centers and cattle ranching, with large areas of forest between the regions. Landscapes associated with those in the organization who would prefer to see the parceling of the collective title into household-owned lots (the egalitarian perspective) include a much larger number of relatively small clearings separated by relatively small areas of forest, as each family has some land in gardens, some in fruit trees or fallow, and some in relatively untouched forest. Maps of land cover that I have created using aerial photographs and satellite images provide a unique lens into which of these two camps was most successful in pursuing their particular vision at various points in time (Erazo 2011). Hand-drawn maps of property lines produced by Rukullakta's residents add the perspective of the conservatives and show the patchwork quilt of property sizes and shapes as of the late 1990s.

Ideas about Land and Tenure That Predate the Cooperative

Prior to the changes brought about through the two agrarian reforms, most Upper Napo Kichwa spent significant amounts of time in homes that they constructed in the forest. Engaging at least part time in subsistence horticulture, hunting, and fishing in forested landscapes was considered a central component of Kichwa identity (distinguishing them from whites and mestizos, who spent more of their time in towns and cities). Most Kichwa moved between their town life and forest life during the year (Macdonald 1979; 1981). The dual residence pattern can still be seen in land cover patterns as of the early 1970s, as interpreted from aerial photographs taken of the region in 1973, a year after the road from Quito to Archidona was completed (see map 3.1). Areas west of the Hollín River were used relatively intensively, and homes were a short walk apart (although typically not so close that they were visible from one another). Clearings east of the Hollín River (where second homes were located) were separated by large areas of forest cover, which were used for hunting and fishing.[1]

The forest, however, was not an open area, available for everyone to use. Rather, Kichwa heads of household claimed and actively defended hunting and gathering territories, and they had well-established ways of demonstrating claims, although these claims were occasionally contested (Macdonald 1979, 43–45). Initial claim to an area began when someone cleared land for a *chakra*, or garden, giving the site a degree of permanence and providing its occupants with de facto claim to the land.

The planting of domesticated peach palm trees (*Bactris gasipaes*, or *chonta*) would signify property claims far beyond the limits of the home garden, ensuring the availability of sufficient space to accommodate the shifting cultivation, hunting, and fishing that the local people practiced. Trees were not planted in lines to denote the limits of property. Rather, each tree exerted a presence like a candle, encompassing the area around it, although the precise distance from each tree that was included within the land claim was open to dispute.[2] Sometimes, clearer markers such as rivers or footpaths created a greater level of certainty as to what was inside and what was outside a particular claim. Any member of the extended household could utilize the forest resources within the household's territory (Macdonald 1979, 35,

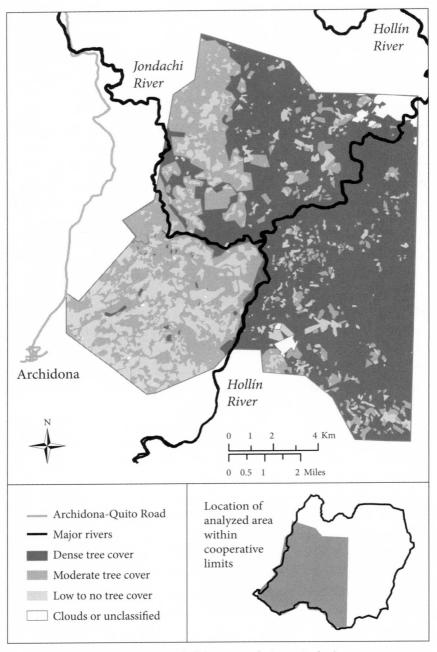

Jondachi
River

Hollín
River

Archidona

Hollín
River

N

0   1   2   4 Km

0   0.5 1   2 Miles

— Archidona-Quito Road

— Major rivers

Dense tree cover

Moderate tree cover

Low to no tree cover

Clouds or unclassified

Location of
analyzed area
within
cooperative
limits

MAP 3.1 Land cover in western Rukullakta, September 1973. Author's interpretation
of black-and-white aerial photographs, 1:32,000. Photos available through the Instituto
Geográfico Militar, Quito.

53). Others could gain access to an area by requesting permission from the owner, but Udo Oberem, an anthropologist who spent time in the Upper Napo region between 1954 and 1956, commented that "if someone hunts in someone else's property [without permission], he sets himself up for a good beating" (1980, 30; see also Wray 1996, 68).

When I asked Jorge Aguinda, one of the people who continues to claim a large parcel within the collective title as his own, how he managed to get such a large parcel, he related the following story: "In those times, shamans controlled most of the land. My father went to a powerful shaman with gifts — some calves, some liquor — and requested some land. The shaman was impressed, saying that most people feared him, hated him, saying he killed a lot. Because my father was not afraid to approach him, he gave him land. Since then we have defended our rightful ownership of this land" (interview, June 20, 2009).

I have asked at least twenty people over the past twelve years why it is that Aguinda has managed to maintain claim to his disproportionately large piece of land (about 200 hectares). Many begin by saying that he will need to give most of it up, but they go on to offer reasons why he has maintained it for as long as he has: he has it well marked with peach palm trees, he defends it well, or he "has the face of a shaman." Although the latter remark is meant as a joke, there is a clear, underlying connection between personal power and the ability to defend land, even within an organization that has had state-backed authority to redistribute it for over thirty years.

The Collectivists and Their Landscapes

Early leaders of the cooperative formation movement hoped that members would be willing to change where they resided and worked within the collective title, based in part on models of zoning presented to them in cooperative-formation training courses. They wanted all members to live closer to one another in what they referred to alternately as a populated center (*centro poblado*) or a commune (*comuna*). This center would include a few public and administrative buildings as well as small lots, where each of the members would build a house. Because of protests from members that living in one populated center would make access to subsistence gardens overly difficult, this plan was later revised to include five smaller centers, which came to be known as subcenters (*subcentros*).

The five original subcenters were all located west of the Hollín River, which roughly divided the cooperative's land in half. The western half of the land was already more densely populated than the eastern half and included some space for family-owned, subsistence-oriented gardens (*minifundios*). Leaders hoped to turn the eastern half into collectively owned and managed land, calling it latifundio (large property). Shelters would be constructed in this zone, and members would reside there periodically, when it was their turn to plant pasture or take care of the collectively owned cattle. Earnings from ranching activities would be used to fund social programs and infrastructure development within the cooperative.

The first leaders elected to office were those most in favor of centrally managed agricultural projects and collective land management. For example, Carlos Alvarado, the first president of the cooperative, has argued consistently that only a minimal portion of the land should be divided into privately owned areas and that the vast majority should remain under collective management, firmly stating that "dividing up the land will be the beginning of the end of the cooperative" (interview, March 26, 2000). Collectivists looked to the strong, centralized territorial government for funding for social programs, agricultural credit, and construction materials for infrastructural projects for the cooperative's members; help managing its finances, including substantial agricultural loans that the state development bank had given it; and help organizing members' labor schedules for both ranching and public works. The landscape-shaping projects thus celebrated both members' collective accomplishments and the importance of the territorial government in their lives.

Like the peach palm trees and other signs of domestication that Kichwa used prior to the formation of the cooperative to designate land claims, designers of these collectivist landscapes intended them to radiate their ideological influence far beyond their boundaries. Unlike the periodic peach palms that stood among naturally occurring trees, the landscapes that collectivists constructed constituted a dramatic change in what and whom people viewed as they went about their everyday activities.

One of the first landscape-changing projects that collectivists pursued was the clearing of hundreds of hectares of rainforest and the planting of pasture grasses for the collective cattle ranch east of the Hollín River in a region known as Lupinu. This collective ranch is easily seen in a satellite image taken in 1977 (Erazo 2011) and appears even more clearly in aerial photographs taken in 1982 (see map 3.2). When members went to the ranch to

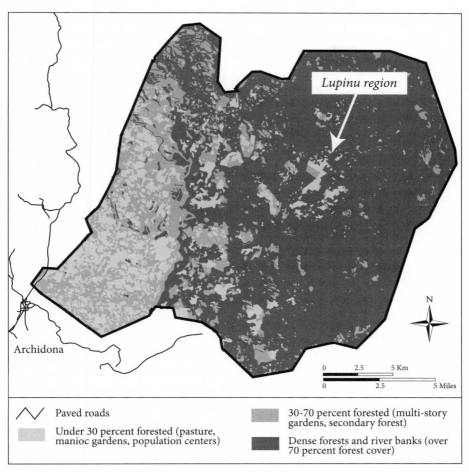

Lupinu region

Archidona

N

0   2.5   5 Km

0   2.5   5 Miles

Paved roads

Under 30 percent forested (pasture, manioc gardens, population centers)

30-70 percent forested (multi-story gardens, secondary forest)

Dense forests and river banks (over 70 percent forest cover)

MAP 3.2 Land cover in the Rukullakta Cooperative, August 1982. Author's interpretation of infrared aerial photographs, 1:60,000. Photos available through the Instituto Geográfico Militar, Quito.

contribute two weeks of their labor to the collective endeavor, the relatively open expanses of the cattle ranches were a potent reminder of how much could be accomplished in a relatively short amount of time when working together. When hundreds of cattle (on loan from the state development bank) were added to the landscape, cooperative formation and collective labor became associated with wealth, progress, and a new era in which indigenous people could run their own large-scale ranches.

Simultaneously, leaders sought funding and organized collective labor days for what was called the urbanization of the populated centers (*centros poblados*). Living in these centers was a dramatic shift from previous ways of living, in which houses were situated out of sight of other houses. The new populated centers that cooperative leaders promoted included, at the very least, common open spaces for playing sports, a school, and a few homes (see figures 1.2, 1.3, and 1.4 in chapter 1).[3] Collectivist leaders attempted to create landscapes and living patterns that would increase mutual intercourse among members, thereby (the leaders hoped) increasing unity and political organization.

Since most if not all of the land within the cooperative's borders had been claimed previously by one extended family or another, some individuals came forward and offered some or even most of their lands to the collectivist enterprise of constructing community centers. Everyone in today's subcenters knows who made this sacrifice on behalf of the collectivist project, and the person is heralded as a founding father of the subcenter. Although current leaders are much less committed than their predecessors were to the large-scale, collectivist economic projects such as ranching, the twelve new subcenters that have formed since the original five were established have all set aside land for collective management, particularly areas for community centers closely modeled on those constructed in the five original subcenters. Thus, the ideal of indigenous people working together toward common ends under indigenous leadership is now closely associated with a particular kind of landscape — one that includes a school, an assembly hall, and common open space for playing soccer and other sports.

Conservatives and Their Landscapes

Other members of the cooperative never accepted the early leaders' calls to think of the territorial space as collectively owned and centrally managed. They participated in the formation of the cooperative not because they were attracted to the ideal of collectivist agriculture, but because state representatives made it clear that this was the surest way to gain title to a large piece of land. Some of these conservatives have managed to prevent their relatively large landholdings within the cooperative's collective title from being divided up among other members, in some instances by running for and obtaining a position on the cooperative's administrative council. The continued presence of undivided landholdings has dampened the effects of collectivist landscapes and challenged the attempts of those elected leaders who sought to change previous property regimes. Jorge Aguinda—whose story of how a shaman gave his father land is quoted above—has long been one of the primary voices opposing land redistribution. He has served as president of the cooperative twice. He explained his situation to me this way:

> In my case, I have about 200 hectares of land in the cooperative. I'm the owner—that land is from before the cooperative formed. It's from before the making of the cooperative. So I've got my kids. If we start dividing the land among the members, all that land that is under my power, I wouldn't like to cede it to another member. I'm always jealous that nothing happens; rather it should stay with me, with my kids. Therefore, my kids affiliate [with the cooperative] and we'll situate them. So I remain calm that all that land, which I struggled and fought for so much, isn't for nothing. Rather [I want to ensure] that it stays with the kids. . . . So everyone thinks like that—no one wants to let go. . . . So you can't enter in a fair legalization, as cooperativism dictates, that everyone is the same, every member has the same rights, the same obligations. You can't apply that because we are an organization of traditional landholdings. That is the most problematic point that exists in the cooperative. . . . Always in our culture, one respects others, whether they have more or have less, each person's natural boundaries are respected, and if one wants something, he has to speak to the *compañero* to ask him to cede a few hectares. Always with dialogue. And if not, they enter into fights, hatred, and vengeance. So we have respected that. Well, until now we've respected it, even though we have replicated like crazy [referring to high birth rates and population growth]. (interview, March 1, 2000)

Aguinda speaks of "natural boundaries," referring in part to the way in which trees, hills, rivers, and other natural features were used to demarcate land claims, but also implying that it is natural for families to own differently sized parcels of land. He also argues that although people were willing to allow others to hunt or fish on the land they claimed, it was always with prior permission (and with the general understanding that the person requesting permission was taking on the obligation to return the favor in another way later). He justifies his claim by referring to the work he has invested in defending his land claim. Finally, he prioritizes previously existing social bonds and obligation, specifically within patrilineal kinship groups, rather than any obligations associated with citizenship in Rukullakta.

Without the same level of state funding enjoyed by the collectivists, conservatives did not engage in bold modifications to the landscape as the collectivists had done. Rather, they frequently sought to hinder attempts to redistribute lands they considered to be theirs. The *Actas* report several attempts to install a more egalitarian land tenure system, including discussions about how many hectares each member would receive. The first is described in the meeting notes from June 21, 1975, which record that the Administrative and Vigilance Councils voted and decided that no member could have more than 40 hectares of land, and that those who had less would receive a 40-hectare plot. In December 1976 that amount was raised to 50 hectares per member, although there was still debate about the proposal: "Solution to the land problem. To which the President of the Cooperative [Jorge Aguinda] referred to the accord we had in the other session to receive individual lots. In that sense, those who have 30–40 hectares in their first lot would also receive 50 hectares in a second lot. Various *compañeros* and members did not approve the previous accord. Rather, we want 50 hectares for each member in equality. Those who have 30–40 hectares in their first lot will receive 20–10 hectares to complete the 50 hectares" (*Actas*, December 14, 1976). As can be seen, Aguinda attempted to allow those with large claims (including himself) to maintain at least some of their disproportionate holdings. Later, the leaders reduced the amount that would be distributed to those with no land to 30 hectares, and, with the help of IERAC topographers, they actually measured and distributed 30-hectare lots to all members of two of the smaller subcenters in January 1979 (the lots were on lands previously claimed by people who had agreed to redistribute them after the cooperative was formed). In the work plan for 1982, however, the leaders returned to the goal of 50 hectares per member, resolving that "so that each member can have an individual lot, it is planned to resituate the members who are currently living in the extremely populated areas . . . , benefiting the ten subcenters that conform the Cooperative with individual lots of 50 hectares for each one of the members" ("Plan de Trabajos, San Pedro de Rucu-Llacta" 1981). The general resolve for making the landscape truly egalitarian by forcing those with large claims to give up much of their land, however, remained weak. In May 1983 the membership decided in an assembly meeting that "if by chance [a member] has more than 100 hectares, he will be given only 10–20 hectares [more]" (*Actas*, May 25, 1983). Division discussions appear in the *Actas* throughout the late 1980s. In practice, however, little was accomplished to resolve the debates.

Part of this indecision was related to the fact that older ideas of property remained strong. This was not just an instance of a few members trying to hold onto their land when most members were against them. Rather, land claims that preceded the formation of the cooperative provided a strong connection to one's ancestors and were therefore tied to one's sense of personhood and identity. When the early leaders first envisioned a cooperative landscape divided into family gardens, collective cattle ranches, and collectively held forest, they were thinking of the land abstractly, divorced from kinship-specific histories tied to particular areas of land. They had asked cooperative members to think of various parts of the cooperative as generic and relatively interchangeable; members would get enough land to meet their needs, but the location of this land was of secondary importance to establishing collective ranches in areas thought suitable to that pursuit. This perspective was part of the leaders' modernist and collectivist, state-like plans described in chapter 1.

However, those who claimed large areas of land claimed it in particular places, rather than simply asserting rights to lands anywhere within the cooperative (or even attempting to obtain particularly fertile land, or lands close to roads or other amenities). Thus, despite the early cooperative leaders' attempts to get members to think in terms of abstract *space*—number of hectares, ecological suitability, and locations based on collectivist social goals (such as bringing people together spatially) — members continued to assert claims to particular *places*, linked to their own histories and their patrilineal ancestors' histories of hunting and fishing.[4] Some regions had particularly potent histories attached to them, closely linked to senses of identity. For example, Yawar Urku (Blood Mountain) is located in the northwestern region of Rukullakta's territory, and it is known as a site of resistance to Spanish invaders. Carlos Alvarado, Rukullakta's first president, documented some of the stories Kichwa residents told about the region's history in *Historia de una cultura . . . a la que se quiere matar* (The history of a culture . . . that they want to kill; 1994). The book includes the following story that Francisco Shiguango and Teresa Catalina Narváez told Alvarado about Yawar Urku:

It was announced that the Spanish were arriving and that they [our ancestors] should not go anywhere, otherwise they [would be killed] from firearms, [and] persecuted with dogs wherever they went. For that reason, a group from the Shiguango family, composed of 80 persons, escaped in the middle of the night, without leaving footprints, toward the green heights of the Sumaco Volcano. Men, women, and children walked for four to six days continuously. . . .

The escape of the Shiguango family provoked the Spanish invaders to call all the *caciques* or heads of the other groups to collect them in a plaza and punish them. They brought together men, women, children, the elderly, etc. The Spanish killed hundreds of our ancestors and they hurled them in the rivers. They [the gathered Kichwa] paid with their lives for the brothers and sisters who did not let themselves be dominated.

Many years of slavery passed. The number of Spanish *conquistadores* kept rising. They found out that in the region of Sumaco a group of natives lived. The Spanish and *criollo* soldiers organized themselves and threw themselves into conquering the zone. . . .

[After the soldiers killed one member of the Shiguango family, alerting the rest to their presence] the group prepared itself for the defense; the high part [of the mountain] has only one place to climb. This was favorable for locating tree trunks. . . . The logs plastered the battalion of bearded Spanish as they passed. They faced off for an entire day and a night. The soldiers were left without munitions and others tried to return. There they [the Shiguangos] killed them [the soldiers] with spears, stone axes, clubs, big sticks, etc. Upon seeing that all the soldiers were without life, with their bodies destroyed, [the Shiguangos] climbed to their houses, observing that the heights were bathed in blood on all sides. From that time it was baptized with the name "Yawar Urku," which means "Blood Mountain." (quoted in Alvarado 1994, 16–17)

The story expresses many social values that are important to those who hear it, including resistance to domination and the cunning of indigenous people in contrast to the savagery of the colonists. It also carries additional significance for the Shiguango family, for they were able to successfully defend themselves against the Spanish. Francisco Shiguango, one of the elders Alvarado interviewed, concluded the story with the following comment: "When we organized the San Pedro of Rukullakta Cooperative, we attended a General Assembly. There we heard that each subcenter should have a name from its origin. For me that word [suggestion] was sufficient, and as we are from that sector, in the first session we agreed to put that name. From that time we are and belong to the Yawar Urku community" (quoted in Alvarado 1994, 18).

Shiguango states that he selected the name Yawar Urku because of its historical significance to his family. However, he simultaneously made claim to part of what was supposed to be collectively held lands, according to the original land divisions devised by leaders. There is a subcenter called Yawar Urku, which is located in the populated southwestern quadrant of the cooperative, just north of the Rukullakta community. However, the mountain after which it is named is quite far away, in the northwestern region of the cooperative, in what was thought of as collectively held lands. Claim to the mountain and the lands surrounding it were made clear through the name that members chose for their subcenter. This very place-specific history thus became attached to a claim to a portion of Rukullakta's land ("we are and belong to the Yawar Urku community"), creating links across space and time between their subcenter and the distant mountain where their ancestors had fled. Indeed, Yawar Urku's citizens were among the first to have 30-hectare parcels assigned to them in January 1979, and these parcels were situated on the flanks of Blood Mountain.

An Intermediary Understanding

As can be seen from the story above, even as central leaders attempted to replace residents' complex understandings of property to one in which everything outside of the southwestern quadrant was centrally managed, people still retained strong connections to the lands they had historically used to escape exploitation and to hunt, fish, and gather food, medicinal plants, and other useful products. After the central leadership experienced great difficulties in organizing the care of cattle in Lupinu (as described in chapter 2), they increasingly assigned cattle to subcenters rather than attempting to manage the animals' care centrally. Subcenter leaders, in turn, started having their members clear pasture on the lands that their founding members had previously claimed, creating an understanding of property as claimed and managed by subcenters, rather than the central government of the cooperative. Subcenters typically had a populated center located near Archidona, and a much larger area located farther away for cattle ranching or other collectivist activities. The precise boundaries of these lands claimed by subcenters were often in dispute, as will be explained below. However, in 2007–8, the Rukullakta government decided to move toward the acceptance of more permanent boundaries by mapping these lands using GPS technology, taking advantage of the assistance from University of Texas researchers described in the introduction. The resulting map helps illustrate the "intermediary" understanding of property that melded some aspects of the collectivists' vision with that of the conservatives (see map 3.3).

The map shows how most of the original subcenters (such as Lushianta) claim a small area in the southwestern quadrant, where members have a home and a small garden, children can attend a local school, and getting to and from Archidona and Quito is relatively easy due to convenient access to roads and public transportation. However, these subcenters also claim a larger area in the northern or eastern halves of Rukullakta, where members can engage in agriculture, hunting, and fishing.

Despite leaders' attempts to fix boundaries, map 3.3 illustrates the difficulty in doing this. The large area in the southeastern-most area continues to be claimed by three communities. These three communities were originally a single subcenter, but when they divided, they were unable to decide how to divide the lands that their ancestors had claimed in the southeastern region of Rukullakta. For example, claims by those who decided to join a new subcenter may be interspersed with those who stayed in the older subcenter, making a clean split impossible. In other cases, there is more agreement today after several years of controversies, as is the case between Lupinu and Lushianta (in the middle of the map). However, despite this long sought-after consensus, the resulting configuration means that Lupinu's lands divide Lushianta's eastern lands into two separate sections.

Furthermore, despite the increasing dominance of subcenters as organizers of both collective labor and managers of collective lands, the central territorial government continued to have some degree of ultimate authority in determining who could do what and where within Rukullakta's territory. In part, this was because it was the only legal entity officially recognized by the state. This became clear when one family sought to withdraw what they saw as their patrilineal claim from the collective title in September 1980. The family was displeased with how the cooperative was being run and found an ally in a new indigenous federation that was attempting to gain members by offering to assist them in obtaining individual legal titles to land. This new federation, the Federación de Organizaciones Campesinas e Indígenas

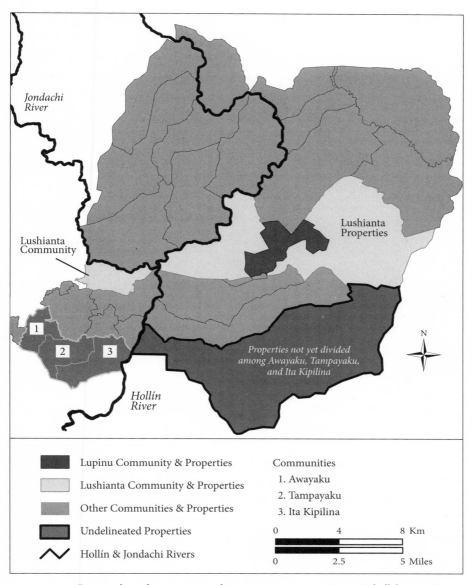

Jondachi
River

Lushianta
Community

Lushianta
Properties

Properties not yet divided
among Awayaku, Tampayaku,
and Ita Kipilina

1

2

3

Hollín
River

N

Lupinu Community & Properties

Lushianta Community & Properties

Other Communities & Properties

Undelineated Properties

Hollín & Jondachi Rivers

Communities

1. Awayaku

2. Tampayaku

3. Ita Kipilina

0	4	8 Km
0	2.5	5 Miles

MAP 3.3 Property boundaries corresponding to various communities in Rukullakta, 2008.
Adapted from Rukullakta's 2008 Management Plan.

de Napo (Federation of Peasant and Indigenous Organizations of Napo, or FOCIN), had formed two years earlier with the encouragement of the Josephine missionaries as an alternative to FOIN. The older organization, which had formed in 1969, had long been engaged in various disputes with the Josephine Mission over land, and the missionaries were probably eager to weaken it by fostering the growth of competing indigenous organizations.[5]

Early FOCIN leaders spent the first few years of the federation's existence trying to convince Rukullakta and other indigenous organizations to shift their alliance as complete organizations, leaving FOIN and joining FOCIN. At a general assembly on February 2, 1980, Rukullakta's members voted to continue their allegiance to FOIN rather than switching. FOCIN persisted, however, and began to offer loans and individual property titles to each person who affiliated with the federation. The promise of individual title was appealing to many agriculturalists because without private title to a piece of land to use as collateral, they could not apply for their own line of credit to invest in agricultural or other income-generating pursuits, and thus they had to wait for the cooperative to obtain credit as an organization. The possibility that indigenous people could lose their land if they used it as collateral was one of the reasons why FOIN supported community-level titling, and why Rukullakta's leadership resisted decentralization. As a FOIN leader put it, "when land is legalized individually, many *compañeros* are deceived by the colonists into selling their lots, but when legalization is done at the community level, the lots that each family has cannot be sold [or lost to the bank]" (FOIN n.d.).

In Rukullakta, an emergency assembly was called on September 13, 1980, in which the accounts manager related the events of a meeting that he had had in the offices of the state land-titling agency (IERAC) with one family from the cooperative. This family had decided it would rather affiliate with FOCIN and thereby regain access to the land that it had claimed since before Rukullakta's formation. These separatists had formed the "May 1st Pre-Association" to pursue these ends. According to the *Actas*, the accounts manager said: "These members claim that the cooperative made them join through deception and promises . . . by deceiving the members they [the leaders] got the collective land title, to which the majority did not agree. That is why FOCIN wants to divide it up for them. FOCIN will give each one of them their own land title. Furthermore, [the separatists charge that] none of the resolutions passed in the assemblies and Administrative Council meetings represent the desires of the members, but rather those of the leaders" (*Actas*, September, 13, 1980). This account is second-hand, coming from a leader rather than the separatists themselves, but it seems that the separatists had two principal complaints. First, they opposed the leaders' continuing drive to maintain the cooperative's lands as a collectively owned and centrally managed territory. Their second complaint referred to a perceived distancing between members and leaders. One of Rukullakta's leaders responded to the charges in the following way:

> You had four years since the cooperative delineated the collective land title to complain; after all the work we did asking IERAC to give [us] the collective land title, after receiving the title, and even after that, you did not express any complaints. Now, just because the organization FOCIN wants to divide [us by] giving individual titles, now because they want to divide the cooperative just as they divided FOIN. As far as we are concerned, we are not going to give up the title because for us it has been an enormous sacrifice to delimit and to obtain the collective title for the 41,888.5 hectares. The cooperative has never deceived members with [false] promises. Indeed, the cooperative is calling on us to unite, and in this way to demand our rights and confront through solidarity the problems that present themselves on a daily basis. Let us defend our lands through the proper authorities of the Ecuadorian Amazon so that the colonists do not come to exploit them. (*Actas*, September 13, 1980)

In this response, the leader refused to acknowledge the distinctions the May 1st Pre-Association was making between leaders and members, choosing rather to speak about "the cooperative" as a unified whole in the following phrases: "the cooperative has never deceived members" and "the cooperative is calling on us to unite." As in one of the three understandings of the state in Kazakhstan described by Alexander and quoted above, the territorial government is equated with its citizens, and "that which is state-owned is therefore owned by the people — a Hegelian-Marxist conception" (2004, 253). In the speech, Rukullakta's elected leader also implicitly equates FOCIN with the colonists, emphasizing the need to defend the title against enemies of Kichwa collectives.

The regional director of IERAC, who had had a long history of collaborating with Rukullakta's government, sided with the leaders. He boosted the collectivists' authority by first repeating some of the same arguments that the cooperative's leaders had made, firmly stating that "as an institution IERAC cannot enter and divide up lots for each of you as you are requesting. It is too late, the day has passed. Before, each of you had four years to repudiate [collective ownership]. Because both the work of IERAC and that of the Cooperative has been a large sacrifice. Now, we cannot undo the title; if the Cooperative authorizes you as an institution, IERAC could make the lots. If it does not authorize, no institution can do anything" (*Actas*, September 13, 1980). The IERAC representative's language depicted the cooperative not as an organization dependent on the state for its legitimacy, but as an entity more akin to a sovereign nation, with full autonomy over what happened within its borders. With this unequivocal support by a government agency, the leaders demonstrated that they had the oratorical skills and powerful connections with state institutions to stand up to the separatists. Central leaders were willing to devolve some aspects of managing collectively held lands to the subcenters, but they were not willing to allow a subcenter or an extended family to gain separate title to lands that belonged to the Rukullakta Cooperative. Through his unequivocal support of the status quo, the government official also reminded Rukullakta's citizens that they had received something very important from the formation of the organization and the work that certain individuals had put into it: title to a substantial area of land and a significant amount of protection from those who wanted to take it away from them. Even if leaders were no longer granting loans the way they had in the past, this fundamental accomplishment could not be denied. As the leaders' legitimacy to make decisions about the collectively held land was reinforced by state agencies, so was the collectivist perspective on land ownership.

The Egalitarianists

A third model existed for how tenure should be divided in the cooperative, in which the majority of the cooperative would be internally divided into equally sized, household-managed plots. Although this model had existed from the early days of cooperative formation, it became increasingly popular in the mid- and late 1980s, when the state greatly reduced financial support for cattle ranching and, as stated in the introduction to this chapter, Rukullakta's central government was by this point no longer managing cooperative ranching or agricultural projects. Due to both the maturing of large families and in-migration (through marriage and even some external applications for membership), the number of men living in Rukullakta who were heads-of-household (and thus wanted to make claims to land) had increased substantially by 1980 and continued to grow. One estimate in the archives indicates that there were about 500 households by 1987 (up from the 207 founding members of the cooperative in 1974). The growth in the number of families seeking land added to the concerns about the limited availability of land.

Furthermore, by the 1980s, most residents had been convinced that they needed to send their children to elementary school, and many aspired to send at least some of their children to secondary school, which required money to pay for transportation, uniforms, and school supplies. Money was also needed for the ongoing expenses of clothing and household items, as well as for periodic rituals such as weddings. Residents began to increase their involvement in cash crop agriculture, which required less initial monetary investment than ranching. Yet many families still had no land for such endeavors. Younger families typically began cultivating land that had belonged to their kin prior to the formation of the cooperative. However, if their fathers had given most of their lands to the cooperative government for cattle ranches, or if they had failed to defend the lands from takeover by other families, members of the next generation did not have this option. Many people in this position moved out into areas that appeared to be unclaimed or at least unused. Conflicts over boundaries were common.

In response to an earthquake in 1987, the Ecuadorian government began construction of a new road just north of the cooperative, known locally as the "Hollín-Loreto Road." Shortly after that, soldiers entered the northeastern corner of the cooperative to lay an access road between the Hollín-Loreto Road and the Galeras Mountain Range for a military station (see map 3.4).

Lands surrounding this military road were, under the cooperative leadership's initial vision, part of the organization's collectively owned and centrally managed forest reserve. However, given the promise of access to markets that would be provided by the two roads, some residents made a bold move. They entered the area surrounding the planned military road and demarcated lines for twenty-five-hectare parcels, as can be seen by the narrow, roughly rectangular land claims just south of Papanku's community center in map 3.5. The founding members who had claimed the land prior to the formation of the cooperative were willing to allow them to do this, but

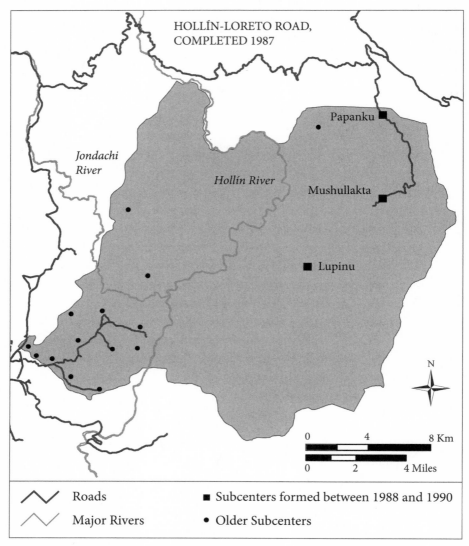

Jondachi
River

Hollín River

Papanku

Mushullakta

Lupinu

N

| 0 | 4 | 8 Km |

| 0 | 2 | 4 Miles |

⋀⋁ Roads   ■ Subcenters formed between 1988 and 1990

⋀⋁ Major Rivers   ● Older Subcenters

MAP 3.4 Location of new road and the subcenters created between 1988 and 1990 in relation to older subcenters.

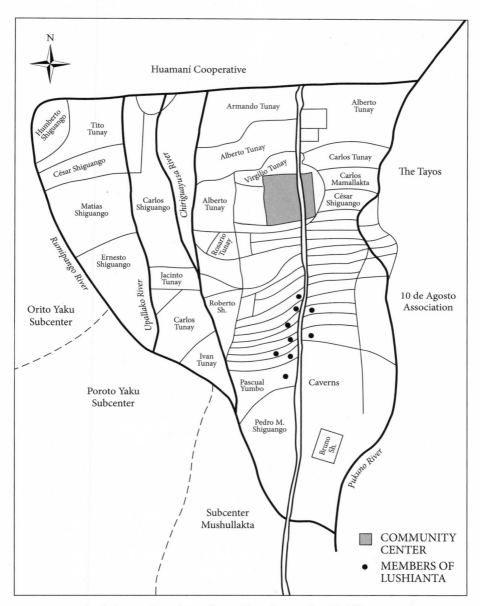

N

Huamaní Cooperative

Humberto Shiguango

Tito Tunay

César Shiguango

Matias Shiguango

Carlos Shiguango

Ernesto Shiguango

Jacinto Tunay

Roberto Sh.

Carlos Tunay

Ivan Tunay

Pascual Yumbo

Pedro M. Shiguango

Rumipuango River

Upallako River

Chiriguayusa River

Armando Tunay

Alberto Tunay

Virgilio Tunay

Alberto Tunay

Rosario Tunay

Alberto Tunay

Carlos Tunay

Carlos Mamallakta

César Shiguango

The Tayos

Caverns

Bruno Sh.

Pukuno River

Orito Yaku Subcenter

Poroto Yaku Subcenter

Subcenter Mushullakta

10 de Agosto Association

◼ COMMUNITY CENTER

● MEMBERS OF LUSHIANTA

MAP 3.5 Land claims in Papanku as of 1999. The collective claims held by surrounding subcenters and associations are also marked. Adapted from a community-drawn map created during workshops with the Ecuadorian NGO Desarollo y Autogestión.

the cooperative leaders were very opposed. They protested frequently during Administrative Council and Assembly meetings (*Actas*, January 2, 1990; May 19, 1990; May 24, 1990; January 30, 1991).

The earliest land claimers ignored the cooperative's governance institutions and engaged in cash crop agriculture without worrying about upsetting the central leaders. This is demonstrated by Papanku's subcenter history, which states, "Carlos Tunay's family and a few other families were the only people who lived in the Papanku region before the road to Loreto was built [these were the families with claims to this region before the formation of the cooperative]. The lands in Papanku were reserve lands for the subcenter Purutuyaku [under the intermediary understanding described above]. With the planning and arrival of the road, a few members of Purutuyaku took over 25 hectare lots in Papanku in 1990" (Desarollo y Autogestión 1998–99). In this short passage, it is possible to see how the three understandings of land ownership could coexist for the same area of land. First, Carlos Tunay and a few other men had had recognized claims to the region even before the cooperative was formed, and they continued to defend their claims by living in the region. Second, with the distribution of centrally managed cattle to the subcenters, the region that was previously understood as collective cattle ranching and forested lands, managed by the cooperative, began to be understood more as divided up among the subcenters (as in map 3.3; this is why the quote says "the lands in Papanku were reserve lands for the subcenter Purutuyaku"). Third, the history states that when the road was built, some members of Purutuyaku felt that they could claim plots of this "reserve land," controlled by the subcenter, for their families in an egalitarian fashion. Carlos Tunay and the others living in the zone did not prevent them.

Nowhere in this short passage is it stated or even implied that the central government of Rukullakta had control of these lands. Indeed, once a few families from Purutuyaku had successfully established themselves there, residents from other subcenters attempted to do so in Papanku, too, even though under one of the understandings of property, these lands supposedly "belonged" to Purutuyaku. Map 3.5 indicates where members of Lushianta claimed their twenty-five-hectare parcels in Papanku, despite the fact that they had no reasonable claim to these lands except as citizens of Rukullakta. Essentially, the coexistence of multiple understandings of land tenure allowed more aggressive individuals to assert stronger claims than less aggressive individuals, and the cooperative-level government was unable to stop them.

Lupinu's subcenter history demonstrates some of the rapid and sometimes confusing ways in which new subcenters were coming together in what cooperative leaders considered to be collectively held and centrally managed lands. Those who formed the new subcenter described its formation in the following way: "Initially, six people met to speak in a spot called Ruyak Lupinu and Yana Lupinu. On September 18, 1990, in the middle of the forest, they decided to form a school. On the following Sunday, they decided to construct the school and, with only six people, began to clean the area [of vegetation] the following day. In the afternoon, twelve more people arrived to help with the *minga*" (Desarrollo y Autogestión 1998–99, Lupinu section). In this instance, planning for and constructing the school occurred even before the clearing of agricultural fields or before those constructing it had any assurance that they would be able to claim agricultural lands nearby. Only once the school was operating did they attempt to make a formal break from the subcenter where they had been living (Lushianta) to form a new governing entity within the cooperative. As illustrated in map 3.3, Lupinu's lands are situated right in the middle of Lushianta's claim.

The residents of Lushianta who stayed behind protested the actions of the Lupinu agriculturalists during a cooperative assembly. The centrally elected leaders joined them in their criticism, seeing the devolution over land distribution as a challenge to their authority (*Actas*, April 16, 1991). The protests continued over the next several years, and the central government did its best to mediate the conflict. In the end, the territorial government decided that the members of the newly formed Lupinu Subcenter who wanted to claim part of Lushianta's reserve lands for their new subcenter should pay the Lushianta Subcenter government for the land (with a small percentage also going to the cooperative's central treasury), and created a land commission to assist in determining the borders between Lushianta's reserve lands and Lupinu's members' lands (*Actas*, August 5, 1994).

The activities of the residents of Papanku, Lupinu, and a third new subcenter (Mushullakta) affected the distribution of forests in Rukullakta (Erazo 2011). Although in many areas of Rukullakta, the patterns and the extent of agricultural activities in 1992 are very similar to those in 1982, a few areas are quite different. The first is the northeastern corner of the Rukullakta, where the new subcenters were located, and where a thin line of cleared gardens followed the military road by 1992. Those members who claimed twenty-five-hectare parcels between 1988 and 1990 planted cash crops, particularly *naranjilla* (*Solanum quitoense*, a fruit in the tomato family used primarily to make juice in Ecuador and Colombia), both to take advantage of new commercial outlets and to solidify their claim to the parcels.

The second area, the southwestern quadrant (previously the most intensively used), was being used less intensively by 1992, as members spent more time in their fields located outside of this quadrant and less time in meetings and *mingas* associated with the development boom period of the 1970s (Erazo 2011). Finally, the collective ranches in the Lupinu region returned to dense forest because they had been abandoned (although, as related above, a small number of agriculturalists were just beginning to settle there). Thus, both areas that were previously used intensively—and that were most associated with the collectivists' desires for developed and vibrant community centers and for large, collectively run ranches—became more forested as people moved farther away from them to engage in cash crop agriculture.

Unlike the older subcenters, formed in the 1970s, where the school, meeting hall, and public plaza were seen as the center around which subcenter residents would construct their houses and garden plots, the three new subcenters that formed between 1988 and 1990 (shown in map 3.4) organized themselves around roads or paths for transporting products to market. Residents of the new subcenters created new community centers with a school, soccer field, and assembly hall, demonstrating the lingering effects of this model. Yet these new public centers were constructed relatively far from one another in a linear fashion (stretched out along the road, separated by several farms) rather than a more circular fashion (radiating out from the community center). This meant that adults spent much less time in the community centers than those living in older subcenters did, and children had to walk up to three hours each way to attend school.

Although it is easier to maintain one path than many, eventually the distances grow so great that it would be quicker to create a second line of homesteads "behind" (to the east and west of) the first, but the homesteaders did not do that. One of the main reasons can be seen in map 3.5, which shows property claims drawn by Papanku residents in 1999. A relatively small number of kinship groups (the Tunays and, to a lesser extent, the Shiguangos) continued to claim large areas of land based on their holdings before the formation of the cooperative, having given up claim only to those lands that abutted the road. The conservatives who maintained the claims they had had before the cooperative had a certain amount of legitimacy in controlling what happened within these lands (especially in this period of reduced legitimacy of the cooperative's elected leaders). Older claimants did not allow aspiring homesteaders to ignore the land ownership history, but some did allow parts of their claims to be carved up into modest parcels, with public centers established intermittently among these parcels. Thus, they were able to maintain claims to relatively large areas of land, while still fulfilling some of the obligations of citizenship in the territory that other citizens expected — namely, permitting those who had no land to have access to twenty-five-hectare parcels along the road.

Managing Conflicts

As may already be clear, by the early 1990s, the idea that substantial areas of land should be set aside for collectivist economic pursuits had lost much of its appeal, and most residents were satisfied with relatively small areas being dedicated to collective use, including schools, sports fields, and community centers. Most disputes in the 1990s were between those claiming land based on the conservative viewpoint of ancestral connection and those arguing for a more egalitarian division. When disputes arose between subcenters over the locations of particular boundaries, the central leadership created land commissions to resolve the conflicts. Parties that participated in the mediation proceedings typically accepted the decision made by the land commissions, demonstrating that the central Rukullakta government still remained important in resolving land tenure disputes. For example, in 1994 three subcenters became involved in a property clash, making the following claims to a land commission appointed by Rukullakta's Administrative Council:

> The representatives of Orito Yaku maintained that since the beginning of the Cooperative, this [disputed] place was designated for Orito Yaku, even the ranching work for the Communal Ranch Lands. For that reason, we want to maintain possession.
>
> Whereas the representatives of the Villano Subcenter maintain that they want to possess [it] because [the land] is the possession of the[ir] grandfathers.
>
> At the same time, the representatives of Purutuyaku said that [the dis-

puted] place is positioned for the subcenter and was provisioned a long time ago [to Purutuyaku] and that it will maintain possession based on the number of [subcenter] members [there], since those of Villano are a small group. Futhermore, they [the Villano families] have various possessions, and for that reason, we do not want them to situate themselves in said place. (*Actas*, August 15, 1994)

Three distinct claims are made on the disputed area. Orito Yaku makes its claim based on historical use, dating back to the stage of the cooperative's history when subcenters managed cattle collectively. (Orito Yaku, located in the center of the northern region, used to be the subcenter-managed ranch for Rukullakta Subcenter. Over time it gained acceptance as a separate subcenter, occupied by those former Rukullakta Subcenter members who did not have salaried positions near Archidona and who therefore wanted access to more land.) Villano attempts to make a claim based on a more distant history, when the subcenter's members' grandfathers hunted and fished there. Purutuyaku makes a claim based primarily on equity: it has many more members than Villano does, and Villano has lands elsewhere within Rukullakta's territory. Therefore, Purutuyaku does not want to relinquish its claims to Villano simply because the latter claimed the lands before the cooperative was formed. It does not appear that Orito Yaku's and Purutuyaku's claims overlap, but rather that Villano is the primary force contesting both of the other two subcenters' claims, citing the tenure of its members' ancestors as its primary justification.

The land commission made a very swift judgment in the case after reminding the representatives of a phrase used frequently in the period of cooperative formation, "only united will we overcome" (*sólo unidos venceremos*), emphasizing the importance of maintaining social ties despite the anger that had accumulated among the three subcenters:

In the first instance, the members should open a trail from the polygon [that delimits the cooperative's collective title], taking into account the distance of 1000 meters on either side of the path. On it [the path], continue situating the members at distances of 250 meters' width, and 1000 meters' depth [from the path for a total lot size of 25 hectares], until you complete the number of members of Orito Yaku. Continue to situate 10 *compañeros* members from the subcenter Villano with the same dimensions, until the point that you find yourself within the possessions of the subcenter Purutuyaku. In the case that there is a leftover lot, situate one member more from Villano, following the request of said subcenter. And if the leftover lot is at the edge of the river banks, it will remain with the *compañero* member who finds himself the possessor of that lot. (*Actas*, August 15, 1994)

In its decision, the land commission gave slightly more weight to the claims that had been established since the beginning of the cooperative, based on contributions to collective cattle ranching, since the first members to be situated in the disputed place are those from Orito Yaku. Purutuyaku's land claims are respected in their entirety, indicating the commission's agreement with the argument that subcenters that had more members needed more land. However, the commission also afforded some legitimacy to the older historical claims, granting ten to eleven lots to Villano's members (it seems that the commission was uncertain about how much land was actually available).

Importantly, the commission stopped short of explaining some of the details of its directive. Once the commission had set the borders of each subcenter's claim, the subcenter leaders were left to determine who would get which lot or, in the case of Villano, who would be denied a lot. In this way, the commission deflected some of the responsibility for resolving the dispute, hoping to thereby maintain the legitimacy to resolve future disputes between subcenters.

Conservation Tips the Balance

Starting in the 1990s, conservationist-oriented organizations increasingly funded development projects that were primarily geared at discouraging Upper Napo Kichwa from practicing cash crop agriculture and cattle ranching. Unlike the government agencies and international donors of the 1970s and early 1980s, which pushed for increased clearing of the forest and its conversion to pasture, these new development organizations tried to convince indigenous people to stop clearing the forest and to engage in completely different economic endeavors, particularly ecotourism. Largely unaware of existing debates over property in Rukullakta, conservationists saw only that farmers growing cash crops were breaking up what the conservationists perceived as pristine forest (even though some of it was in the same locations where cooperative members had previously practiced cattle ranching)[6] and sought to prevent the members from continuing what the outsiders labeled forest destruction.

In one instance, which will be described in detail in chapter 4, these conservation organizations supported the efforts of one family to use its ancestral lands, located in an area that overlaps Rukullakta's territory as well as those of two other indigenous territories, to pursue a family-run ecotourism operation. Economic and political support of this family's claim to a very large area of land presented a threat to cooperative legitimacy very similar to that represented by the FOCIN incident described earlier in this chapter. In most instances, however, conservationists collaborated with indigenous territorial governments to create what were known as community-based development projects. These projects required community-owned land to operate and therefore bolstered the collectivists' preferences for managing a significant portion of the territory centrally.

During my summer 2009 visit to Rukullakta, Nelson Chimbo, president at the time, proudly showed me Geographical Information System analyses of land cover within Rukullakta's borders. He pointed to one map in which approximately 11,000 hectares (of the total 41,888.5 hectares) had been set aside for conservation. He planned to use the fact that Rukullakta was conserving so much land to attract conservation-based development projects. I asked him how he planned to prevent people from claiming land and clearing forest there. He said: "It was part of the document they signed when we switched from being a cooperative to the PKR [an organizational switch that members voted on in December 2006]. They signed it, they have to follow it." Soon after my visit, he gained official state recognition for the 11,000-hectare reserve through the Socio Bosque (partner forest) Program, run through the Ministry of Environment. The central Rukullakta government receives US $39,500 annually to continue protecting the land (the program is further discussed in chapter 4).

The officials who run the program in the Ministry of Environment presumably think that the central leaders of Rukullakta determine what occurs within these reserve lands, or that a consensus was reached among all of the members to enter a contract to conserve the reserve. As of 2011, tensions over the contract were already starting to develop, as the reserve overlapped with the properties claimed by just eight of the seventeen communities in Rukullakta, and central leaders were using the funds for territorywide initiatives rather than favoring members of those eight communities in spending decisions. This issue will be further described in chapter 4, but for now it is worth emphasizing that property regimes remain a process rather than a product in Rukullakta, with conflicting claims that speak to the proper relationship among Kichwa people, the proper relationship between leaders and citizens, and the proper relationship between people and the lands they claim.

Conclusion

Given the emphasis on norms, rules, and sanctions in the literature on commonly held lands, perhaps the most surprising aspect of property regimes in Rukullakta is how they have remained so contested for so long. Yet this is only surprising if Rukullakta's territory is imagined as either an ancient territory based on traditional social relations, or as an autonomous political entity, free from external efforts to shape property regimes. As I have argued throughout this book, collective territorial ownership was a legal process in which Rukullakta's members participated because they believed it was the best way — possibly the only way — to defend their access to ancestrally claimed territory subsequent to the agrarian reforms of 1964 and 1973. This dramatic change from household-claimed and defended lands to a centrally administered territory that included 207 kinship groups, and the associated creation of a territorial government that was assumed by outsiders to have the ability to determine land use within the territory's borders, initiated complex controversies over understandings of property, personhood, and obligation.

As this chapter reveals, the formation of the territorial government was only one of several points at which outsiders attempted to persuade Rukullakta's residents to reconfigure these understandings. Since the formation and legalization of the territorial government in the 1970s, a number of external organizations have shifted the terms of debate within Rukullakta, challenging any attempt to establish norms within the territory as well as the ability of territorial residents to make long-term plans based on a belief in the continuity of particular alliances. These entities include the Ecuadorian National Development Bank, through its collectivist cattle ranching projects; an indigenous organization created by Catholic missionaries promoting private, family-held property over collective ownership; the Ecuadorian military, which constructed a road that entered Rukullakta's territory; and environmental organizations and Ecuador's Ministry of Environment, which have funded collectivist pursuits such as ecotourism and large-scale territorial conservation through the Socio Bosque Program. When cattle flowed into the cooperative through state-backed loans, most members were willing to view large areas as collectively owned and centrally managed; when financing for cattle disappeared, most members sought private control over an area in which they could grow cash crops. In the late 1990s, a new force—conservationists and their funds—shifted the balance of power once again toward a more collectivist, centrally managed regime of land tenure, reviving a collectivist system that had seemed to be on the wane.

Although the broader literature on commons regimes has recognized the importance of communities' relationship to the state (Agrawal 2001; Baland and Platteau 1996; Ostrom 1990; Wade 1988), residents of indigenous territories are still often imagined to live in relative isolation from state programs and other relationships that might influence property-related rights and obligations. This image of indigenous territories as isolated can be further solidified in Western minds through the predominant attention that has been paid by scholars to indigenous senses of place (Basso 1996; Escobar 2008; Feld and Basso 1996; García-Hierro and Surrallés 2005; Rappaport 2005a; and Santos-Granero 2005) and traditional ecological knowledge (Ingold 2000; Posey and Balée 1989; Scott 1998).

In this chapter, I have sought to show how internal disagreements about what the cooperative landscape and property-scape should look like have continued, in part because outsiders have continued to try to shape land use and property regimes in Rukullakta. Furthermore, internal disputes are not easily attributed to differences between leaders and other residents, or between modernists and traditionalists. Rather, the three ideals described have been held by both leaders and non-leaders, and all three combine older ideas with ones promoted by the state in the late 1960s and early 1970s. Even when it seems that a particular perspective is becoming more established, residents continue to engage in acts of persuasion to encourage others to adopt their ideas on how much land should be centrally managed and how much should be individually claimed. These acts range from collectivists' efforts to convince government officials and development organizations to fund public infrastructure projects (such as assembly halls) and collectivist development projects (such as collective cattle ranching and community-based ecotourism) to egalitarianists' acts of delimiting twenty-five-hectare parcels for themselves in lands that the territorial government had zoned for collective use.

The viewpoints that Rukullakta's citizens have taken on how the division of land within the cooperative should occur are tied to their perspectives on appropriate relationships among people, including those between citizens and their elected leaders. Those who argue in favor of collective labor projects and land tenure see a strong, centralized organization as critical to improving all citizens' quality of life, including the need to fight periodic battles to maintain control of the title and the need to make the organization attractive to development organizations. As they highlight these benefits to living together in an organized way, they remind their fellow residents that being part of the organization entails responsibilities as well as rewards.

Meanwhile, both those who refused to abandon their claims to the lands they controlled prior to the cooperative's formation and those who sought the equal division of cooperative lands into privately managed family plots distrust the ability of central leaders to manage large, collectivist projects on land that belongs to "everyone" in Rukullakta. People have said to me countless times, "when it belongs to everyone, it belongs to no one." Egalitarianists view their claims to twenty-five-hectare parcels as justified through the work they or their parents did in creating the collective territory, including both the arduous work they contributed in delimiting the land claim with topographers and caring for the collective cattle to show state officials that the cooperative deserved a large parcel of land. Conservatives, on the other hand, emphasize relationships forged and labor exerted even prior to the formation of the territorial organization. The language of relationships and associated rights that is commonly used to talk about property in Rukullakta illustrates the deep connections among property, identity, and reciprocity.

CHAPTER FOUR

CONSERVATION AND ENVIRONMENTAL SUBJECTS

Many aspects of current Western-style conservation run counter to the ways most Upper Napo Kichwa generally thought of the forest in the past. One key example is the modern emphasis placed on wilderness conservation, by which I mean prohibiting almost all human activities in extensive areas of land for the presumed benefit of plants and animals. At the most basic level, when Kichwa from the Upper Napo region speak about the period prior to the 1970s—which brought agrarian reforms, road building, and the extraction of petroleum in the northeast Ecuadorian Amazon, all of which increased the number of colonists homesteading in the region—it is clear that the forest seemed plentiful. According to their recollections of this time, when tensions arose within a family group, it was always possible for people to break away and move to a previously unclaimed area of forest farther from the mission town to build a home, plant a garden, hunt, and fish. Indeed, when colonization in the Upper Napo first began, some Kichwa did this, selling the lands they had claimed earlier to colonists for cattle and taking the cattle farther into the forest to claim new lands and raise the animals there. Thus, it is safe to say that most Upper Napo residents were not overly concerned about limits to the forest before the 1970s. Prior to the construction of new roads and colonization programs promoted by the Ecuadorian government, population levels remained low (Muratorio 1991, 142–45); the market for forest products was minimal (with the exception of gold and *pita*, or agave fiber); and there is no indication that the hunting, fishing, and very limited agriculture and cattle ranching that Kichwa practiced put any species at risk of extinction.

On another level, wilderness conservation and other aspects of Western environmentalist thought are predicated on an understanding of people as having the power to either endanger or protect animals and plants (Milton 1996). In the Upper Napo, most people have not felt that they were in such a position of unequivocal power in relation to nature. Jaguars eat your chickens; anacondas swallow your children whole (or at least so people say); and a host of diseases, fungi, and animals attack your gardens and cash crops. Most people see nature as a powerful force in their lives, not as a fragile entity that needs to be carefully protected.

Furthermore, beliefs and stories that blur the boundaries among humans, animals, and forest spirits abound. For example, Michael Uzendoski (2010) relates two stories that are indicative of many that continue to circulate in the Upper Napo. In one, a river dolphin became a human through shape-shifting and then impregnated a woman, who went on to give birth to two dolphins. In the other, a snake that was really a forest spirit exacted revenge on the man who had turned its skin into a belt. What appears to be a jaguar can in fact be a human, as powerful shamans are capable of shifting shape (Uzendoski 2005). Disease in one's plants and domesticated animals can be caused by the ill will or jealousy of one's neighbor and therefore reflects tensions in human relationships rather than the predatory activities of micro-organisms. Animals can be "locked up" (spiritually kept away from those who want to find them) by people who are jealous of the ecotourism success of their neighbors, so that tourists will be disappointed with their experience (Hutchins 2010, 31). Given these complex understandings of the relationships between humans and the natural and spiritual world, combined with varied understandings of what might cause animals to disappear or die, environmentalists' overwhelming focus on preventing hunting and cutting down trees seems, at best, simplistic.

Like many indigenous peoples (Chapin 2004), Kichwa in the Upper Napo put the need to protect and legalize their own use of their lands at the top of their organizations' agendas (see chapter 1). Since the late 1980s, however, Western conservationists have been a relatively constant part of many Amazonians' lives, and the money and political connections the conservationists possess have been impressive to indigenous leaders. Environmentalists have worked with and through various organizations in Ecuador, including governmental organizations — which means that local leaders hear environmentalist messages from various sources, including the Ecuadorian state, the various schools and universities that they attend, and local municipal authorities. (For example, Archidona Canton, where most of Rukullakta's territory is located, recently designated itself "An Ecological Canton"). The leaders also hear these messages from the larger indigenous federations to which they belong, including those that represent Napo Province, the Ecuadorian Amazon, and the multinational Amazon Basin. This chapter, therefore, traces some of the changes in local Rukullakta leaders, as well as in the larger indigenous federations to which the cooperative belongs. By showing these various sites in which indigenous politics are being shaped and debated, I seek to demonstrate that even though there are multiple perspectives on the goals that environmentalists from the global north have pursued in Ecuador, and even though many conservation-oriented programs are hotly contested and negotiated among indigenous leaders, there has still been a noticeable shift over time toward a more Western way of thinking about the environment and sustainable development. Because indigenous territories encompass significant areas of intact rainforest, this has profound implications for the obligations of indigenous citizenship and leadership, and for the enactment of indigenous sovereignty more generally. In particular, most conservation initiatives both assume and reward strong central governments in indigenous territories, much as the cattle ranching projects of the 1970s did.

The following exchange, documented in Rukullakta's archives of meeting minutes, is indicative of the ways in which conservationists have shaped the development projects pursued by Rukullakta's leaders. One leader, Ramiro Chimbo, a graduate of Quito's Central University, presented a new project to the council of subcenter presidents:

> Food Security Project: On this point it was expressed that the Food Security Project was designed to value or rescue our old sustenance practices, because our grandparents consumed products exclusively from [this] area. For that reason, it is necessary to recover the ability to gain adequate sustenance from the products [of our local environment] including

the animals (birds, fish) as well as seeds of rice, peanuts, beans, corn, and others, as well as egg-laying hens and fish.

[Chimbo continued:] Now the distribution of these animals and seeds is considered to be a form of credit, and we will therefore keep track of the quantity that each member obtains, whether it be animals or seeds. One would have to sign an agreement concerning the exchange, since the objective is to conserve the products.

Then he [Chimbo] asked those present to express their opinions on what he had described. On hearing this proposal, the leader of the community of Pavayaku asked the following: so I cannot eat the chickens because that is the only way that I will conserve the chickens?

In response to that doubt, Engineer [Chimbo] clarified that yes, you may eat or sell [them, but] at the same time you will have to buy [a chick] to conserve the number of chickens received and in that way continue with [the same number of] whatever product you received. (*Actas*, June 23, 2008)

The way in which Chimbo designed the project resonates with several trends in environmentalist thinking. First, planting crops that previously had been an important part of people's home gardens resonates with the local food movement in North America and Europe, which looks to locally grown produce as a source of better nutrition (fruits and vegetables that travel long distances are typically lower in nutrients than those that have not) and as a way of reducing the pollution associated with long-distance transport. Second, the project's appeals to the past and the practices of the people's grandparents resonate with some environmentalists' appreciation of traditional ecological knowledge (often referred to as "TEK" in the scholarly and policy literature).

Finally, based on the products that the leaders list (rice, peanuts, beans, corn, eggs, and fish), most of which have better market potential than some traditionally grown products (such as manioc, plantains, and fruit from trees), the project was presumably also designed to encourage people to change the crops they grow for income. In the 1990s and early 2000s, when the price for *naranjilla* was very high, it became the primary cash crop grown in the Upper Napo. It grows best on recently deforested soils, and many of Rukullakta's residents moved to forested regions of the territory to cut down forest and grow the crop in much more of a monoculture fashion than they usually practice. The combination of forest clearing and monoculture, with the addition of pesticides in later years, helped make *naranjilla* what many environmentalists called an "enemy crop." Conservationist organizations in the Upper Napo, therefore, have sought alternatives that could be grown in areas that were already populated and produce the same income as *naranjilla* without requiring the clearing of forests and subsequent use of pesticides. Chimbo's project fit neatly within that agenda.

In his question about eating the chickens, Pavayaku's president ridiculed the project: what is the point of having chickens (and, by implication, feeding them and taking care of them) if you cannot eat them? After Chimbo finished his succinct response, another long-term leader added a more locally meaningful justification for the project, expressing its benefits in pragmatic and economic terms rather than using Chimbo's rationale of replicating the practices of their grandparents. He said: "We are capable of raising chickens at home and [in this way] abandoning the practice of buying products in the city; let us take advantage of planting, in an orderly fashion, cocoa, corn, rice, beans, and other crops and strengthening our food security. Furthermore, in the future this will help us to create a farmers' market inside the organization" (*Actas*, June 23, 2008). In this addendum, the second leader presented the project as one that could reduce families' expenses for food bought outside of Rukullakta and offered a vision for increasing household income through the formation of a farmers' market.

None of the second leader's ideas were new to farmers; many have grown these products at some point in their lives, and there were already some opportunities in the region for selling them to the residents of Archidona (a nearby town) and Tena (the provincial capital). However, most farmers believe that, with the exception of cocoa, the amount that can be earned from these crops is too low to make growing them for sale particularly worthwhile. And even in the case of cocoa, used to make chocolate, the price fluctuates dramatically based on global markets, making many local farmers reluctant to invest substantial money or labor in growing it.

Following the second leader's explanation, questions were raised about who would finance the project. When Chimbo responded that the German bilateral aid organization GTZ was providing $30,000, and that half of this sum was already in the organization's coffers, the tone of the discussion changed quickly, moving to pragmatic issues of how the project would be implemented. One subcenter president asked whether crops grown at higher elevations were among those being funded, as the members of his community had lands at higher elevations. Another asked what documents had to be submitted for participation. And finally, one community president congratulated Chimbo for his initiative, calling on her peers to provide a model for other organizations in their execution of the project. Once it was framed as an initiative that provided both access to capital and an opportunity to be a model for other indigenous organizations, the leaders approved the project unanimously.

Chimbo grew up in Rukullakta and has spent most of his life living there, but he had become so immersed in Western ways of framing conservation projects (using terms such as "food security" and "rescue our old sustenance practices") that he forgot he would need to translate these development goals into a framework that would be more meaningful to those who had not spent as much time as he had with Western-style environmentalists. This is the tricky terrain that indigenous leaders navigate, a process that Michael Hathaway (2010) terms "transnational work." Hathaway argues against the notion that conservation agendas can be unilaterally imposed. Rather, he demonstrates how they must first gain traction through the efforts of multiple agents, by and through particular social engagements. In the case of Rukullakta, leaders must create projects that will simultaneously be attractive to funders, win indigenous participants, and improve the welfare of participants. If the leaders promote a project that fails in any of these three areas, they lose status as leaders and the members become increasingly cynical about the benefits of collectivist development projects.

In recent years a number of scholars have questioned whether the resources associated with conservation and the long-term engagement between urban environmentalists and indigenous people has had a noticeable effect on the latter's views of the environment. For example, building on work by Benedict Anderson (1983), Arjun Appadurai (1996), James Carrier and Daniel Miller (1998), and Vincent Crapanzano (2004), Paige West argues that conservationists wield the power to shape "the social imaginary, a set of ideas that have come to be taken as common sense by some, and on which those with power act in ways that make the real world conform to the imagined one" (2006, 10). Because environmentalists emphasize the existence and importance of native animal and plant life in certain parts of the world, the people who live in those places are delegated to a secondary position, becoming something that should be managed, rather than playing key roles in determining the policies that will affect their lives. In large part because of this power imbalance, tensions continue between environmentalists and local people in Papua New Guinea, West argues. In her analysis, conservationists have been able to shape the way that government officials and distant development funders have understood indigenous New Guineans and the region where they live but have not been as successful in converting indigenous New Guineans into Western-style conservationists.

In a very different part of the world, the Canadian Yukon, Paul Nadasdy (2004) has examined the ways that Kluane leaders' understandings of the land and wildlife have changed. He suggests that the bureaucratic burdens placed on the leaders as part of their land claims process (having to sit in offices and attend meetings with Canadian ministry officials during much of the day, over the course of several years, in order to gain secure title to their ancestral territory) has greatly reduced the amount of time they spend outdoors and hunting. This has, in turn, reduced their intimate knowledge of the landscape and wildlife behavior. Other processes initiated by the Canadian government, such as forcing young people to attend boarding schools in the mid-twentieth century and constructing a road through Kluane territory, have also contributed to dramatic changes in the way most Kluane understand land and animals, Nadasdy argues. These many changes have also contributed to different patterns of exchange, as people no longer share hunted meat as much as they used to.

Finally, working in yet another part of the world, Arun Agrawal (2005) has argued that the creation of community-based forest councils in India, charged with setting policies regarding the use of collectively held forests, has led to a change in understandings of the forest among forest council members. Given the responsibility for ensuring the long-term survival of the forests (and threatened with the loss of access to those forests if the Indian Forest Department determines that they are not fulfilling this role), forest council members have come to see the forest as something that is limited and fragile and must be actively protected by people. They see themselves as carrying the obligation to protect the community forest for future generations, a dramatic shift in subjectivity that Agrawal terms "environmentality."

All three of these perspectives have something to offer in understanding what has occurred in Rukullakta and the Ecuadorian Amazon more generally. First, environmentalists have undoubtedly played a key role in shaping worldwide understandings of the Amazon as a hot spot for biodiversity and as a place where indigenous people live in harmony with this biodiversity. This has affected not only the way that schoolchildren in the United States imagine the Amazon, but also the way schoolchildren in the Ecuadorian Amazon understand their home and themselves. Thus, as West argues, through more than two decades of environmental education and investments in "conservation as development," environmentalists have succeeded to some extent in making "the real world conform to the imagined one" (2006, 10). This does not mean that young people in the Upper Napo never want to eat hunted meat or want to limit themselves to owning a single pair of shoes in the name of conservation, but it is now very common to hear both children and young adults talk about the Amazon rainforest as something precious, beautiful, and threatened, as well as about their own responsibility to ensure its conservation.

Second, similar to the lands claims professionals whom Nadasdy describes, a group of indigenous sustainability professionals (including Ramiro Chimbo, quoted above) has been created in the Upper Napo, partly by the financial resources associated with conservation. These professionals, like those indigenous individuals who have made careers out of working for political parties and running for political offices (described in chapter 5), typically think of themselves as leaders of the indigenous community. They sometimes run for political office themselves, as it is generally believed that the connections they have forged and the experience they have gained working for conservation-driven development projects have also prepared them to fill governance roles in the municipality and in the territory. For example, members of a prominent political party in the region convinced Jaime Shiguango, a university-educated agronomist from Rukullakta who has held managerial positions in multiple sustainability projects, to run for mayor of Archidona.[1] These professionals spend much less time farming, hunting, and fishing than other indigenous people in the region, given the responsibilities of the various posts they hold. Has this led them to lose touch with the territorial citizens they are elected to govern? This is one of the questions that will be explored through the historical analysis provided in this chapter. An overlapping question, stemming in part from Agrawal's arguments concerning the shifting subjectivities emerging from the practice of governance in forest councils, is whether Rukullakta's population as a whole has come to think of nature as limited and needing protection through the policies and restrictions set by the territorial government.

Regional Indigenous Organizations and Conservation

Increased international attention to both the Amazon as a vital ecosystem and to the plight of the indigenous people who live there inspired environmental NGOs and bilateral development organizations alike to provide new financial resources for indigenous organizations in the 1980s. Mac Chapin dates this shift to 1989, after the Coordinadora de las Organizaciones Indígenas de la Cuenca Amazonica (Coordinator of Indigenous Organizations of the Amazon Basin, or COICA) made an appeal directly to "the community of concerned environmentalists" at the international level, proposing that they form an alliance "in defense of our Amazonian homeland" (2004, 19). The appeal also included the following statement:

> We, the Indigenous Peoples, have been an integral part of the Amazon Biosphere for millennia. We have used and cared for the resources of that biosphere with a great deal of respect, because it is our home, and because we know that our survival and that of our future generations depends on it. Our accumulated knowledge about the ecology of our home, our models for living with the peculiarities of the Amazon Biosphere, our reverence and respect for the tropical forest and its other inhabitants, both plant and animal, are the keys to guaranteeing the future of the Amazon Basin, not only for our peoples, but also for all humanity. (quoted in Chapin 2004, 19)

Although Chapin may be correct in that the quantity of resources dedicated by the largest conservation organizations to collaborating with indigenous organizations increased dramatically after this statement was issued, the language used in COICA's appeal — including words such as "biosphere" and appeals to the concepts of traditional ecological knowledge and reverence for the tropical forest — indicates that they were already engaged with Western environmentalism. This does not mean that the writers were being deceptive, for they did want to protect their lands and wanted environmentalists' help in keeping out extractive industries, gaining title to lands for indigenous peoples, and other such projects. But, similar to the way in which Chimbo (the engineer described at the beginning of the chapter) was able to gain agricultural credit through an application that framed his project as one that would increase biodiversity and provide an avenue for the continued use of traditional ecological knowledge, COICA was able to make an appeal that simultaneously addressed its own goals and was attractive to potential allies.

The decade that preceded COICA's appeal corresponded with the forging of new indigenous organizations in Ecuador that spanned larger areas than past groups had, incorporated people from various ethnicities, and strove to pursue political projects at the national and international levels. The Confederación de Nacionalidades Indígenas de la Amazonía Ecuatoriana (Confederation of Indigenous Nationalities of the Ecuadorian Amazon, or CONFENIAE) was formed in August 1980, when leaders from FOIN; the Organización de Pueblos Indígenas de Pastaza (Organization of Indigenous Peoples of Pastaza), the newly established Kichwa organization for Pastaza Province, just south of Napo; and the Shuar Federation, from the southern Ecuadorian Amazon, held their first congress. The influence of these organizations' engagements with environmentalists during the early 1980s can be seen through an analysis of the issues the delegates discussed during CONFENIAE's biannual congresses prior to the appeal cited by Chapin. At the first congress in 1980, there was little evidence of environmentalists' influence. The only issues pertaining to the environment included in the resolutions were gaining more lands for indigenous peoples and pursuing both agricultural intensification and cattle ranching projects to improve their income (CONAIE 1989, 100).

In the next three conferences, held in 1982, 1984, and 1986, there was a steady increase in the number of issues discussed that pertained to the environment. In the 1982 congress, delegates continued to talk about gaining additional lands for indigenous people. Kichwa and Shuar representatives who had attended the first congress had invited delegates from the less formally organized indigenous nationalities in the Ecuadorian Amazon — such as Cofán, Siona, Secoya, and Huaorani (also spelled Waorani) — to join them in the congress and prioritized assisting these groups in their land claims. The congress issued resolutions that urged the reduction of negative impacts associated with petroleum extraction, mining, and African palm plantations on indigenous lands, indicating a growing awareness of the environmental contamination each of these caused — particularly the damage caused by petroleum extraction in the northeastern Ecuadorian Amazon (where Cofán, Siona, and Secoya live).

By the fourth congress, in December 1986, delegates were discussing several new issues concerning the environment. For the first time at this congress, they also addressed the perceived need to be more proactive in conserving forests and their flora and fauna. Specifically, the 1986 resolutions included a call to reforest indigenous lands and the suggestion that communities control hunting and gathering of animal and plant species. Resolutions under the heading "Defense and Utilization of Natural Resources" included the following:

1. That CONFENIAE will create a project to conserve, utilize, and take advantage of timber resources.
2. That the federations, with the support of CONFENIAE, will generate reforestation campaigns in all of the communities.
3. That CONFENIAE will create development projects in the areas of agriculture, fish farming, and livestock according to the communities' conditions.
4. That the communities will control the utilization of faunal, floral, and fish resources in their territories.
5. That CONFENIAE will promote cultivation programs for traditional products.
6. That CONFENIAE will contract with technical personnel and assistants to create projects in defense of natural resources in indigenous communities. (CONAIE 1989, 106)

With these resolutions, the delegates demonstrated a continuing commitment to increasing the welfare of their constituents through strengthening territorial control and increasing production. This is clear in the title of the section: "Defense and Utilization of Natural Resources." However, the resolutions also included various conservationist goals and a corresponding shift toward recognizing the limited quantities of natural resources. For example, there were mentions of reforestation (so that trees would be available to future generations), planting of "traditional products" (it is unclear if this is directed at improving nutrition and food security, conserving cultural practices, increasing income from marketing these products, or some combination of the three), and greater centralized control over the use of floral and faunal resources.

Finally, it is also clear that congress participants were increasingly seeing collaboration with environmental organizations in terms of job creation. If conservation organizations typically prioritized the drafting of management plans (Chapin 2004, 21), indigenous organizations could improve the welfare of at least some of their constituents by ensuring that the "technical personnel," or at least "the assistants," came from their constituents, with salaries provided by the conservation organizations. There was also an explicit recognition at the 1986 conference that forming alliances with external organizations brought power as well as funding, and congressional participants took pride in having "won a space in the national stage, as well as having consolidated a position in the international camp, especially with organizations that are concerned with indigenous issues" (CONAIE 1989, 104).

Importantly, the points that overlap with conservationist goals and the recognition of the power and funding achieved through collaborations with environmentalists are framed in such a way that they could also be understood as improving the welfare of constituents, rather than robbing them of their rights to use resources. Even the idea that the communities should "control the utilization of faunal, floral, and fish resources in their territories" could be read as a call for stronger, centralized management of indigenous territories and greater efforts to keep outsiders out of the territories, rather than as a call for indigenous people to stop using these resources.

Despite the continuing commitment to increasing production, a new perspective has taken hold: that natural resources have limits — even the term "resources" indicates a Western-inflected approach to nonhuman living things — and thus the resources must be collectively managed. Furthermore, the resolutions reflect the perspective that humans, including marginalized peoples, have a role to play in managing the use of natural resources. These framings do not emerge in the summaries of the first three congresses, but they firmly underlie the resolutions made during the fourth congress, indicating that by the mid-1980s, engagement with Western environmentalists was strongly shaping leaders' understandings of the environment in which they lived.

Conservation in Napo Province in the 1990s

Conservation organizations also became key supporters of FOIN, the provincial-level organization to which Rukullakta belonged, during the 1980s. FOIN entered into conservation-oriented development projects with multiple international organizations such as the World Wildlife Fund, and these projects soon became a critical source of funding for FOIN (Perreault 2003, 598). The importance of these funds became particularly pronounced after an earthquake on March 5, 1987, that caused substantial damage to roads in the Ecuadorian Amazon, cutting off several Upper Napo communities from the national transportation grid. The earthquake simultaneously cut off access to Ecuador's oil fields, which lie about 150 kilometers northeast of the Upper Napo region. To reduce the possibility of a future interruption in access to these fields, the Ecuadorian government decided to construct an alternative road to connect the oil region to other national roads. According to the plan, the new access road, referred to as the Hollín-Loreto Road, would pass within a few kilometers of the entire northern border of the cooperative (see map 3.4). At the same time, the national government declared the 100,000-hectare area surrounding the proposed road a "Forest and Vegetation Preserve" in an effort to protect important watersheds in the area. Also in 1987, the Fundación Natura, Ecuador's largest environmental NGO (which was receiving substantial funding from the World Wildlife Fund at the time), recommended including the area within the national system of protected areas (which would have implied a greater level of protection than currently existed), although the state did not change the designation then (Larrea 2001).

The 1987 earthquake and the road-building plan were vital in bringing the region surrounding the cooperative to the attention of a variety of international and national organizations. One of the first organizations to arrive was Cultural Survival (a US-based organization that promotes indigenous rights). Noting that the construction of the new road made indigenous communities vulnerable to land grabs by colonists, Cultural Survival and FOIN produced a joint report called "The Legalization of Indigenous Lands and Management of Natural Resources in the Zone of Influence of the Hollín-Loreto Road" in 1988 (Perreault 2000).

Environmental groups provided a new idiom and institutional structure through which FOIN and other indigenous organizations could make claims to land and natural resources (Perreault 2003, 598), as well as emphasize the importance of strong indigenous territorial organizations and governance. For example, in a letter to a Dutch organization, the Humanistic Institute for Cooperation with Developing Countries, FOIN requested funding for its 1992 congress (the same year as the famed Earth Summit in Rio de Janeiro, Brazil). The request stated: "We believe that the best investment for protecting the global resources, which our tropical rainforest produces for the whole planet, is to invest in the strengthening of our institutions and to support the indigenous people of the rainforest who love and sincerely respect our Pacha Mama (Mother Earth)" (quoted in Perreault 2003, 598). Along the same lines, the stationery for the Programa de Uso y Manejo de Recursos Naturales (Project for the Management and Use of Natural Resources), administered by FOIN and funded from 1988 to 1998 by Cultural Survival and the World Wildlife Fund, included a drawing of a tree and a deer and the words "Región Amazónica, pulmón verde del mundo" ("Amazon region, green lung of the world") (Perreault 2003, 599).

Rukullakta, both as FOIN's largest member organization and through its geographical location just south of the new road, also received some attention from environmental organizations after the earthquake, but less than FOIN itself did. Fundación Natura, which had proposed placing the region under protected status in 1987, first appears in Rukullakta's archives on August 10, 1990, when the foundation invited two representatives from the cooperative to participate in a two-day environmental education seminar it was holding in Tena. In 1991 Ayuda en Acción (Help in Action), a development NGO from Spain, began working along the Napo River on sustainable development projects and visited Rukullakta a few years later (*Actas*, October 23, 1993).

Despite this exposure, there is very little evidence in Rukullakta's archives to indicate that its leaders were concerned about conservation or interested in conservation programs or messages that were being promoted by the environmental NGOs visiting the region in the early 1990s, even though CONFENIAE and FOIN were actively reaching out to environmentalists. Prior to the 1990s, the only restriction that Rukullakta's leaders had attempted to enforce through conservationist appeals was a ban on using a natural poison, *barbasco*, for fishing, arguing that it "destroyed the rivers" (*Actas*, October 2, 1976; February 9, 1985).

The other way in which Rukullakta's leaders promoted conservation, albeit indirectly, was through their efforts to prevent and slow the dividing into parcels of the northeastern quadrant of the cooperative (described in chapter 3). During the discussions over the homesteading activities of some of the members, leaders also began to express concern over logging that was occurring within the cooperative's boundaries and the need for the leadership to exert some control over the practice:

The *compañero* President of the Land Commission of the Cooperative F...S... manifests that the *compañeros* [three names are listed], without respecting the decisions of the Cooperative leaders, continue destroying wood [cutting down trees], and working without previous authorization, and they do not fulfill the obligations that we as members have with the Cooperative, [nor] to the [sub]center to which they belong. For this reason, in the Assembly they resolved to expel them from the Cooperative, given that they are not residents within the perimeter of the Cooperative [they had moved outside of Rukullakta's territory, but were logging inside it]. (*Actas*, May 19, 1990)

In this quote and others from this period (see, for example, *Actas*, April 16, 1991), the leaders' primary concern was that the people who were benefiting from the fine woods in the northeastern region of the territory were not active members of the local subcenter or the cooperative. The primary argument was that the denounced individuals were not fulfilling the obligations of citizenship, and therefore they should not enjoy the benefits of citizenship. Thus, the proposed solution was to expel them from the list of organizational members. Although some sense of the limited quantity of valued hardwoods can be inferred from the fact that the logging was even brought up at a meeting for discussion, there is no mention in the archives of habitat conservation; the damage that logging can cause to wildlife, soils, or rivers; or any other such Western environmentalist framing. The individuals were "destroying wood," not destroying "the rainforest" or "wildlife habitat," or even "trees." It was the economically valuable resource — wood — that needed to be defended against those who were not active citizens of the territory. Thus, it seems that leaders were not particularly worried about the issues that were concerning environmental NGOs at the time this discussion took place.

Rukullakta's Harsh Wake-Up Call

Shortly after this discussion, however, leaders were directly confronted with the growing power of the international conservation movement in the region, ironically through actions taken by one of Rukullakta's own members. In 1991 Casimiro Mamallacta, one of the cooperative's founding members, formed an NGO, at first calling it the Fundación Mamallacta (the Mamallacta Foundation) and later changing the name to the Fundación Izu Mangallpa Urcu (Foundation Izu Mangallpa Urcu [Mountain of the Land of the Jaguar], or IMU)[2] (Rogers 1996, 85). Through the NGO and the legitimacy recently afforded to conservation-minded indigenous peoples by international organizations, the Mamallacta family asserted claim to a large area of land for conservation and ecotourism. Of the 18,000 hectares the family claimed, 3,000 fell within Rukullakta's borders (*Actas*, September 19, 1992).

Part of the initiative for forming the NGO can be traced to Mercedes Mamallacta, Casimiro's daughter and another founding member of IMU. She had worked at a research station called Jatun Sacha (Kichwa for "big forest") that was dedicated to biological and ethnobotanical research in the rainforest. Through this job, Mercedes encountered the international ecologists and conservationists who run it and others who resided there for research visits of varying lengths (Rogers 1996, 84). Jatun Sacha also serves as an ecotourism destination; visitors arrive daily to go on guided or self-guided walks in the rainforest, observe gardens of ethnobotanically important plants, and even volunteer to assist with ecological research projects. Through the confluence of Mercedes's exposure to conservation-minded projects and her father's reputation as a shaman, the idea emerged to form a foundation dedicated to the following objectives:

1. Protect the "ancestral" lands of the Mamallactas "which are under their control and possession" and maintain their rights to them "so that they will remain in their natural state";
2. Promote, coordinate, and carry out "research relative to the conservation, use, and development of forest resources"; and
3. Maintain the legends, traditions, and religious myths of the "aborigines" of the "zone of the sacred Galeras mountains." (quotes and paraphrasing from Rogers 1996, 85)

The Mamallactas supported their claims to the land by tracing a historical claim, passed through patrilineal descent within the Mamallacta family (not unlike the claims of the property conservatives described in chapter 3) and tied to their shamanic powers. In a letter to the cooperative leadership dated February 23, 1994, they wrote: "Those of us who form the Center for the Mamallacta Family, are conscious of our justified claims; we are not invading lands nor dividing the cooperative; rather, we want to live united as an ancestral *ayllu* [patrilineal family] in the territories of our fathers, grandfathers, and great grandfathers." Thus, the justification presented to Rukullakta's leaders, unlike that presented to tourists and potential funders, emphasizes traditional Kichwa understandings of property and power (see chapter 3).

Many international conservation organizations were sympathetic to indigenous claims to land, especially when they were based on a history of stewardship. That fact, along with the Mamallactas' apparent demonstrated commitment to conservation (based on the relatively pristine state of the forest at the time and the objectives stated in IMU's charter) constituted a strong case for collaboration. In 1992 the Ministry of Agriculture and Ranching gave IMU official governmental recognition as a foundation and designated its staff as Honorary Wildlife Inspectors in the Field of the Conservation of Nature and Its Wild Plant and Animal Resources. This official designation opened the door for collaboration with the Quito-based NGO the Center for the Investigation of Tropical Forests, which agreed to provide economic and technical assistance to IMU to delineate the boundaries of "their" forest preserve, develop a model botanical garden on the Mamallactas' property, and train personnel in the management of tropical forests (Rogers 1996, 90). The Austrian embassy in Quito also reportedly provided IMU with funds (*Actas*, June 8, 1993).

When IMU interacted with government agencies and with NGOs in Quito, it often limited its claims to the portion of "their" land that was part of the state-owned forest lands, not areas that were legally part of existing indigenous organizations, including the Rukullakta Cooperative (Rogers 1996, 99). However, IMU concurrently attempted to lay claim to lands within the cooperative, as well as to lands within three other legally recognized indigenous territories (the Asociación 10 de Agosto, the Asociación Santa Rosa de Arapino, and the Asociación Las Galeras). The cooperative's leadership reacted strongly to the attempt, arguing that the land was "for other organizations, not for one family" and that "we Organizations have the right to our forest patrimony; they should go where there are free lands" (*Actas*, September 19, 1992).

During an emergency cooperative assembly meeting, the president of FOIN expressed the federation's support of the Rukullakta Cooperative in the dispute with IMU, promising to pursue appeals with the larger indigenous federations to which it belonged, specifically the national-level indigenous rights organization Confederación de Nacionalidades Indígenas del Ecuador (Confederation of Ecuadorian Indigenous Organizations, or CONAIE) and the Ecuadorian Amazonian organization CONFENIAE. However, in the same speech, the president encouraged cooperative leaders to "take care of it [the southwestern region of Rukullakta] as a protected forest," indicating that FOIN was also cognizant of changing international and national priorities toward environmental conservation.

A representative from the state agency IERAC then added that "IERAC does not compete for this [mountain] range, it belongs to the state, and for that reason to you five organizations [FOIN plus the four indigenous territorial organizations listed above]. Organize yourselves and take care not to cut down the trees. The lands are better suited for ecology and reforestation." Then a representative from the Ministry of Agriculture and Ranching (which had previously given the Mamallactas the title "Honorary Wildlife Inspectors") chimed in: "We agree, and I am leaving the forestry promoter in charge so that you all plan the natural resource management plan and in this very way coordinate with the organizations in order to be able to maintain [as is] the protected forest of the Galeras [Mountain] Range" (*Actas*, September 19, 1992).

In this series of comments, cooperative leaders were made well aware of the fact that the views of the Ecuadorian government had changed significantly since the 1970s, when it had supported cattle ranching and even made obtaining land titles dependent on clearing a certain amount of forest for pasture or agriculture. Some of the unspoken messages even imply that it was not enough to hold legal title to the land that the Mamallactas were claiming; Rukullakta's leaders also had to show their commitment to conserving the forested areas to which the Mamallactas were laying claim.

Placed in this difficult position and recognizing that IMU had been very successful in obtaining national and international resources in pursuit of its purportedly conservationist goals, cooperative members then resolved to submit requests for assistance to FOIN, which would then appeal to CONAIE and CONFENIAE, so that IMU "would remain under the control of the Organizations that empower it" (*Actas*, September 19, 1992). The battle continued for several years, with the Mamallactas constructing ecotourism cabins within the cooperative's borders and sending various aggressive notes to the cooperative leadership, insisting that they were going to gain title to 3,000 hectares of the cooperative's lands, even if it meant destroying the cooperative (*Actas*, February 8, 1993; February 11, 1994; March 14, 1994).

Cooperative leaders held firm to their land claim and slowly began discussing their own plans for developing ecotourism within the cooperative. These discussions indicate that the leaders were starting to see ecotourism as something that could potentially provide income to what they saw as legitimate indigenous organizations (including their own), rather than posing a threat to them. In another example of these shifting understandings of ecotourism, when Rukullakta received a memo from FOIN on September 9, 1993, regarding the promotion of ecotourism in the Upper Napo region, the subcenter presidents and centrally elected leaders approved the idea unanimously (*Actas*, October 8, 1993).

From the perspective of Rukullakta's leaders, there was a fundamental difference between FOIN's proposal and the Mamallactas' project. In the latter, benefits accrued to one patrilineal family. In the former, projects were seen as belonging to, operated by, and benefiting multiple patrilineal families. Thus, after an initial defensive response to the actions of IMU, the cooperative leadership attempted to subsume it within FOIN and within the four indigenous territorial organizations that held legal claim to the land IMU was attempting to claim as their own. The Rukullakta leadership was willing to accept IMU's ecotourism activities if IMU remained "under the control of the Organizations that empower[ed] it." When the Mamallactas refused to subject their activities to these organizations' control, the cooperative continued to contest IMU's land claims, stating explicitly that the project should not solely benefit one family. Collectivism that extends beyond kinship groups has been a long-standing, central feature of Rukullakta's leaders' vision for indigenous empowerment (see chapter 2).[3]

At no point were concerns expressed about the restrictions on other uses of the forest that ecotourism would imply. Rather, forest conservation and other environmental concerns had entered the cooperative's understanding of ways to improve the welfare of its members and of increasing indigenous empowerment more generally in an inclusive way, with the focus on benefiting multiple families and respecting the territorial jurisdiction of the various indigenous governments.

Ecotourism and Other Conservationist Initiatives in the 1990s

In another example of this attitude toward ecotourism, in 1994 one of Rukullakta's subcenters, Mushullakta, located in the northeastern region, requested permission from the cooperative's central leadership to pursue ecotourism near the military road that extends southward into the cooperative from the Hollín-Loreto Road (described in chapter 3). The leaders decided to allow a land commission to make an inspection of the lands that Mushullakta hoped to use for this purpose (*Actas*, June 10, 1994). The commission did not act immediately, however, and on July 13, 1994, Mushullakta once again submitted a request to the Administrative Council, requesting that the leaders authorize them to begin ecotourism work, "to continue to defend the forest so that the petroleum companies do not damage this zone" (*Actas*, July 15, 1994). Although petroleum companies posed no immediate threat, this particular framing indicates that the initiators of the project felt that engaging in conservation-oriented development would help create the ties to powerful international organizations that could help prevent any future problems with extractive industries. In the end, the cooperative leadership agreed to set aside over 1,000 hectares of land for conservation. Cooperative leaders gave the subcenter permission to both control access to those lands and to implement an ecotourism initiative there.

In this instance, Rukullakta's leaders were directly confronted with the issue of designating land that could have been used for agriculture (forty families could have been assigned twenty-five-hectare plots in the area) and decided to set aside the land for ecotourism, in large part because of the way in which Mushullakta presented its case. First, it approached the cooperative's leaders and sought their approval before beginning any activities. Second, the subcenter representatives presented ecotourism as an activity that would help defend the territory's lands from claims by petroleum companies. Finally, they presented the project as something that could generate earnings for the multiple families living in Mushullakta and for the cooperative's government, and thus could be used to fund projects that would benefit hundreds of families, unlike the IMU project. All of these arguments were directed at demonstrating that the Mushullakta project would improve the welfare of the cooperative's members as a whole.

Beyond the setting aside of conservation areas and ecotourism, Rukullakta's leaders have discussed various other policies that indicate that they have become very aware of the limited extent of the territory's lands. For example, in 2001 leaders proposed (but as of 2011 had not yet implemented) a measure that would allow only two children of any family to have access to twenty-five-hectare parcels within Rukullakta's territory. This would significantly slow the growth in the number of citizens with rights to land, as many families have four or more children. Such discussions could be interpreted as resulting at least partially from the leaders' exposure to environmentalists. Although in the years soon after the cooperative's formation there was substantial sense of amazement that they had secured 41,888.5 hectares from the state, when they had originally been hoping for 10,000 hectares, this sense of vastness has diminished substantially.

A Biological and Cultural Diversity Hot Spot

Throughout the 1990s, even more dollars streamed into Ecuador for conservation. For example, the Global Environmental Facility (GEF), established in 1991 as a collaborative effort of the World Bank and the United Nations, favored Ecuador in its projects. One of GEF's first initiatives (beginning in April 1992) was a US $7.2 million project for biodiversity conservation in Ecuador. Ecuador was also the site of ten single-country GEF biodiversity protection projects, totaling US $39.2 million in grants, and five climate change projects, totaling US $7.64 million in grants, between 1992 and 2002. And it shared five regional grants (either for Amazonian nations or for Latin America) for biodiversity protection during that decade.

Both GEF and various bilateral funding organizations working in Ecuador, such as the US Agency for International Development and the German GTZ, positioned indigenous Amazonians as stewards of the rainforest during this time. The projects they funded were generally directed at conserving both tropical forests and indigenous cultures, although the former was given a higher priority than the latter. For example, the executive summary of the World Bank's 1990 discussion paper, *Ecuador's Amazon Region: Development Issues and Options* began with this question: "Why single out a national region for specific analysis as part of the Bank's country economic studies?" (Hicks 1990, ix). The first answer supplied for this question was: "Ecuador's Amazon Region has several unique features, among which are the extreme fragility of the region's natural resources, its rich biological diversity, its significant native populations, and its large, but diminishing, petroleum reserves" (Hicks 1990, ix). Shortly thereafter is a section that explains why readers should be concerned about the region's inhabitants:

> The region is home to approximately 85 thousand to 100 thousand native peoples that have retained a relatively autonomous life style. Over the past years, some of these indigenous groups have remained isolated; others have retained their cultural identity while incorporating some services (e.g., education, health care) offered by the broader Ecuadorian society. The opportunity for preservation of cultural choice (including sophisticated ecological knowledge and resource management strategies)

for the Amazon's native populations is another of the region's unique characteristics. (Hicks 1990, ix)

In this paragraph, indigenous people are described as an integral part of the biologically diverse ecosystem in the Amazon, with sophisticated knowledge about it. They have "retained their cultural identity" essentially unchanged despite some participation in public education and health care projects. The executive summary does not acknowledge the widespread cattle ranching projects of the 1970s or the political activism of indigenous organizations, although both are mentioned briefly later in the report. Although it could be argued that indigenous people are empowered to maintain or regain title to land by this positioning as environmental stewards, especially when compared to their mestizo neighbors, there are also risks associated with being portrayed as "ecologically noble savages" (Redford 1990). In this construction, to be indigenous means being a caretaker of the Amazon forest. Residents of indigenous areas are then constrained to acting in particular ways if they hope to sustain this privileged political position (Brosius 1997; Conklin 1997, 2002; Conklin and Graham 1995). In another example of the linking between conservation and indigenous peoples, the Belgian government decided to forgive Ecuador's US $7.5 million debt in 1993 on the condition that 48 percent of the money be converted into a fund destined for social projects, with an emphasis on "reforestation programs and the provision of services to indigenous communities" (quoted in Rogers 1996, 88).

Given the financial incentives involved, Ecuador took several steps to demonstrate that it was worthy of international conservation investment, including setting aside large areas as national parks and ecological reserves. By 1998, 39 percent of the country was under some sort of conservation status, the highest proportion of any nation in the world (Lewis 2000, 111), with at least 16 percent of the country in national parks or biological reserves, the highest level of protection (Varea et al. 1997). In a related development strategy, it changed the rules for registering as an NGO, making it easier for them to be recognized as nonprofit organizations (Lewis 2000, 112). This, in effect, increased the number of people in Ecuador who were engaged in seeking international funding, much of which was linked to conservation and other forms of alternative development, at negligent economic cost to the state. In 1995 GTZ became the largest financial player influencing the direction of development in the Upper Napo region.[4] In collaboration with the Instituto Ecuatoriano Forestal y de Areas Naturales y Vida Silvestre (Ecuadorian Institute of Forests, Natural Areas, and Wildlife), GTZ began the Proyecto Gran Sumaco (Great Sumaco Project), named after the Sumaco Volcano, just north of Rukullakta. The concept guiding the project was to seek "a harmonious relation between human beings and nature through maintaining the integrity of the natural areas and their genetic materials, and the improvement of the quality of life of its population" (Knoblauch 2001, 3).[5]

Soon after beginning its work, the project sought to attract greater international attention to the region by applying for its designation as a "United Nations Biosphere Reserve." Project staff began the lengthy process of compiling the necessary information and developing cross-organizational collaboration (with state agencies and local organizations, including indigenous ones) to be able to submit an application to the United Nations Educational, Scientific, and Cultural Organization (UNESCO). GTZ worked to win broad local approval of the biosphere reserve through several mechanisms, including the sponsoring of periodic meetings with local leaders from the area; financially supporting some of the NGO activities that were seen as promoting environmental sustainability; and conducting pilot projects of what were seen as environmentally and economically sustainable market pursuits, such as the cultivation of oyster mushrooms and silkworms, neither of which is native to the area, as well as various wild fruits that are native to the region.

The application was accepted by UNESCO, and the region was officially declared a biosphere reserve on November 10, 2000. The reserve covers 931,215 hectares, with a core area of 205,249 hectares and a buffer zone of 178,629 hectares. The entire Rukullakta Cooperative fell within the reserve, and about two-thirds of the cooperative was in the buffer zone—which implied that agriculture would be severely restricted there (the other third is within the boundaries of the reserve, but not in either the core area or the buffer zone—see map 4.1). According to the project's application for biosphere reserve status, the buffer zone "presents a minimum of human intervention, containing characteristic ecosystems, in which moderate use is permitted, for scientific ends, tourism, forest management, and wildlife" (Ministerio del Ambiente 2000, 18). Thus, according to the zoning at the time the application was submitted, agriculture was prohibited in most of Rukullakta's territory.

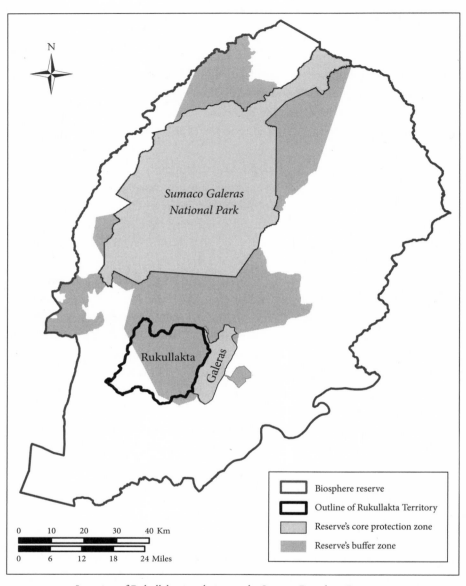

MAP 4.1 Location of Rukullakta in relation to the Sumaco Biosphere Reserve.

One of the primary activities of the Great Sumaco Project during its early years was to study the soils that exist within the biosphere reserve to predict what types of agricultural activities might or might not be sustainable in particular areas. Throughout the plan for the March 2001–February 2002 project year (Larrea 2001), there are calls to advance the "territorial ordering" (*ordenamiento territorial*) of the lands within the reserve based on technical criteria such as soil suitability, and justifications as to why the ordering had not advanced further since the implementation phase of the project began in March 1998. Specifically, project officials asserted that there was a "lack of agencies specifically for planning and little acceptance of the act of planning" (Larrea 2001, 9). Furthermore, "new authorities present new plans that are not necessarily continuous with the processes of the previous authorities," and there is "weakness in the legal frame surrounding territorial ordering" (16). Behind all of these rationalizations is the assumption that central authorities controlled land use throughout the biosphere reserve, including within the Rukullakta Cooperative, and these lands were thus available for top-down land use plans in the first place. At no point is there any evidence that the planners took into consideration the property regimes within indigenous-owned lands that preceded their work in the region (such as those described in chapter 3). The assumption appears to be that territorial residents can simply move their homes, gardens, and agricultural fields to areas that are deemed to have the right soils for those purposes, and that the territorial governments located in the reserve had the authority to make them do so.

Regardless of what the progress reports state, most indigenous people in the region saw the Great Sumaco Project as a source of funding for sustainable development, not as an entity that was telling them to stop engaging in agriculture in certain places. Prior to its termination in 2010, the project invested a significant amount of resources in finding alternative products that held the potential to increase the earnings of the people who produced them. In Rukullakta it paid for an oyster mushroom production project; helped an Ecuadorian NGO that promoted agricultural development projects such as moderate-scale chicken raising (with pens holding a hundred chickens each), pig farming, fish farming, and the production of coffee and cocoa; and, as described at the beginning of the chapter, financed the Food Security Project. In effect, the Great Sumaco Project attempted to entice people toward conservation, experimenting through dozens of pilot projects to see what types of income-earning activities might be attractive to and economically viable for local people, while improving prospects for biodiversity conservation. Through hundreds of meetings with indigenous leaders, women's groups, and government agencies, it attempted to promote a particular way of seeing the forest and the environment in general. Despite its failure to fully impose rational land use in terms of soil suitability, it was a key actor in shifting indigenous leaders' views toward more Western environmentalist understandings of human-environment relationships.

Rukullakta, CONFENIAE, and COICA in the New Millennium

In 2007, with funding from the EcoFund Foundation Ecuador and the assistance of Rodrigo Sierra from the Center for Environmental Studies in Latin America at the University of Texas at Austin — as well as a number of additional experts in Geographic Information Systems, soils, plants, and ornithology — the leaders of Rukullakta began an eight-month process of creating a land management plan. In my subsequent conversations with leaders who had been active in the drafting process, it was clear that they saw the plan both as useful in guiding their own governing activities, and as a critical document to present to potential project financiers. The document is full of numbers on the population, including average family size and education level. It also includes eleven maps of Rukullakta, portraying everything from political boundaries to tree cover and community-level land tenure. Several of the statements are quite startling, such as the following: "If the average family size [in Rukullakta] is eight members per family and this continues in the next two decades, the population could easily pass ten thousand people by the year 2028. This means that an equitable distribution of the territory in the year 2028 would give each member [*sic*][6] approximately 4 hectares" (Plan de Manejo, Pueblo Kichwa de Rukullakta 2008, 49). This was not the first time the leadership had compiled a management plan (there was another one in 1981), but this plan includes substantially more numerical and geographical data than the previous one did, and these representations change the way managers conceptualize the forest. As Agrawal argues, forests' "existence, value, role, importance, and place in the national economy; demands for their protection and management; and concerns about the effects of human interventions can be appreciated only inadequately in the absence of numbers and the use of numbers to represent social facts"

(2005, 33; see also Latour 1987, chapter 6). With these documents and data in hand, Rukullakta's leaders gain a particular kind of knowledge that will contribute to long-term decisions. These decisions stand to have greater impact on territorial citizens' access to land than any other arrangement made since the legalization of the territorial boundaries.

The introduction to the management plan begins with a succinct statement of the leaders' vision for the future: "The communities that make up the Kichwa People of Rukullakta recognize the importance of natural resources which are found in their territory as the base of their economic and social development, and furthermore constitute their natural capital which generates goods, direct and indirect user services. For this reason, they are conscious that these need to be managed sustainably to guarantee the economic and social development of future generations, and that they are a critical element in the participation in new markets of goods and ecological services, taking advantage of green markets and fair trade" (Plan de Manejo, Pueblo Kichwa de Rukullakta 2008, 15). As with the change in CONFENIAE's agenda described above, in which leaders' engagement with environmental NGOs and the more conservationist leanings of state agencies such as IERAC has contributed to their understanding of the scarcity of land and natural resources and the need for long-range planning, this document illustrates that Rukullakta's leaders are increasingly articulating their vision of the future as one in which the territory has limited resources and thus is in need of a stronger level of management.

Also similar to CONFENIAE's shift is the way in which the leaders' concept of the welfare of their population has expanded to include the possibilities of benefiting from the priorities of international conservation-driven organizations and consumers, including such initiatives as organic and fair trade certifications.[7] Interestingly, Rukullakta's leaders do not use the well-rehearsed references to "Pacha Mama" (Mother Earth) and "Lungs of the Planet," both of which were frequently used by other indigenous leaders in the 1990s; rather, the leaders use more scientific concepts such as "ecosystem services." After two decades of exposure to (and for some, salaried positions within) environmental organizations, the leaders comprehend and make use of the sophisticated idioms that conservation biologists and development professionals use to justify the conservation of watersheds. Finally, the management plan demonstrates an openness to experiment with some of the sustainable development projects most in vogue at the time, including direct payment for conservation and obtaining organic and fair trade certifications for agricultural products.

Although the plan reveals significant changes in the ways in which the Rukullakta leaders envisioned their territory and presented it to the outside world, these were not as dramatic as the change in thinking that is implied by setting aside significant areas of the territory for wilderness protection, a trend that has been growing since the 1990s. As described above, in 1994 the community of Mushullakta convinced the Rukullakta leadership to set aside 1,000 hectares for the specific purpose of conservation, and as a potential site for ecotourism. In 1999 the community of Purutuyaku set aside 75 hectares of its community lands for "wildlife reproduction." And in 2008, after a process of thirty-five separate workshops — held in each of the seventeen communities — with members to discuss the issue of conserving land, Rukullakta's membership reached a consensus that there should be a sizeble reserve protected from agriculture so that future generations would be able to experience the forest. Shamans present at the workshops also expressed their opinion that access to forests was important for continuing their work. Based on this consensus, Rukullakta's leaders worked with the researchers from the University of Texas to delimit an 11,000-hectare conservation zone in the southeastern portion of Rukullakta. The reserve occupies about a quarter of the entire territory (and includes the 1,000 hectares that Mushullakta had set aside for conservation in 1994).

Shortly after these meetings were completed and consensus was reached, a representative from the Ministry of Environment visited Rukullakta and described the Socio Bosque (partner forest) Program to its leaders. The latter saw the program as a way of demonstrating the immediate benefit of the reserve, providing them with a better justification for halting encroachments into the area by people who were still unconvinced of the value of setting aside the land. The leaders presented the program to the assembly of members for a vote, and participation was approved (Nelson Chimbo interview, June 16, 2011). Compared to the broad participation in the thirty-five community meetings, a relatively small number of members attended the assembly meeting. Therefore, many did not participate in the vote to sign the contract with the Ministry of Environment. Still, the concern about the potential loss of the forest does seem to be widespread among people in Rukullakta.

If Rukullakta's citizens break the twenty-year Socio Bosque contract with

Ecuador's Ministry of Environment by deforesting any of the 11,000 hect-ares within the first five years, they must return all of the money they had received until that point; within the first ten years, 50 percent of it; and within the first fifteen years, 25 percent (Jaime Shiguango interview, June 13, 2011). Given the financial risks associated with the penalties and length of the contract, there probably would not have been as widespread a consensus on signing up for the program as there was on setting aside a reserve, which carried no obligation to the Ecuadorian government. With the contract and the possibility of having to pay a hefty fine, obligations of territorial citi-zenship have now grown to include the responsibility to protect the forest in this zone, controlling not only one's own agricultural practices but also those of fellow members.

As described at the beginning of this chapter, wilderness conservation re-quires a perspective on nature that is significantly different from the Kichwa ways of thinking about land and living things that were predominant in the first half of the twentieth century. It also goes against long-standing ideas about property, under which one demonstrates ownership through working the land — establishing gardens, planting peach palms, creating trails, and other such actions. When there is no sign that a person is actively using an area of land, even if simply for hunting and fishing, someone else will often claim it for him- or herself. This has continued to occur even after the legal-ization of collective territories in the 1970s. For example, in 2009 the oldest son of Juan Shiguango, the man most often credited with creating the social movement that became the Rukullakta Cooperative, explained to me that he had been granted twenty-five hectares of land in the eastern region of the co-operative. However, he had not been using it or defending it from takeover due to the fact that he held a salaried position in town, and someone else started to farm there, effectively establishing a claim to the land. Thus, the oldest son of the man heralded for securing almost 42,000 hectares of land for Rukullakta's members does not currently own any significant amount of land in Rukullakta's territory beyond the small area where his house and household garden is situated. After telling me this, rather than complaining about his loss of land and the economic security it entails, he simply said: "That is the custom here."

Given these deep-seated understandings of property, members' willing-ness to set aside such a large reserve even before the Ministry of Environment offered financial incentives to do so suggests that Western environmentalists' framings of the forest as fragile and limited have had a strong influence on Rukullakta's members' understandings of their territory. Leaders' willingness to enter into a twenty-year accord with the Ministry of Environment indicates that "autonomy without resources" (Stahler-Sholk 2005, 37) continues to shape the alliances that leaders forge. It also illustrates that the leaders in power at the time were willing to put a high level of faith in the Ecuadorian government. This contrasts sharply with the way in which other indigenous peoples have reacted to programs that offer direct payments for conservation, as will be described below.

Since the signing of the accord with the Ministry of Environment, there have been complaints from various groups in Rukullakta about it but not, as of June 2011, any organized attempts to renege on the contract. The major stimulus of existing complaints has been associated with property boundaries within Rukullakta (see chapter 3). The reserve that receives funding through the Socio Bosque Program overlaps with the property holdings of only eight of the seventeen communities in Rukullakta (see map 4.2). Thus, the members of some of those eight communities see themselves as making a bigger sacrifice than their neighbors and have complained that the funds received through the program should benefit them more than other members of Rukullakta.

Despite what appears to be a conservation "success story," it is important to note that the faith that Rukullakta's government has placed in Ecuador's government institutions to respect their control over land has not been universal among indigenous organizations in the Ecuadorian Amazon. Participation in a program that overlaps substantially with the Socio Bosque Program in Ecuador, known as Reducing Emissions from Forest Destruction and Degradation (REDD or REDD+), has been highly controversial.

REDD+ is one of the pillars of the international approach to climate change. Recent research shows that the combined contribution of deforestation, forest degradation, and peatland emissions accounts for about 15 percent of anthropogenic greenhouse gas emissions, roughly the same as the transportation sector (van der Werf et al. 2009). Under current conceptions, the money for REDD+ would come not only from multilateral organizations and governments in the global north but also from polluting industries: through carbon trading markets, polluting companies would pay forest communities to actively conserve the forests within their territories, thereby presumably reducing global levels of carbon. Many governments,

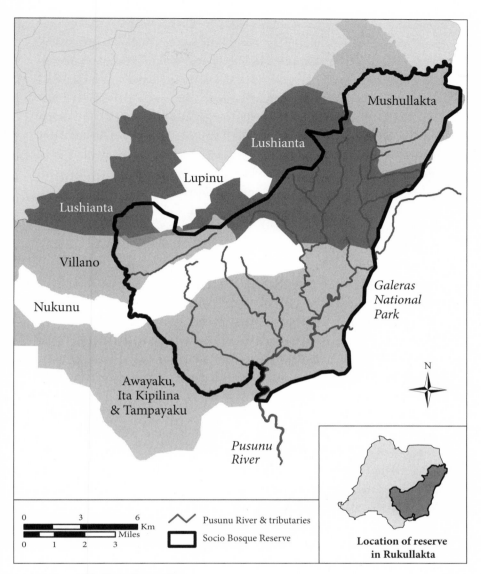

MAP 4.2 The Socio Bosque Reserve.

dominant environmental organizations, and international financial institutions are therefore heralding the possibilities of creating partnerships between polluting industries based in North America and Europe and developing countries that have significant areas of forest, under which the latter would actively protect their standing forests. For example, the United Nations Collaborative Programme on Reducing Emissions from Deforestation and Forest Degradation in Developing Countries (UN-REDD) states: "It is predicted that financial flows for greenhouse gas emission reductions from REDD+ could reach up to US$30 billion a year. This significant North-South flow of funds could reward a meaningful reduction of carbon emissions and could also support new, pro-poor development, help conserve biodiversity and secure vital ecosystem services. Further, maintaining forest ecosystems can contribute to increased resilience to climate change. To achieve these multiple benefits, REDD+ will require the full engagement and respect for the rights of Indigenous Peoples and other forest-dependent communities" (UN-REDD Programme 2009).

Despite UN portrayals of the program that paint it as a clear win-win situation, many indigenous groups have protested against it. Fears that such programs are an initial step toward disenfranchising indigenous peoples exist in the leadership as well as among territorial citizens and extend to indigenous organizations at the regional and national level. The International Indigenous Peoples Forum on Climate Change has argued that "REDD/ REDD+ will not benefit Indigenous Peoples, but in fact will result in more violations of Indigenous Peoples' rights. It will increase the violation of our human rights, our rights to our lands, territories and resources, steal our land, cause forced evictions, prevent access and threaten indigenous agricultural practices, destroy biodiversity and cultural diversity and cause social conflicts" (quoted in Goldtooth 2011, 18). A recent alliance between COICA and the US-based NGO the Environmental Defense Fund (EDF) to create a project funded by international organizations also created very public and pointed arguments between COICA and CONFENIAE about REDD. Under the agreement, EDF channeled REDD funds toward indigenous communities in the Amazon. This incited CONFENIAE to issue a statement condemning the collaboration, which was distributed to various NGOs in the global north in English and Spanish (see appendix 1).

CONFENIAE's statement compares REDD and its implications multiple times to petroleum extraction and mining. By drawing that stark comparison, CONFENIAE's representatives are expressing their fear that participating in agreements such as REDD are analogous to signing over the titles to their territories, allowing environmentalists and carbon traders to gain control of the areas whose legal titles they fought so hard to obtain. The International Indigenous Peoples Forum on Climate Change's statement expresses similar fears. It even appears that the drafters of the CONFENIAE declaration were under the mistaken impression that COICA had already signed over their territories through their collaboration with EDF.

Despite CONFENIAE's harsh assessment, COICA has continued its collaboration with the EDF and signed an additional $1 million REDD technical cooperation project with the Inter-American Development Bank on March 18, 2011, to pursue a series of activities in the Amazon Basin. However, unlike the Ministry of Environment's Socio Bosque Program, the agreement that COICA made with the Inter-American Development Bank highlights training and jobs for indigenous people over simply being paid not to use the land, showing that COICA was able to insert some of its priorities into the collaborative projects. The Inter-American Development Bank website described the project in the following way:

> With a two year period of implementation, the project will support capacity building for indigenous leaders and their communities so that they can more effectively participate in the consultation processes, negotiations and decision-making relating to climate change agendas in the Amazon basin as well as better manage the impacts of climate change on their communities. The project also supports pilot projects and monitoring and evaluation. . . . It will also provide technical assistance for carbon mapping and land management planning, which will become more important as voluntary market mechanisms such as REDD continue to be developed and implemented. (Inter-American Development Bank 2011)

Subsequent to initiating the project, the COICA website went into great detail about how Component 1 of the project involved educating indigenous people about REDD and training them in forest management skills such as measuring trees and using a global positioning system (GPS). Component 2 involved attending international conferences in which funders of REDD would be present. Component 3 was the pilot project component, in which "COICA, the IDB [Inter-American Development Bank], and associated NGOs would work with indigenous communities that have participated in Component 1 [training], to identify the communities with the environment and adequate conditions (such as secure land tenure, capacity, property rights over carbon or agreements for distributing earnings, adequate carbon reserves, community support, etc.)" (COICA 2011). Thus, at least in the way the agreement was presented on the COICA website, many communities from throughout the Amazon Basin could benefit from training in the measurement of carbon storage potential and use of a GPS. Only subsequent to receiving this training would they have to demonstrate that they were willing and able to enter into a carbon trading agreement. The COICA website also included multiple photographs of indigenous people being trained to measure tree diameters at breast height and use a GPS, and being taught other forest management skills.

Similarly, a blog maintained by Chris Meyer, project coordinator of the Amazon Basin for EDF, included the following statement concerning EDF's collaborative work with COICA:

> Instead of having outsiders come in and measure the carbon in the community's trees, indigenous communities can measure it themselves, earn good wages, and learn to value another resource in their forests: carbon . . . The training workshop, which has been adapted for numerous other indigenous groups in the Amazon Basin, teaches and empowers indigenous peoples with technical skills needed for measuring carbon trapped in forests, like using a GPS to find specific coordinates; measuring out a 40 x 40 meter "parcel" of forest; and measuring the diameter of each tree in that area . . . indigenous peoples with forest carbon measuring skills will be able to generate not only **good jobs for locals based on conservation**, but also generate important information regarding the amount of carbon in their lands that will **help them make better land management—and conservation—decisions** for the future (Meyer 2010). (boldface type in the original)

Thus, it seems that COICA, like Ramiro Chimbo in the Food Security Project described at the beginning of the chapter, tapped into international concerns about the environment to obtain resources for indigenous communities — in this case, training in forest inventory skills and short-term salaried work as technicians. Additionally, COICA's leaders saw the collaboration as a way of increasing their participation in international climate policy discussions rather than a way in which more powerful organizations would gain control of indigenous lands. According to the Inter-American Development Bank website, Juan Reategui, COICA's project coordinator, made the following statement during the official launch of the project: "Participation in international events will allow us to have our voice heard and to share successful experiences and lessons learned about our relationship with our mother nature" (Inter-American Development Bank 2011). Through their collaborations with international organizations, COICA's leaders were able to shape the two programs into ones that they believed would increase the welfare of participants. Like Chimbo, indigenous leaders played an important role in designing the programs and thus were able to include priorities such as creating jobs and training people to perform them. Once the agreements were drafted, these leaders evaluated them as having benefits that outweighed the risks involved, including the risk that environmental and multilateral development organizations were attempting to control what happened within indigenous territories.

For its part, EDF is helping fund the training of indigenous forest technicians in the hope that measuring carbon storage will turn unimproved forest land into a commodity, whereas according to older Kichwa ways of thinking, unimproved land belonged to no one and was available for the taking. For EDF's Chris Meyer, the act of measuring trees and translating those measurements into a carbon absorption capacity makes one more conscious of the value of resources. This increased commodification of the standing forest (as opposed to the value of timber or new farmland) will, he hopes, make indigenous participants more likely to pursue conservationist policies. This reasoning parallels Agrawal's (2005) analysis of India's community forest councils, in which he argues that participation in the governing role of the councils contributed to council members' increasingly seeing themselves as caretakers of the forest, with the forest then positioned as something that was fragile, limited, and in need of human management.

The controversy between CONFENIAE and COICA is not a controversy about whether conservation is inherently good or bad. It is a debate over what constitutes the welfare of indigenous populations. COICA sees global concerns over climate change as an opportunity to obtain something most indigenous communities say that they want (job opportunities and training in skills relevant to life in their particular environment). CONFENIAE, on the other hand, denounces the REDD program as the first step on what could become a road to indigenous peoples' territorial disenfranchisement.

Conclusion

After three decades of interactions with environmentalists, and a longer history of fighting to maintain land in indigenous hands, leaders in Rukullakta — and in the Ecuadorian Amazon more broadly — have come to see nature as limited and in need of protection by and from human beings. These ideas do not appear to have received much credence prior to the mid-1980s, although certainly defending land from takeover by others is a priority that has existed for a much longer period of time. In Rukullakta, there also appears to be a broad consensus among all members that the territory's lands are limited, and that the central leadership has a role to play in long-term planning, including the designation of a conservation zone within the territorial boundaries.

As previous chapters have argued, being forced to form a singular political entity in the 1970s (the cooperative) and the government's promotion of migration from other parts of the country into the Amazonian region has established fixed boundaries to potential property ownership. This contributed to people's having a stronger sense of the limits to land in the 1970s and after. Increasingly, the existence of statistics; maps; and summarized data on soils, elevations, aspect, forested areas, and tenure regimes allow territory to be apprehended quickly and unambiguously, and thus the limits to land are made even clearer in the minds of Rukullakta's leaders. Although the leaders have engaged in centralized management since the 1970s, "seeing like a state" (Scott 1998; see chapter 1), now they see like a different type of state — one that views conservation as a key strategy for improving the welfare of its population. They are thus increasingly looking toward relatively sustainable economic pursuits, such as ecotourism and cocoa production, rather than agricultural pursuits that environmentalists have criticized, including growing *naranjilla* and raising cattle.

It is true that today's leaders might not have the hunting, tracking, and forest survival skills of other Rukullakta residents and may never even visit the conservation zone they helped establish. Nonetheless, a convenient overlap in interests has allowed them to identify "middle ground" (Conklin and Graham 1995) with the Socio Bosque Program. These interests include their constituents' desire to ensure the availability of the forest for their own uses, the territorial government's need for financial resources to fund its operations and development priorities, and the relatively recent environmentalist focus on carbon storage to slow global climate change. Under the latter project, monies have become available for groups willing to commit to leaving trees standing, without some of the restrictions on hunting and the collection of nontimber forest products that earlier projects sought. Under these earlier projects, environmentalists envisioned strict wilderness protection as the only method of ensuring the protection of biodiversity (a view that critics often termed "fortress conservation"). This vision was difficult to reconcile with indigenous people's desires to live in their ancestral lands and use forest products to support that life. The types of collaborations that have emerged in recent years, including that between COICA and EDF, suggest that many environmentalists have also been shaped through their engagement with indigenous leaders. In this region, at least, these individuals and organizations have been willing to incorporate some indigenous priorities into their projects rather than pursue fortress conservation, even as they actively work to shape international, national, and local social imaginaries regarding the Ecuadorian Amazonian region, thereby making "the real world conform to the imagined one" (West 2006, 10).

CHAPTER FIVE

EVERYDAY FORMS OF TERRITORY FORMATION

There have been a few times during the history of Rukullakta when its citizens downplayed their deeply felt differences in order to present a unified front against threats to their territory. One of these occurred in 1987, when some non-indigenous families formed a civic association (*junta cívica*) in the nearby town of Archidona to take possession of Rukullakta's lands. A state plan to build a road that passed roughly parallel to the northern border of Rukullakta (the Hollín-Loreto Road, shown in map 3.4) made lands that had been difficult to access easier to reach by car and truck, increasing their value substantially. The non-indigenous association was formed specifically to gain control of those lands.

Members of the association met with officials from the two state colonization agencies (IERAC and INCRAE), the Tena Development Bank (a state-owned bank to which Rukullakta still owed money for cattle loans), and the Ministry of Agriculture and Ranching to convince them that the leaders of the cooperative were "irresponsible, lazy, and incapable of paying their debts" (*Actas*, June 4, 1987). They requested the expropriation of the cooperative's lands and the awarding of the lands to a new cooperative, which they would form. Rukullakta's archives document the following response by the public agencies: "Stemming from this meeting, the Director of INCRAE and the Regional Director of the same propose the dissolution of our Cooperative, and on the basis of that, to resituate all of the inhabitants into individual lots so that they can function with the Development Bank through individual credits and mortgages" (*Actas*, June 4, 1987). In this passage, the development officials tempt the cooperative's residents with the possibility of owning their own plot of land. Having title to an individual parcel would allow them to gain access to individual loans directly from the bank (using their parcel as collateral), rather than having to go through indigenous organizations (many of which, including the cooperative, had yet to pay off their previous collective loans and were therefore considered too risky to qualify for new ones). This proposal was aimed at making whatever remained of the cooperative's lands after parceling them out to residents available to the new cooperative that the civic association planned to form. The *Actas* continue with the following impassioned comments, in which members were asked to remember and reaffirm their sense of identification with the Rukullakta Cooperative:

> Carlos Alvarado [the cooperative's first president, who served from 1970 to 1973] asked for the floor and said that . . . "they are trying to finish [us] with the dissolution of our cooperative, which cost us so much sacrifice to organize and legalize; this is what INCRAE wants. IERAC has the right to adjudicate [award the land] to whatever interested party, perhaps leaving those of us who are the authentic owners marginalized. For that reason I reject INCRAE's proposal, and if it is necessary I will spill my blood in defense of the organization, and of the territories of the Cooperative, which is the patrimony of all of those who make ourselves members of this first exemplary organization in our Amazon," he concluded.
>
> The *compañero* M . . . S . . . requested the floor and said: "Despite the fact that I am not a [cooperative] member, but as the son of an active member,[1] we will never allow the abuses of the colonists. For that reason, I unite myself with the words that preceded mine, and would give my life in defense of our lands and of the Cooperative." For that reason, he said that the San Pedro of Rukullakta Cooperative will end when the world ends, not when someone distant from our interests says so. . . .
>
> The *compañeros* presidents of Tampayaku and [Ita] Kipilina [subcenters in the cooperative] say that they are in agreement with defending

[Rukullakta] until the final consequences together with the members and leaders of the Cooperative.

The *compañero* C...P...asked for the floor and maintained that all of these territories belong to our valiant, heroic men, to Waskar, Atawalpa, ...Tupak Yupanki [all of whom were part of the Incan royalty] and Jumandy [who led a revolt against the Spanish in 1578; see chapter 2]. For that reason, it naturally belongs to all of us, and in that respect we will never allow abuses by the colonists who attempt to form phantom [fake] cooperatives. (*Actas*, June 4, 1987)

These declarations continue for several pages, as representatives of each of the subcenters and several other individuals express their interest in defending the collective land title and the cooperative as an organization, linking its survival to their own. Their references to a shared indigenous history of resistance represent an effort to get members to see beyond their particular quarrels with the territorial leadership and with one another, and to recognize that this attempt to divide up the land is a new chapter in a longer history of land usurpation by outsiders. The fact that not only leaders but several members contributed to the discussion indicates that feelings of nationalism (or, perhaps more correctly, territorialism) were very high, at least in the face of this threat. The statements also indicate a strong connection between a broad indigenous identity and the collectively held territory (as opposed to a collection of parcels controlled by extended families).

In an even stronger demonstration of unity and shared identity, the members resolved to pay off the remaining loan as a collective and to settle the issue of debts held by particular individuals in the cooperative at a later date:

The *compañero* Accounts Manager, after thanking the *compañeros* for their massive attendance, said, "I have the privilege of bringing to your attention the fact that about six months ago we paid 5,000,000 *sucres* [about US $11,000], leaving about 2,000,000 *sucres* [left to pay; about US $4,400]. For that reason, I ask the favor, not for me but for the good of the Cooperative, that all of the [sub]centers that have cattle from the program offer one cow, and that the [adult nonmember] sons of members [pay] 3 or 5 thousand *sucres* [US $7.50–11], with the goal of paying, in its totality, [the debt to] the Tena National Development Bank." To this request, after various discussions, it was approved that each center would bring in one head of cattle to the hands of the leaders, and that they [the leaders] would be the ones to negotiate and pay the Bank. In light of this resolution, *compañero* B . . . C . . . said that he proposes that the Assembly make an additional effort, [with each member] paying something like 3,000 *sucres* with the goal of paying first to the Bank, and later we will charge the indebted individuals, since it is an Internal problem. In response to this suggestion, it was resolved by the majority that each member pay 1,000 *sucres* [US $2.50] by June 16 at the latest, and to the Bank by the 20th of this month. (*Actas*, June 4, 1987)

Through this appeal, cooperative leaders asserted that verbally supporting the organization against external threats was important but not sufficient. Territorial citizenship was not only an issue of identity but also one of sacrifice and coordinated effort, particularly when the territorial land title was at risk.

As previous chapters have shown, this collective outcry was not indicative of the harmonious, organized living that early leaders had imagined. At the time that this challenge to the collective territory occurred, internal conflicts were common, attendance at assemblies was often not enough for a quorum, and central leaders were at an all-time low in their ability to rally members to contribute their labor to collective projects. Indeed, the commitments to provide the territorial leadership with one cow per subcenter and $2.50 per member paled in comparison with the sacrifices that members had made in the early days of the organization.

Still, when the tempting offer to divide the land into family-owned plots was presented (something most members had been pleading Rukullakta's leaders to do for years), members chose to keep the organization intact in spite of their short-term economic interests. This is particularly impressive given that many people were suffering economically compared to the previous decade, due to the neoliberal reforms that began in the early 1980s. Yet all the people quoted in the archives chose to support their territorial organization even though that meant sacrificing the opportunity to gain legal title to a parcel of land for their family. The strong statements made at the meeting indicate that the Rukullakta Cooperative had a symbolic importance in the hearts and minds of its members. The territory's integrity had become strongly connected to both deeply felt sentiments of lowland Kichwa identity, members' sense of who they were as persons, and indigenous rights more broadly.

How was this achieved, and how has Rukullakta maintained its ability to bring members together to fight major battles in subsequent decades? In this chapter, I argue that even though most citizens of Rukullakta did not participate in meetings or collective work projects in the 1980s and early 1990s, they worked in other ways to maintain a minimal level of legitimacy for the territorial government, helping create the types of leaders that they wanted to have. One of the key sites of this organizational legitimization was in the area of conflict resolution: members turned to leaders to resolve conflicts they had with other members, rather than using the older method of avoiding conflict by moving away. Leaders' acts of mediation contributed to their raison d'être and thus boosted the importance of the territorial government in members' lives. This has been the case particularly with resolving accusations of sorcery, as will be described below.

Furthermore, in the final years of the 1990s and the early 2000s, leaders have sought new ways to create more engaged territorial citizens. It is their belief that such engaged citizens are key to the territory's ability to confront new challenges, such as oil exploration in the Upper Napo region. In chapter 2, I argued that in the early years of the territorial government, leaders created and administered new "governable spaces" (N. Rose 1999, 31–34), becoming increasingly involved in shaping territorial residents' lives. These "spaces" included not only physical sites (such as collectively run cattle pastures or schools) but also realms for intervention (such as collective agriculture or bilingual and intercultural education).

In this chapter, I examine how Rukullakta's citizens' actions played an important role in creating and modifying these spaces in subsequent decades, and I demonstrate how citizens have employed their own techniques to shape leaders. Rukullakta's residents do not coerce their leaders. Rather, like the World Bank project designers described by Tania Li (2005), residents act on leaders' actions, using the fact that most leaders want to be seen as powerful and effective at governing to guide them in the direction residents prefer. For example, when members fail to attend meetings that NGOs schedule to procure public participation, fail to contribute their labor to collective work projects, or fail even to show up to receive a free vaccination or dental checkup (provided by professionals who walk hours through the mud to provide their services in the more distant communities), it is the territorial leaders who suffer the embarrassment and loss of status, not the citizens themselves. In these and many other ways, citizens "conduct the conduct" (Dean 1996, 47) of their leaders, demonstrating their distaste with leaders' activities (or lack thereof). When citizens use distance as a strategy to shape leaders, they are not simply resisting the government's projects, they are practicing "government through distance."[2]

When faced with these clear rejections of their various projects, leaders who want to enjoy high status are forced to recapture citizens' interest in the territorial government. After two decades of open criticism by most territorial residents during the 1980s and 1990s (except for a few brief periods, such as that described above), leaders greatly increased their efforts to energize citizens. Their desire to do so was bolstered by new opportunities for indigenous leaders that were associated with neoliberal decentralization at the national level. Increasingly (and under pressure by international lending institutions), the Ecuadorian government devolved development monies and decision-making powers to local governments, including municipalities. When Archidona became a new municipality in 1996 (having reached the minimum population for that designation), and the indigenous Rukullakta resident Nelson Chimbo was elected its first mayor, new possibilities opened up for those willing to dedicate themselves to governing roles. More people started to see becoming president of Rukullakta not simply as a burdensome, thankless task, but as an apprenticeship — an opportunity to demonstrate leadership skills in the hopes of being elected to a well-paid and higher-status post in the future, such as mayor. The sacrifice one made as president of Rukullakta, working without a salary for two to three years, could now be justified as a temporary one in the name of building one's status and leadership experience. But, for the sacrifice to pay off, Rukullakta's leaders had to show voters that they were good leaders — which, among other things, included getting voters excited about the various development initiatives that the leaders were pursuing.

The projects initiated by the leaders in the late 1990s and 2000s were much smaller in terms of the possibilities for economic improvement for territorial citizens than the cattle ranching projects of the 1970s. The funds and resources that development agencies and organizations made available during the later period were relatively limited, and leaders had to do more with less. Some of the funds that were available were connected to state and international interest in promoting indigenous cultures and multiculturalism more generally. Leaders used these funds to promote identity-affirming arts among youth, such as traditional music and dance competitions, art competitions that celebrated lowland Kichwa identity, and public speaking competitions that encouraged Kichwa-Spanish bilingualism. They took these steps in an effort to boost people's sense of pride in being a citizen of Rukullakta, an indigenous territory, building on the sense of commitment that was already present in the civic association incident.

The interplay between leaders' and citizens' efforts to shape one another can be understood as "everyday forms of indigenous territory formation," to build on Gilbert Joseph and Daniel Nugent's edited volume, *Everyday Forms of State Formation* (1994a). The book's editors argue that a critical component of understanding state formation is the "quotidian process whereby the new state engaged the popular classes and vice versa" (Joseph and Nugent 1994b, 12). Both the members' efforts to turn leaders into conflict mediators and the leaders' efforts to increase members' levels of territorial pride can be thought of as these everyday sites in which leaders and members engaged one another.

I will examine three additional forms of indigenous territory formation in the second half of this chapter, all of which have been used to strengthen senses of citizenship and improve the practices of leaders since 2000: a public speaking contest for young women; an organizational reinvention, designed in part to involve more people in governance; and pioneering work in the field of informed consent, developed as a way of confronting attempts by the Canadian oil company Ivanhoe Energy Ecuador to establish oil wells in Rukullakta's territory. In each of these sites, Rukullakta's leaders have worked to create better informed and more active territorial citizens in the hope of constructing a more unified territory better able to resist threats, but the leaders have simultaneously made themselves more vulnerable to citizens' criticism. Taken together, I argue, citizens' acts to shape the duties of their leaders and the leaders' attempts to shape the obligations of citizenship have contributed to the solidification and legitimization of the territorial government over time.

Conflict Resolution

As mentioned above, the 1980s and early 1990s were a period of low legitimacy for the leaders, partly because the state had substantially reduced development funding for the Amazon and international development investment was also relatively low, compared to the situation in the 1970s. Elected leaders felt powerless to affect change without the funding that these outside entities had provided. The following quote from a speech given by the president who ended his three-year term on January 9, 1988, illustrates this point: "The leaders who were elected in the General Assembly on February 9, 1985, as the Administrative Council and the Vigilance Council have not collaborated at any moment, failing to meet our entrusted duties and obligations. . . . Principally, the President and Accounts Manager have [instead of initiating new projects,] faced all of the problems, such as [negotiating payments with] the Tena Development Bank; the issue of lands owned by nonmembers; [and] members' issues of sorcery, requests, divorces, and deaths, etc." (*Actas*, January 9, 1988). In the speech, the outgoing president dismisses duties such as dealing with sorcery as minor. Certainly, mediating conflicts among members is not as awe-inspiring as being able to take credit for bringing a development project with tens or even hundreds of thousands of dollars' worth of donations or credit, as leaders had been able to do in the mid-1970s (see chapter 2).

Yet dealing with accusations of sorcery has been an important function that members have wanted leaders to perform. When members approach leaders to mediate their conflicts with other members, it gives those leaders status and legitimizes the organization. Dealing with sorcery, therefore, is one of the key sites of "everyday territory formation." Just as scholars have interpreted the religious wars against sorcery in both the New and Old Worlds as part of the establishment of the authority of the state (Griffiths 1996; Whitehead and Wright 2004), indigenous leaders' efforts to mediate sorcery accusations are part and parcel of their efforts to solidify and legitimize their own authority over citizens of their territories. Unlike the wars that colonial governments conducted against sorcerers long ago, Rukullakta's leaders did not pursue the role of mediation willingly until relatively recently. Rather, members pushed them into this role through their many requests for assistance.

Sorcery in the Upper Napo region is quite different from what many Westerners might imagine. Perhaps not surprisingly, it is strongly connected to a form of knowledge that Western science does not recognize, specifically the knowledge of spirits and how to use the power of the spirits to obtain desired outcomes. However, it is also strongly connected to the quality of interpersonal relations among people living close to one another, and therefore to the ability of leaders to govern communities. It is extremely difficult for leaders to bring members together for a collective work activity or even a meeting if those members are feuding with one another, and these feuds are more often than not connected to misfortune believed to have been caused by shamans.

A shaman, or *yachaj* (one who knows), is thought to possess an extraordinary amount of *samay* (spiritual knowledge or power) and is thus able to mediate between the spiritual world and human society. With this power, a shaman can cure or cause sicknesses, help or prevent the catching of forest animals and fish, and defend or avenge other Kichwa whenever necessary. There is a power hierarchy among shamans, depending on their degree of knowledge and experience as well as their perceived effectiveness. Only a shaman who is capable of invoking the spirits and putting them at his service is known as *sinchi yachaj* (a wise and powerful person). The most powerful shamans are typically men (so I will use the male pronoun), but there are exceptions, and women can also strive to improve their personal power. The hierarchy among shamans makes the profession dangerous to the shaman and his family, as all shamans face attacks from other shamans attempting to assert their superiority (Rogers 1995).

What motivates people to hire shamans to cause harm rather than to heal? As indicated above and as described for other Amazonian groups (see, for example, Wright 2004), envy and resentment are oft-cited reasons. For example, if someone does not live up to his or her part of an exchange, or when someone is known to have spoken malicious gossip, these actions may incite the wronged party to hire a shaman in retribution. Additionally—as in many other societies characterized by an egalitarian ideology—greater visibility, prestige, wealth, or knowledge (such as that acquired by successful leaders), even when acquired by hard work, can make someone vulnerable to envy and thus sorcery (see also Buchillet 2004, 120). Sometimes, my informants have told me, acts of sorcery are not even actively pursued or sought by the jealous or angry party. Rather, a shaman will sense jealousy or anger and send misfortune on his own. His hope is that the injured party will then pay him for a cure, and possibly even for revenge against the envious individual(s) who unknowingly inspired the shaman to act.[3]

Illness and death are not the only possible repercussions of sorcery. Many Kichwa in the Upper Napo region believe that sorcery causes sickness in animals; conflicts between people, including land disputes; and even arguments between husbands and wives (Muratorio 1991, 222–23). Mark Rogers (1995) found records of thirty-four denunciations of sorcery in the Archidona sheriff's office for the period between 1987 and 1993. The cases ranged from serious accusations of murder or destruction of property via sorcery to complaints of threats from alleged sorcerers. In some cases, accused sorcerers had gone to the authorities as a preemptive measure, hoping to convince authorities that the accusations that were to be made against them were unfounded. Most of the cases occurred between people who knew one another, including neighbors and even relatives (Rogers 1995, 193–94).

Belief in sorcery is very common in Rukullakta among leaders as well as other residents. A few people do not believe in it, but those exceptions are not necessarily the individuals who have had the most Western education or the most immersion in Western development projects. In other words, beliefs do not necessarily progress from "superstitious" to "scientific" with increasing exposure to Western science or health practices. I came to know one Rukullakta president who had worked for a long time for health-related, international development projects (such as vaccination campaigns), and he told me emphatically in 2000 that he did not believe in sorcery. Five years later, I had a long conversation with him in which he told me that he had changed his mind entirely. His wife had gotten very sick, to the point at which Western-trained doctors had told him that she would probably not survive much longer. Desperate, he decided to hire a shaman, and she was quickly cured. He went on to tell me about several other incidents that had confirmed his growing belief in the power of shamans. Thus, even individuals who spend most of their days collaborating with foreigners and working in leadership roles can simultaneously have, or develop, strong beliefs in sorcery.

When members approached Rukullakta's leaders with a dispute believed to involve sorcery, the leaders would often act as mediators rather than attempting to determine guilt, listening to both sides and seeking a solution that was acceptable to both parties. When the dispute involved land boundaries, the president would appoint a commission to resolve the dispute, especially starting in the 1990s, when these types of disputes among members became more common (see chapter 3). Parties that participated in the mediation proceedings typically accepted the decisions the land commissions made, demonstrating that the elected leaders and organization enjoyed some legitimacy.

But leaders' efforts to mediate conflicts were not always simple or straightforward. Elected leaders sometimes asked state authorities to step in when the conflict was too difficult to mediate themselves. In one case in Ruku-llakta, a man had died, and his family hired a shaman to determine who was to blame for the death. The shaman named a member of the same subcenter as the culprit. The family then brought the case to the leaders of the co-operative, who subsequently passed it on to the sheriff's office (Rogers 1995). Most leaders see involving the sheriff's office as a last resort, however, and there is a strong preference for resolving internal tensions internally.

Even though leaders gained some power in their efforts to mediate dis-putes, they frequently spoke about the damage sorcery caused to the well-being of their citizens and strongly discouraged them from hiring shamans to harm others. For example, in 1994, the leaders resolved that "regarding sor-cery, in subsequent occasions, there should not be problems between mem-bers. If it occurs, they [the instigators] will be summoned to the Cooperative and at the same time to competent authorities [such as the sheriff]" (*Actas*, August 15, 1994). Leaders frequently complained about being tired of re-solving disputes believed to be fueled by shamanism in the early 1990s and threatened to report the involved parties to the Archidona police. However, resolving these disputes internally constituted a key raison d'être for the gov-ernment and for themselves as leaders in this period of low external invest-ment by the state and international development organizations.

The importance of conflict resolution in increasing leaders' authority became clear in a 2008 incident, when someone who believed that he had been harmed by a shamanistic attack approached an outside organization to resolve the incident rather than going to Rukullakta's elected leaders. The outside organization was the Association of Indigenous Shamans of Napo (ASHIN), which had been founded by two Shuar shamans in the nearby pro-vincial capital of Tena in 1997 and which reportedly had 363 members by 2000. The original idea had been for the organization to grant identity cards to shamans who had earned the respect and certification of their commu-nities for their powers to cure illness and misfortune, and to rescind iden-tity cards from those who had been accused of causing harm. When I inter-viewed ASHIN's leaders in 2000, the organization's members were meeting every one or two months to discuss accusations against members.

In the 2008 incident, the president of the Purutuyaku community (pre-viously the Purutuyaku subcenter) approached the president of Rukullakta, complaining that one of Purutuyaku's members had gone to ASHIN rather than seeking his help or that of Rukullakta's central government. His comments indicate that he felt it was an affront to Rukullakta's government when people sought external assistance:

> The gentleman responsible for the problem went to the organization ASHIN, which has nothing to do with our organization; rather, all of the problems that exist should be solved within our organization. With these words, he [Purutuyaku's president] asks the President of the PKR Government for authorization to create a set of internal rules for the Purutuyaku Community and to make people respect them inside the community. In the same way, all of the [community] presidents present revealed that they all have problems in their communities for the same reasons — Shamans and territory [that is, sorcery associated with conflicts over land ownership within the collective territory — see chapter 3].
>
> The President of the Government of the Kichwa People, listening to this petition and after several deliberations with those present, authorizes all 17 Presidents of the communities, and all those who have the capacity to help, to elaborate the associated internal rules for the communities, specifically referring to TERRITORY and SHAMANISM. (*Actas* March 21, 2008; capitalization in the original)

Purutuyaku's leader's status comes partially from being able to mediate tensions within his community, and he was upset when one of the parties involved went to ASHIN, an outside organization. He then approached Rukullakta's president (whose own status as central leader was reaffirmed through the process of requesting his permission) to ask if he could set up new policies that would require community residents to approach elected officials to mediate disputes before seeking help elsewhere. The administrators agreed to allow him to do so. Unlike in the 1990s, when leaders received so many requests for conflict mediation that they sought to reduce this aspect of their offices, in 2008 (subsequent to indigenous victories in municipal political races), many leaders appeared interested in becoming more involved in conflict resolution as a path toward gaining experience and boosting their legitimacy as leaders.

Elected leaders' status thus rises and falls according to how well their constituents believe they deal with tensions among members. If an elected leader is not a good mediator, members will stop seeking his or her mediation and thereby reduce both the responsibilities of and the respect for that leader. This dynamic resembles processes Robin Wright observed in his work with a Baniwa community in the northwest Amazon. Wright has "noted the ways in which community elders may actively prevent witchcraft from taking hold by reinforcing a community sentiment of 'happiness' while also downplaying discussions of witchcraft incidents. The great Baniwa prophets of the past . . . centered their messages and actions precisely against witches and sorcerers who provoked discord, revealing their nefarious intentions in public — thus reshaping community sentiment toward a much-desired harmony and unity" (2004, 91–92). Although leaders clearly see sorcery accusations and associated social rivalries as a hindrance to both organizational strength and the possibility of people's living harmoniously together within a bounded territory, these accusations also form one of the ways in which leaders maintain legitimacy during periods in which there is no immediate threat to the collective title and no major development projects that allow them to "engender collective fantasies of progress" (Coronil 1997, 5; see chapter 2). As Frank Salomon argued in his analysis of the relationship between the Spanish colonial state and lowland shamans in Ecuador, "The shaman stands in opposition to the statesman as an exponent of a contrary kind of power. But the two roles are functionally complementary" (1983, 422).

Engaging Young People in Territorial Governance

Starting in the late 1990s and continuing through the first decade of the twenty-first century, leaders have sought new ways to shape the citizens of Rukullakta. One reason was to counteract citizens' general lack of enthusiasm about participating in the territorial government and their vocal criticism of leaders' actions. Another reason, as described above, is associated with the potential rewards for being considered a good leader, as the Ecuadorian state has devolved development funds to municipalities and indigenous leaders have successfully run for municipal office. Leaders have sought new ways to encourage their citizens — particularly young people — to become more engaged, in an effort to convince them to become impassioned enough about the territory to participate in collective work projects, rallies, and other political activities.

A dramatic example of this surfaced in an unexpected place — a local competition for the title of Miss Purutuyaku (the most populated subcenter within Rukullakta's territory) in 2001. The competition was modeled in part on the ubiquitous beauty contests that occur throughout Ecuador (and beyond), but it focused less on appearance than it did on the contestants' ability to speak about difficult political issues in both Spanish and Kichwa.[4] Subcenter leaders asked me to serve as a judge in the competition, hoping that I would be more impartial than others.

In the question-and-answer portion of the competition, the three contestants each answered one of the following queries: "What did the recent indigenous uprising in Quito mean to you?"; "How can we convince more families to send their children to Purutuyaku's bilingual high school rather than the Hispanic schools in Archidona?"; and "If elected *Purutuyaku Warmi* [Miss Purutuyaku], what would you do to improve people's health in this zone?" Answering these questions in both Spanish and Kichwa counted for over half of the contestants' scores, indicating the priority that pageant planners placed on public speaking and bilingual fluency. Two of the three contestants deferred to the indigenous elected officials' opinions and expertise in their answers, saying little more than that they would collaborate with officials in instituting campaigns and programs to produce the desired outcomes. The competition's winner, however, answered the question on the bilingual high school and offered several concrete suggestions on how the school could be improved, including increasing the number of specialties (or tracks) that students could select.

I later learned that competition planners typically give the contestants the questions ahead of time (with the particular question that they are asked to answer chosen randomly at the competition). This gives the young women the opportunity to practice their responses, but it also invites them to reflect more deeply on issues of governance. The competition is a big event, and many people attend. As the audience listens to the contestants' answers, many individuals probably also think about how they might have answered the questions. These pageants are therefore key sites in which leaders invite residents to reflect on what could be done to improve the territory, and to become more involved in territorial governance.

In another sign of the ways in which Rukullakta's leaders have begun to see the contests as key sites for forging more active citizens, the *ñusta* (Incan word for princess) of Rukullakta, winner of a competition similar to the one described above, now takes a prominent seat at assemblies alongside the kuraka (president) and other top officials. When Rukullakta was still a cooperative (prior to 2006), the leaders always invited Rukullakta's pageant winners to participate in administrative meetings, but the young women who had won rarely did so. The fact that their successors today do participate

FIGURE 5.1 Sisawa Shiguango, Rukullakta's *ñusta* (princess), wearing her feather crown and sash, and Nelson Chimbo, the cooperative's kuraka (president), during a rally against petroleum exploitation, April 16, 2010. Photo courtesy of Medardo Shiguango-Cerda.

reflects two things. First, by giving the winner a prominent seat at assemblies and asking her to come attired in an attention-grabbing way (often with a feather crown and satin sash announcing her title — see figure 5.1), leaders are encouraging the young women to feel pride in being a part of shaping Rukullakta's future. This includes being more informed about the issues the organization faces.

Second, there have been policy changes at the national level that have opened up new career possibilities for women in politics. In the 2000 election, a new Ecuadorian elections law required that at least 30 percent of the candidates on political party lists be women. Implementation of the new law left political parties in Napo Province scrambling to find women who were both respected by their communities and effective public speakers.[5] This situation created incentives for Rukullakta's leaders (nearly all of whom were men) to increase opportunities for Kichwa women to gain leadership experience. Having women from the territory who were prepared to run for office increased the leaders' chances of having one of "their own" elected to positions in the municipal and provincial governments. By taking a place of distinction at political gatherings, Rukullakta's young *ñusta* is gaining experience in politics and being groomed to run for political office in the future. These changes in male attitudes toward female leadership have occurred not only in Rukullakta, but also in surrounding communities. For example, Dr. Rosa Alvarado was the first woman to fill the role of president of the primary provincial-level indigenous rights organization in Napo, the Confederación de la Nacionalidad Kichwa de Napo y Orellana (Confederation of the Kichwa Nationality of Napo and Orellana, or CONAKINO), formerly called FOIN. She served between 2004 and 2007, shortly after the amendment to the elections law took effect. Having served successfully in that role, she ran for mayor of Archidona in 2008. Although she did not win, she was nominated by a prominent party and ran a very promising campaign. When young women see examples such as Dr. Alvarado, they can imagine themselves entering politics as a career, and what previously were thought of as beauty pageants take on new meanings. Although Rukullakta's leaders' efforts to make young women think through and speak on issues of governance began before the changes in the elections law, participants are now even more invested in the speaking component of the competition than they were previously.

Broadening Government

In the early 2000s, leaders started imagining a very different sort of organization, inspired by the need to reinvigorate their citizenry and as a way to present themselves differently to the outside world. In part, they felt that the term "cooperative" did not reflect what they were: they were not a for-profit organization, and they had not engaged in large-scale collectivist economic projects since the 1970s. They also felt that their name should emphasize the fact that they were an indigenous organization. They hoped that changing the name to highlight citizens' indigeneity would attract more development funding than they had been receiving, and it would better reflect the type of citizen that the leaders were trying to create. They settled on the name Pueblo Kichwa de Rukullakta (PKR). "Pueblo" is usually used in this area to refer to a town, such as Archidona. However, Nelson Chimbo, who was Rukullakta's president during the legal reclassification, emphasized that their use of "pueblo" is meant to signify something more akin to "politically joined populace," such as when a politician addresses "the people" of a nation, state, or town. Thus, the new name emphasizes that they are the Kichwa people of a territory. As former president José Shiguango put it, "cooperatives are part of colonization; we are not colonists. We identify as a people, as Kichwas" (interview, June 21, 2009).

Perhaps even more interesting, those who drafted proposals for the new governance structure greatly increased the number of people directly involved in territorial governance. The new central government would include five representatives from each subcenter, or community (rather than just the president of each community, as was the case in the past). The main government would also include Rukullakta's kuraka (president), the director of economic development, the director of sustainable human development, the director of territory and natural resources, and the director of organizational strengthening. In all, this meant that the government grew from roughly fifteen to twenty individuals (the number varied somewhat from year to year) to a total of ninety individuals.

The designers of the new government also imagined additional branches of government, in particular a Council of Amautas. (According to informants, this term—*amauta*—implies practicing sorcery for the good of the community; in contrast, *yachaj*, the more common term for sorcerer, describes a person engaged in both healing and causing harm.) This judiciary board, made up of powerful shamans, would be charged with evaluating and settling charges of shamanistic attack. As of 2011, this part of the plan had not yet been implemented, indicating the complicated nature of engaging shamans in formal governmental structures designed to discipline their practices.

Planners also incorporated new rituals into the territorial government that temporarily reversed the positions of leaders and members. The most dramatic one permitted members to physically castigate their leaders in public spectacles when they were unhappy with the way those leaders were carrying out their duties. In particular, the planners chose a practice that parents had long used to punish their children—rubbing the fruit from the *ají* plant (a hot pepper) in their eyes. The practice is thought to increase children's strength and resilience against the temptation to act inappropriately. With the change in government from the cooperative to the PKR, and partially as a result of efforts by indigenous organizations throughout Ecuador to increase community forms of justice rather than relying on the state police and penal system, PKR's government decided to start allowing members to use *ají* to punish leaders at organizational assemblies. The practice was used in April 2009 against Rukullakta's kuraka, Nelson Chimbo, and the president of CONAIE, Marlon Santi. Chimbo had wanted to invite representatives of the petroleum company Ivanhoe Energy Ecuador to come and speak at an assembly. Some members felt that this was a dangerous first step that might lead to a later collaboration, and they rubbed *ají* in Chimbo's and Santi's eyes in an act intended to make them more resilient to the threats these companies posed.

The *ají* ritual reverses the typical hierarchy that has long existed in Rukullakta, where elected leaders sit at the front of the assembly hall on a raised stage and do most of the talking (although members are free to interject their opinions). In the ritual, members are briefly and dramatically allowed to become governors of their leaders, effectively treating them like children. Children have much to learn in life, and leaders are reminded that they must listen as well as speak and open their minds to contradictory ways of seeing issues as well as alternative ideas on the best way to behave and move forward. The creation of the new ritual clearly demonstrates that leaders are attempting to incorporate members into their own governance by inviting them to become leaders, even if only for a short period.

The social and governance changes that accompanied the change in legal designation brought a noticeable energy to the people involved, particularly in the first few years after the creation of the new organization. As Fausto Shiguango (the son of Juan Shiguango, the first vice president and second president of the cooperative), put it, "it was a very rapid change. Inside, we were destroyed. Now, there is more help from the government and foreign organizations. There is more credibility. There are pessimists [within Rukullakta], but they are few. Before, only a few people became members [the rest chose to continue living in Rukullakta's territory without ever paying membership dues or otherwise participating in citizenship duties]. Now, we are more than 2,000 [registered members. Multiple adult members of a household, not just its head, can become members now]. There are more people who want to be members" (interview, June 16, 2009). By 2011 some of the initial excitement had worn off, but Rukullakta was successfully presenting itself as a community rather than a cooperative to foreign NGOs.[6] This appeared to make Rukullakta more attractive to these NGOs, and several collaborations were under way, from funding for market-oriented projects to legal assistance in confronting Ivanhoe Energy Ecuador.

Just as elected officials have worked to shape members into what they consider to be good citizens, members have worked to make Rukullakta's elected officials into what they perceive to be good leaders. Both leaders and members distinguish between two types of people — those who *siempre co-laboran* (always contribute or collaborate), and those who work for *intereses personales* (to benefit themselves) (see also Wilson 2010, 230). Those in the former category gain status and approval, while those in the latter category are marginalized or (in the case of leaders) deposed from office. In these acts of shaping, both leaders and members have contributed to processes of territorial government formation. Even acts of removing leaders from office are acts of citizenship, part of the everyday process through which Rukullakta's government "engaged the popular classes and vice versa" (Joseph and Nugent 1994b, 12). As the Native American scholar Scott Lyons has argued, "civil disobedience is when the citizen tries to improve the nation by ridding it of some evil, and should be distinguished from resigning one's citizenship, or for that matter being a do-nothing sort of citizen" (2010, 173). If Rukullakta's territorial government had no validity, members would not even bother attending assembly meetings, reverting to "do-nothing" citizens. By incorporating new governance roles and instituting new rituals that attract attention, leaders are shaping themselves into people who are individually and collectively more responsive to their citizenry.

Pioneering Work in Informed Consent

The third type of territory formation that has emerged through leaders' and citizens' efforts to shape one another is related to a petroleum company's recent interest in drilling in Rukullakta's territory. Ivanhoe Energy Ecuador signed a contract with the Ecuadorian state on October 8, 2008, for services related to the development, production, and processing of heavy crude in an area known as Pungaracu, a 647.5-square-kilometer (250-square-mile) oil field that stretches from just north of "Kilometer 24" (the intersection between the Hollín-Loreto Road and the major north-south road — see map 3.4) to the town of Puerto Napo to the south (see map 1.1). Much of the central part of the oil field lies beneath Rukullakta's territory, and industry-sponsored tests indicate that the entire field contains between 4.5 and 7.0 billion barrels of "oil-in-place."[7] The field also lies beneath the Great Sumaco Biosphere Reserve. The oil was not of interest to oil companies until the twenty-first century because it is a particularly heavy form of crude, but

Ivanhoe wishes to use a new upgrading technology, which the company calls HTL (heavy to light).

As in much of Latin America, the state maintains ownership of below-surface resources and therefore is able to issue contracts for their exploitation. However, the 2008 Ecuadorian Constitution includes language that requires the informed consent of indigenous communities prior to mining or oil extraction from under their lands. This was a major victory for indigenous activists, as previously there were no official requirements to obtain informed consent. Ivanhoe completed an environmental impact assessment and presented it to the Ministry of Environment at the end of May 2009, a prerequisite for digging exploratory wells. According to Rukullakta's president at the time, Nelson Chimbo, the minister approved the assessment overnight, even though it was a document of approximately 1,500 pages, which enraged members of Rukullakta and the surrounding region (interview, June 16, 2011). Rukullakta issued a formal denunciation of the contract and the approval of the environmental impact assessment, stating that it roundly rejected the contract and environmental license awarded by the Ministry of Environment "for being Un-consulted and Unconstitutional" (*por ser Inconsulta e Inconstitucional*).

Despite the seeming solidarity in the pronouncement and in later assemblies and marches on Quito and Archidona, there was still discussion and debate among Rukullakta's leaders and citizens. The petroleum deposit apparently covered a large area. According to one way of analyzing the question of drilling, those landholders who agreed to have wells constructed on their property would stand to benefit most from any earnings, while the entire region could potentially bear the costs of pollution associated with extraction or potential spills. Thus, some residents reasoned, they might as well permit the company to drill in Rukullakta, rather than allowing another individual or organization to reap all of the benefits.

Ivanhoe offered to construct a road to Pitayaku, which would have created better access for the farmers whose land was located close to the planned road. According to Chimbo, most members wanted the road. Those with lands close to it thought they might be able to get away with allowing the company to construct the road and dig an exploratory well, and then reject any plans to extract petroleum on a longer-term basis.

Chimbo thought that this was unlikely to work, and he saw three viable options for Rukullakta. First, citizens could make a united protest, taking to task all of the state, provincial, and cantonal officials and governmental agencies for not fighting Ivanhoe after so many years of promoting conservation as the best path toward development for Archidona Canton. Second, they could allow drilling to take place in the territory, making an arrangement under which a small percentage of petroleum earnings would go to Rukullakta; this, Chimbo estimated, could have provided thousands of dollars daily to the organization. The third option was for Rukullakta to enact a moratorium on drilling, agreeing to wait ten to fifteen years before making a decision, during which time leaders could encourage Rukullakta's high-school students to obtain college degrees in mining and petroleum sciences so that they could serve as more informed mediators in negotiations. At first, explained Chimbo, most members seemed to lean toward the protest option, but when he tried to organize a protest, only about a dozen people came. After that, he once again felt that he did not have a clear mandate (interview, June 16, 2011).

Shortly afterward, Rukullakta held elections, and a new kuraka replaced Chimbo. In the very first days of his administration, the new kuraka was confronted with the issue of whether he should sign a contract with Ivanhoe to dig an exploratory well in Pitayaku or not. Given members' desire to have the road built and his failure to convince Transsepet (which Ivanhoe had hired to obtain the necessary permissions from landholders) to pay Rukullakta $60,000 for permission to dig the well, the new leader had to make a decision. When Transsepet offered him $1,000 to act as liaison and reiterated the offer to build a paved access road, he accepted. Rukullakta's members then confronted him, accusing him of acting against their wishes, but he claimed the signature was a forgery and denied any wrongdoing. The fact that he denied signing the contract even though witnesses had seen him leave in a taxi for the meeting with Transsepet angered members even more, and they deposed him. Even so, the signed contract was in Transsepet's hands.

On October 29, 2010, I received an e-mail message from one of the leaders of Rukullakta, which stated:

Esteemed Friends:

I am attaching an urgent pronouncement from the Kichwa People of Rukullakta (PKR) in PDF format. Please forward it to all of your friends, institutions. . . .

The ancestral People of Rukullakta are willing to receive the solidarity against the deeds occurring with respect to the petroleum company IVANHOE ENERGY of Canada, and its partner COMPAÑIA TRANS-SEPET S.A., which has the concession for the Pungaracu Block of Ecuador — Amazon — Napo. www.ivanhoeenergy.com/s/Home.asp.

[Signed] PKR

Attached to the message was the official "Statement Issued by the Government of the Pueblo Kichwa de Rukullakta (Kichwa People of Rukullakta)" (see Appendix 2). Notably absent from the statement were two signatures — those of the president of Rukullakta, as members had yet to name a new one to take the place of the one they had deposed, and of the community president of Lushianta, which is the community to which the deposed president belonged. The extended kinship networks present in each of Rukullakta's seventeen communities still play a major role in the side people take when a dispute arises in the territory.

Rukullakta's strongest legal argument, given the state's ownership of below-surface resources and articles in the constitution concerning informed consent, was that its members had not been properly consulted. Specifically, the company appeared to be trying to obtain permission solely from the organization's president, rather than from "the community." Roderigo Varela, a lawyer with the Ecuadorian NGO Fundación Regional de Asesoría en Derechos Humanos (Regional Foundation for Assistance in Human Rights, or INREDH), has followed the case and reported on it on the NGO's website. According to Varela (and confirmed by leaders from Rukullakta), Rukullakta's leaders decided to pioneer a new model for community consultation, in which they invited representatives from Ivanhoe and its Ecuadorian ally Transsepet as well as ecologists to participate in meetings in each of the seventeen communities that make up Rukullakta. In these meetings, each of the industry representatives and ecologists would make presentations, and Rukullakta's leaders would, according to INREDH, "explain the . . . life plan designed for Rukullakta, based on conservation, human development and investment in ecotourism" (quoted in Saavedra 2011). The process of consultation would be followed by a secret ballot in which every inhabitant of Rukullakta would be allowed to vote, in the presence of international observers, government officials, and indigenous leaders. According to Varela, "detailed information, participation by all actors involved and, above all, support from indigenous leaders, will allow for the realization of a genuine consultation where, if the indigenous side loses, it would be [*sic*] lost fair and square, and not through misleading or deceptive processes. And if they win, the people of Rukullakta will stand their ground on the victory attained during the consultation" (quoted in Saavedra 2011).

In its pioneering efforts to set an example for processes of adequately consulting communities prior to pursuing mining or other extractive activities on their lands, Rukullakta is likely to draw the attention of many potential allies from Quito and abroad, especially those concerned with promoting human rights. The move can be seen as strategic, since in attracting allies, the leaders strengthen their ability to resist oil extraction if members decide that is what they want to do. Rather than simply adding themselves to a long list of indigenous peoples who face environmental threats to their lands, another David confronting Goliath, they are positioning themselves as innovators on a key legal question. They have already convinced the lawyers at INREDH that this is the case: Varela stated that "Rukullakta's internal consultation will be an example of how the state should handle prior consultation, with binding results and total respect for the rights of indigenous peoples, and not as it is now, a consultation where the outcome does not matter, but rather what the president [of Ecuador] decides does" (quoted in Saavedra 2011).

Leaders are also using the controversy as a way of demanding more active and informed citizens rather than "do-nothing" citizens who refrain from attending meetings and complain about not being told about the decisions leaders are making in their absence. After the poor attendance at the centrally organized protest described by Chimbo, leaders are working to bring political activity to the communities, closer to where people live. The secret ballot they describe is another stage of broadening government, in which leaders are strongly encouraging members to inform themselves and take a stand. Rather than allowing outsiders to select amenable members of Rukullakta and present them as representing all members, as oil companies have done in other regions of Ecuador (see Sawyer 2004), the leaders who are forging ties with INREDH and other human rights organizations are exposing the opinions of their citizens to the outside world in a pioneering act of transparency.

Conclusion

Rukullakta's leaders and members have long been engaged in the "permanent provocation" that Foucault argues is constitutive of government rather than antithetical to it (1982, 790). As leaders attempt to shape citizens and members attempt to shape their leaders, both contribute to a more institutionalized territorial government, even while it must remain dynamic to survive both recurring external threats to the territory's integrity and changing landscapes of potential allies.

In the 1970s leaders' visions of active citizens were strongly influenced by the state's definition of an agricultural cooperative; in order for the territory to be legally recognized and for the organization to receive credit that would allow it to pursue social programs, members needed to donate their labor to help clear forest, plant pasture, and raise cattle. After struggling for a decade to pay off cattle loans and in the face of resistance by members toward the excessive obligations of large-scale, collective economic endeavors, leaders today see such economic collaboration as a much smaller part of what it means to be an active citizen. Rather, Rukullakta's leaders push for citizens to contribute much more modestly in terms of money and agricultural labor, but to simultaneously be fully involved in the political causes and debates affecting the territory. The leaders do this in part through fostering stronger senses of territorial, Kichwa, and indigenous identity. It is their belief that engaged citizens are crucial to the territory's ability to confront new challenges such as oil exploration in the Upper Napo region.

Part of the leaders' efforts have, by necessity, included the recognition that they must constantly legitimate their rule (N. Rose 1999), for members remain free to reject the stipulations of citizenship and ignore leaders' calls for political participation. But citizens do not just reject and resist leaders' projects; they work actively to shape leaders in a number of ways, including demanding conflict resolution services, vocally criticizing leaders whom they think are putting their own interests ahead of those of Rukullakta's members, purposely staying away from some of the meetings and events that leaders ask them to attend, and even punishing leaders as if they were children in public spectacles. In examining these actions, I show how the conduct of conduct is not simply a top-down process in political entities such as Rukullakta. Rather, the binaries of governors and governed and of center and periphery are constantly reworked and even reversed in the process of territory formation.

MAKING CITIZENS, MAKING LEADERS, MAKING TERRITORIES

I began this book with a story about how in 2001, Rukullakta's leaders did not agree with the title I proposed for their history, "Only United Will We Overcome," preferring instead the seemingly more mundane "Our History of Living Together in a Large Group, 1970–2000." Far from mundane, however, Rukullakta's history has been filled with frequent and strikingly different challenges. Yet it has managed to maintain its collective title to its land, and its leaders in particular continue to have high expectations for the enactment of sovereignty.

In the 1970s leaders' notions of active territorial citizens included the hope that members would donate ninety days each year to agricultural labor, community improvement, and governance meetings. Given members' resistance to these heavy obligations, the development projects that leaders pursue today do not demand such high levels of sustained, collaborative labor and debt accrual. Yet leaders still need to finance the basic expenses of running the territory, including everything from the cost of transportation associated with visiting the various communities and conducting official business in urban centers to the expenditures for office supplies and an Internet connection. Rukullakta's leaders therefore engage in a wider variety of more modest development projects to accumulate the needed funds, including small-scale agricultural projects such as the Food Security Project and fee-for conservation programs such as Socio Bosque (partner forest).

Other projects that leaders pursue in Rukullakta are increasingly intertwined with those of larger indigenous organizations representing various constituencies, including the indigenous people of the Ecuadorian Amazon (CONFENIAE), indigenous people throughout Ecuador (CONAIE), and indigenous people of the multinational Amazon Basin (COICA). These organizations promote diverse campaigns, including increasing participation in bilingual and intercultural education, gaining the right to practice local forms of justice and medicine, and improving the process that corporations must follow to obtain informed consent before extracting resources from indigenous lands. For the citizens of Rukullakta, supporting these diverse causes does not necessarily require as much donated labor as leaders requested in the 1970s, but the obligations involved can be just as controversial. Leaders increasingly try to connect members' important life decisions — such as where to send their children to school, whether to report a crime to the police or to community leaders, and how to vote in an election — to their identities as indigenous persons and Rukullaktan citizens.

Sometimes the causes associated with these individual decisions seem distant and obscure to many of Rukullakta's members. Leaders, therefore, must find ways to encourage their constituents to become better informed about the broader campaigns and to act accordingly. They regularly seek new formats in which to do this by forging new "governable spaces" (N. Rose 1999, 31–34), such as the public-speaking component of young women's pageant competitions, and by employing new technologies of citizenship, such as the multistakeholder conferences they plan to hold in each community prior to having people vote on oil exploration in the territory.

Both techniques and the changing vision associated with leaders' governing have emerged through engagements with many outside social movements and organizations, including indigenous ones, but have not been entirely determined by them. Territorial leaders have worked to produce a different type of person than other governing agents sought, and these differences are important to understand if one wants to comprehend changes in indigenous lives, values, and ways of seeing the world. Throughout this book, I have shown how subalterns in general and indigenous peoples in particular (usually seen as only the objects of governmental action) can also be the agents of governmentality.

Part of this demonstration has been my analysis of how citizens have worked to shape their leaders and their governance practices, imposing their own expectations and obligations. Sometimes they do this by simply ignoring leaders' varied calls for engagement and distancing themselves spatially and emotionally. This government through distance has led to the downfall of many leaders and forced others to seek new ways of engaging residents' imaginations and (re)invigorating their loyalties to the collective body. Other times, citizens demand services that leaders would rather not provide, use vocal criticism or public punishment to lower leaders' status, or even collaborate with outsiders to improve their bargaining power in territorial matters.

The last time I was in Rukullakta, in the summer of 2011, controversy was brewing over monies associated with the Socio Bosque (partner forest) Program, through which Rukullakta had signed a contract to conserve 11,000 hectares of its territory in forest for the next twenty years. In exchange for this conservation, Ecuador's Ministry of Environment committed to giving the territorial government two semiannual payments of US $19,750, for a total annual payment of $39,500. As described in chapter 4, the 11,000 hectares placed portions of the lands of just eight of Rukullakta's seventeen communities off limits for agriculture. Some of the most heavily affected of these eight communities felt that they should receive the majority of the money, since they were the ones making the largest sacrifice. The central territorial leadership disagreed, arguing that the money was for the benefit of all citizens. According to one of my friends, at least three of these disproportionately affected communities were threatening to sign a contract with Ivanhoe Energy Ecuador, as the road that Canadian oil company had promised to build would have benefited them more than other communities (the exploratory well that Ivanhoe wants to dig is very close to the conservation area). My friend explained the three communities' reasoning in this way: since they had lost access to some of their land through the signing of the Socio Bosque contract, they could rectify the harm they had suffered by gaining a road that would better connect the rest of their land to markets. These discussions were just beginning, however, and the various explanations I heard from others did not coincide with one another. Thus, in the relatively short time that I spent in Rukullakta in the summer of 2011, it was difficult to know how serious the controversy was.

Three months later, I exchanged a few e-mail messages with the same friend. He said that the debates continued, and that it looked like Ivanhoe might take advantage of the internal dispute to move forward with its plans. Knowing that outsiders have frequently used this divide-and-conquer strategy in their attempts to gain control over resources in other indigenous territories, I was worried. I knew that Rukullakta had worked through similar sorts of controversies in the past, but not knowing how angry the communities affected by the Socio Bosque arrangement were, it was difficult to predict what might happen. When I received an e-mail message that December from a North American volunteer who was living in Rukullakta, introducing himself and offering to help me in my work, I requested that he ask the then-kuraka (whom I do not know) what was happening. He spoke to the kuraka and told me that, from each of the $19,750 semiannual payments, "each community got somewhere around $1,000 (which the kuraka pointed out translated to about 25 cents per person), but [the kuraka] mentioned that all of the communities put forth some land for the reserve, not just a few as you indicated. He also said that the road that a few communities (Tambayaku and Ita Kipilina I believe) wanted Ivanhoe to build was never approved and thus has not been built. He said that Socio Bosque has produced a very minimal benefit for the communities and has required a lot of paperwork." It is not clear why the kuraka did not connect the petroleum road with the Socio Bosque Program in the same way that my friend did. The kuraka may have been reluctant to divulge details of the dispute to the volunteer, or perhaps he simply did not view the two controversies as having anything to do with one another. Documenting history as it is occurring (and from thousands of miles away) can be confusing and difficult. In any case, it seems that my worst fears about the controversy's potential to tear Rukullakta apart were unfounded.

Disputes over property and the associated relationships between the leadership and membership have been among the most hotly contested aspects of territorial citizenship. Deep connections to particular places and the land is what brought members together to form a collective landholding organization in the 1970s, but these same connections have threatened at times to tear it apart, as this recent controversy shows. Understandings of property have also been and continue to be deeply connected to citizens' understandings of themselves as Kichwa persons, their expectations of kinship and exchange, and their notions of the government's and citizens' obligations to one another. Thus, each time leaders attempt to impose new property regimes (often to fit the requirements of development projects emerging from external sources), citizens must try to imagine their implications for many aspects of their lives, not simply assess the loss or gain in hectares that would be under their personal control.

Rukullakta's leaders are motivated by a desire to empower their citizens and to bolster their own status as leaders. Their efforts, combined with those of their citizens, have contributed to Rukullakta's ability to remain a viable and resilient political entity for over four decades. However, as I have shown here, these efforts have also involved new subjectivities, new hierarchies, and new ways of relating to other people and nature. The paradoxical process that began when Rukullakta's residents first formed a collective territory and political body—when its residents needed to change some aspects of their lives and culture in an effort to maintain others—continues even today, creating new controversies and challenges.

Yet the fact that the petroleum road dispute has not led to Rukullakta's dissolution illustrates how, once again, leaders and residents alike have found some advantages in continuing the collective territorial government and subjecting themselves (at least to some extent) to living together "in a large group," within a defined territory, under an elected leadership, and through engagements with select outsiders. They have also found advantages in continually reworking what their sovereignty means. As I argued in the introduction, territorial citizenship is a moving target, one that leaders pursue, members assess, and multiple outsiders attempt to grasp and bend to suit their own political agendas. Territorial leadership is also continually reworked as citizens attempt to make the government meet their own expectations. Although observers of indigenous organizations typically emphasize the importance of tradition, Rukullakta's forty-year history illustrates that change may be as important as continuity in sustaining and strengthening senses of shared ownership and identity.

Appendix I: Statement Issued by CONFENIAE and Distributed to Various International NGOs

Unión Base, Puyo, August 3rd, 2009

CONFENIAE REJECTS ALL KINDS OF ENVIRONMENTAL NEGOCIATIONS [SIC] ON FORESTS AND EXTRACTIVE POLICIES THAT DAMAGE THE TERRITORIES OF THE AMAZONIAN INDIGENOUS NATIONALITIES AND PEOPLES OF ECUADOR.

CONSIDERING

That the Right to Plurinationality and Sumak Kawsay [to live well], enshrined in the Constitution of the [Ecuadorian] Republic, and the Right to Self-Determination of the Ancestral Nationalities and Peoples, consecrated in international instruments like Convention 169 of the ILO [International Labor Organization] and the universal United Nations Declaration on the Rights of Indigenous Peoples, exist to guarantee that human beings and nature live together in a world in suitable conditions, and that they can develop based on the principles of solidarity, reciprocity [and] the conservation of the territorial space as a whole, for the security and survival of the present and future generations; and to guarantee a healthy environment, free of pollution, repression and the imposition of government policies on indigenous peoples;

That all these policies and extractive activities and negotiations on the forests and biodiversity in our Ancestral Territories will have unfathomable consequences, including the extinction of our identity as Ancestral Nations, [our] loss of the control and management of our territories, which would subsequently be managed by the State, foreign countries, multinationals, REDD negotiators or Carbon Traders; which would result in unprecedented misery, hunger and extreme poverty, just like what is happening right now to our indigenous brothers and sisters in the Northern Amazon of Ecuador because of geopolitical, economic and commercial interests; [the reference is to the contamination of soil, rivers, and groundwater caused by petroleum extraction in the northern Ecuadorian Amazon]

RESSOLVES: [*sic*]

1. To warn and communicate to all the grassroots organizations of the structure of the Confederation of Indigenous Nationalities of the Ecuadorian Amazon–CONFENIAE, which is comprised of centers, communities, associations, federations, organizations and nationalities, in the framework of the Resolution and Mandate of the Congress held on May 28–31, 2009, that the Regional Organization of the Ecuadorian Amazon, will not permit interference nor representation, nor allow spokespersons to discuss nor dialogue, let alone take steps to negotiate in national or international forums our Natural Resources that exist in our Territories.

2. The CONFENIAE will not negotiate nor dialogue without the consent of the grassroots on the issues of Oil Extraction Activities, Mining, Hydroelectric Dams, the Socio Bosque Plan, REDD business, Environmental Services, etc., since certain entities, like the Energy, Environment and Population institution, the World Bank and Carbon Traders in alliance with Latin American governments are trying to negotiate the lives of the Indigenous Nationalities and Peoples [and] undermine our Rights to our Territories.

3. We recognize that climate change is a problem and we demand that Annex I countries acknowledge their responsibility for greenhouse gas emissions, [and,] therefore, diminish the burning of fossil fuels, whose extraction has caused deforestation in the Amazon and grave social and environmental problems in our territories.

4. We reject the negotiations on our forests, such as REDD projects, because they try to take away our freedom to manage our resources and also because they are not a real solution to climate change, on the contrary, they only make it worse.

5. We inform COICA, of which we are a part, that, as Ecuadorian Amazonian representatives with the right to voice and vote, that no person, entity, NGO, etc., is authorized to speak on our behalf in favor or against any issue without our knowledge and participation.

Sincerely,

Tito Puanchir

PRESIDENT "CONFENIAE"

Note: See, for example, http://www.redd-monitor.org/2009/08/11/indigenous-peoples-in-ecuador-reject-redd/ (accessed May 17, 2011).

Appendix 2: Statement Issued by the Government of the Pueblo Kichwa de Rukullakta (Kichwa People of Rukullakta)

Rukullakta, Napo Province, October 28, 2010

In the community of Rukullakta, on the 28th of October, 2010, the 17 Kurakas [community presidents] of the Community Government of the Kichwa People of Rukullakta, in defense of its territory, and realizing our objective to defend the territorial integrity of the People, and conforming to Articles 57 and 98 of the Constitution of the Republic of Ecuador, and the Declaration of the United Nations on the Rights of Indigenous Peoples and Convention 169 of the ILO [International Labor Organization], declare the following:

First — The Kichwa People of Rukullakta declares a high state of alert in its entire territory and announces the permanent Assembly of communities.

Second — The Kichwa People of Rukullakta ratifies its position in defense of its ancestral territory and the Natural Resources that exist within it.

Third — The Kichwa People of Rukullakta condemns the attitude of the petroleum company IVANHOE ENERGY ECUADOR and the COMPAÑIA TRANSSEPET S.A. for attempting to divide the people, disrespecting its own form of organization.

Fourth — The Kichwa People of Rukullakta does not recognize any agreement, contract, access, use and servitude and/or signed settlement that has not been authorized by the Assembly; this refers to our collective rights and the constitutional right to resist.

Fifth — The Kichwa People of Rukullakta convenes the struggle of the base communities of the Kichwa People of Rukullakta and Napo Province, to defend the Pachamama [Mother Earth] which is being threatened by petroleum and mining companies.

Sixth — The Kichwa People of Rukullakta calls for solidarity on the part of the national, regional, and international authorities to support our legitimate process of resistance.

In affirmation, the presidents of the communities of the Kichwa People of Rukullakta sign: [signed by fifteen of the seventeen presidents, the chief of organizational strengthening, and the chief of economic development]

Note: I received this proclamation as an attachment to an e-mail message from Medardo Shiguango-Cerda on October 29, 2010.

Preface

1. For insightful explorations of these obligations, see Povinelli 2002, 2006, and 2011.

2. Some of the most impressive accomplishments of the national-level indigenous movements in Ecuador include creating a state-funded bilingual and intercultural education program that allows indigenous students to study in their native language as well as Spanish; blocking the passage of an agrarian reform bill that would have benefited exporters of agricultural products at the expense of small peasant producers for the national market; and playing a key role in the ousting of two Ecuadorian presidents, Abdalá Bucaram in 1997 and Jamil Mahuad in 2000.

3. Although I have not conducted a census, it is clear from my discussions with various residents of Rukullakta that was common in the past for women to have between seven and thirteen children and to begin to have children in their mid-teens. Today, as families increasingly hope to send their children to high school and beyond, family sizes are significantly smaller. Most people strive to have between three and five children.

4. "Pueblo" is usually used in this area to refer to a "town," such as Archidona, but Nelson Chimbo, who was Rukullakta's president during the legal reclassification, emphasized that their use of "pueblo" is meant to signify something more akin to "politically joined populace," such as when a politician addresses "the people" of a nation, state, or town. According to Marc Becker (2011, 5), Luís Macas, a national-level indigenous rights activist in Ecuador, uses "pueblo" to refer to a specific population (such as that of Rukullakta) and uses "nationality" for a group of people who share common customs, a cosmology, and a way of life (such as the Amazonian Kichwa).

5. My interest in obligations was partially inspired by Elizabeth Povinelli's multiple explorations of the topic (2002, 2006, and 2011), and partially by anthropological

works that examine how conflicting understandings of reciprocity complicate development encounters (see, for example, Conklin 2010; West 2006).

6. See, for example, Brysk (2000, 2), Hutchins (2010, 18), MacDonald (2010), and Smith (2005).

7. Unless otherwise noted, all quoted passages from local sources are translated from Spanish by the author.

Introduction

1. I use the word "intimate" to refer to the fact that residents live more closely to territorial leaders than they do to representatives of the state leaders and may even have histories of kinship, friendship, or animosity with the territorial leaders. I am not using the term in the same way that Arun Agrawal does, as he draws attention to how local forest councils are carrying out what are essentially state-mandated plans. Furthermore, although I agree with his point that "intimate government involves the creation and deployment of links of political influence between a group of decision makers within the village and the ordinary villagers whose practices it seeks to shape" (2005, 179), I do not agree with the ways that he formulates subjectivities in terms of calculations of self-interest. I will discuss this point further in chapter 4.

2. An exception to this has been the scholarly work on the Zapatista movement in southern Mexico, some of which describes the movement's efforts to create new subjectivities within the indigenous population there (see, in particular, Stahler-Sholk 2010).

3. "Government through distance" is thus quite different from "government at a distance," a concept used frequently by Foucauldian scholars. The latter concept was first used by Peter Miller and Nikolas Rose (1990) and later developed in additional publications by Rose (1996, 1999) and Rose and Miller (2008). It builds on Bruno Latour's (1987, chapter 6) notion of "action at a distance" and seeks to describe how political programs to increase national efficiency or democracy are translated by multiple, otherwise autonomous, agents into ways of shaping spatially and metaphorically distant persons, places, and processes. In "government through distance," spatial and emotional distance is used as a strategy by nonleaders to structure leaders' possible field of action.

4. Arturo Escobar goes even further, arguing that the fact that indigenous and black groups have always been dominated "makes all the difference" since activists "emerge from this border and . . . conduct their struggle from the colonial difference" (2008, 12–13). As I will show in chapter 1, classifying the residents of Rukullakta as a "dominated group" is problematic, although they certainly exist within multiple power inequities and postcolonial regimes of rule.

5. For Latin Americanists who emphasize that nonstate entities such as NGOs engage in governance, see García (2005) and Postero (2007).

6. People who do not have electricity charge their cell phones when they are on trips

to relatives' homes, Rukullakta's offices, or the nearby mission town of Archidona. They are therefore not able to use them as consistently as people who do have electricity in their homes.

7. For one of these documentaries, see Bennett and Diller (2009).

I. History, Empowerment, and Rule

1. At least twice a year, the Indians were forced to purchase coarse cotton cloth, thread, needles, and a large number of superfluous goods and to repay the debts incurred with agave fiber and gold dust (Muratorio 1991).

2. *Terrenos baldíos* has more complex implications than can be represented in a simple translation. It could mean uncultivated land, but it could also include insufficiently cultivated land. Amazonian indigenous horticultural techniques were extensive rather than intensive, and indigenous people's fields often seemed unkempt and underused to government agents from the highlands. Thus, the law had racist implications as well, suggesting that indigenous people were lazy and that only people who knew the "proper" way of doing agriculture should be able to claim lands. Finally, the term implies that forested land is somehow valueless (since it is "vacant") until converted into agriculture.

3. Some of these plants do not have commonly used English names, so I have kept the Kichwa names. I was able to find some scientific names: *chirimuya* is *Annona chermimola*, *wabas* are *Psidium guajaba*, and *pasu* is *Gustavia macarenensis*.

4. Despite various changes in name, CEDOC has maintained the same acronym. In 1938 the group was the Ecuadorian Confederation of Catholic Workers (Confederación Ecuatoriana de Obreros Católicos); it became the Ecuadorian Confederation of Catholic Workers, Employees, and Artisans (Confederación Ecuatoriana de Obreros, Empleados y Artesanos Católicos) in 1957 and the Ecuadorian Confederation of Christian Workers' Organizations (Confederación Ecuatoriana de Organizaciones Sindicales Cristianas) in 1965. Marc Becker has argued that "the Conservative Party founded CEDOC in 1938 with the goal of stopping communist influence in labor movements and emphasizing a conservative religious spirit in Ecuador's workers" (2008, 157). In 1972, a few years after the courses mentioned in the text, the group changed its name once again — this time to the Ecuadorian Center for Class-Based Organizations (Central Ecuatoriana de Organizaciones Clasistas), indicating a growing separation from any particular religious institution or group of institutions and a move to the political Left.

5. I mention this detail because, several years later, Jorge Aguinda became an important leader in Rukullakta, working against some of the socialist principles espoused in the course (see chapter 3).

6. Jorge Aguinda told me this story during an interview on March 1, 2000. Aguinda's exact words were: "con otra visión, con otra ideología, con otro ánimo de formar la organización misma."

7. The first explicitly indigenous organization in the Ecuadorian Amazon was the

Federación de Centros Shuares, formed in 1964, in large part a product of the Salesian Mission (Perreault 2000). Shuar come from a different linguistic group but occupy an ecological zone similar to that of Amazonian Kichwa.

8. The organization changed its name first to Federación de Organizaciones Indígenas de Napo (the Federation of Indigenous Organizations of Napo, or FOIN) and then to Federación de Organizaciones de la Nacionalidad Kichwa de Napo (the Federation of Kichwa Nationality Organizations of Napo, or FONAKIN) and then to Confederación de la Nacionalidad Kichwa de Napo y Orellana (the Confederation of the Kichwa Nationality of Napo and Orellana, or CONAKINO).

9. The other option for obtaining collective land title, forming a legally recognized community (a *comuna*) had the same two requirements (Pallares 2002, 42–47), but it was not being promoted as vigorously by the state or other actors, and it seemed unlikely to inspire state agencies as much as the prospect of a large cooperative in terms of getting a large area of land, facilitating the processing of paperwork, and meeting other requirements.

10. Although a few of Rukullakta's leaders attended either the Josephine Mission school or a state-funded school in Archidona, well over half of Rukullakta's founding members did not and were illiterate. In the 1960s the Josephine Mission intensified its efforts to extend the reach of its educational system into sparsely populated areas. Within the zone that eventually became the Rukullakta Cooperative, the mission established schools in Purutuyaku in 1963, Tampayaku in 1967, Lushianta and Awkayaku in 1969, and the area of Rukullakta that is closest to Archidona (also called Rukullakta) in 1970. According to a survey conducted in the Rukullakta Cooperative between 1998 and 1999, out of forty-six people (thirty-three men and thirteen women) who were nine years of age or older in 1963 (before these rural schools were formed), over half (twenty-four) had no formal schooling at all; eight had between one and three years of schooling; and only thirteen had more than three years of schooling (Erazo 2003, 57). It is also important to note that some of the survey respondents may have received the formal education they reported after the formation of the cooperative, as adult literacy programs were one of the early leaders' top priorities.

11. In 1972 the group won first prize at an Archidona folkloric festival. Between 1973 and 1978, it performed in cities all over Ecuador, and in July 1978 it represented Ecuador at the IV Sesión Mundial de Teatro de las Naciones (Fourth World Session of National Theater) in Caracas, Venezuela.

12. Of course, this new conception did not totally supplant people's older forms of relating to one another. In fact, the negotiating of obligations between the territorial government and individual members was often complicated by existing relationships between particular members and particular leaders. Members often felt both that the cooperative organization owed them something, and that particular leaders owed them something. For an interesting analysis of the ways in which local people expected both foreign conservation organizations and particu-

lar biologists to reciprocate the efforts they invested in conservation projects, see West (2006, 47).

13. For a similar contrast in the Amazonian context, see P. Gow (1995).

2. Collectivist Utopias

1. As Patrick Wilson has argued for the Upper Napo region more broadly, "development projects represent much more than just an economic opportunity and carry a symbolic weight that is central to understanding the relationships between indigenous leaders and members" (2010, 220). This particular understanding of the role of leaders began, I argue, in the 1970s.

2. It is not clear who the gringos were, although the term is typically used to refer to white people from outside Latin America. In this case, the local people may have been referring to Peace Corps volunteers, who participated in part of the cooperative's delineation process in 1973 and who were working with the Ecuadorian government to establish cooperatives in various frontier areas of the Ecuadorian Amazon (Salazar 1989).

3. Blanca Muratorio notes that Kichwa in the Tena and Archidona area visit the hospital mainly "to die," only after visiting one or more shamans (1991, 222). Although this is still the case for many people, having a local facility where they did not need to compete with white people for the doctor's attention carried significant symbolic importance.

4. For more on sorcery among Upper Napo Kichwa, see chapter 5.

5. The first schools in Rukullakta's territory were formed in the years just prior to the formation of the cooperative. Starting in the 1960s, the Josephine Mission intensified its attempts to extend the reach of its educational system out into sparsely populated areas. One of the priests, known as *Sacerdote* Francisco, traveled around the region and tried to convince Kichwa parents to work together to build schools for the students who lived too far from Archidona to travel there each day, and who were not already living in the Archidona mission school's dormitories. In the region that later became the Rukullakta Cooperative, elementary schools were established in 1963, in Purutuyaku; in 1967, in Tampayaku; in 1969, in Lushianta and Awkayaku; and in 1970, in Rukullakta (see map 2.1 for the locations of the first five subcenters, which were centered on the first five schools). In the case of Tampayaku, the mission purchased four hectares of land for the school, and families living in the surrounding area worked together to construct a schoolhouse, which went on to serve sixty students. In the case of Purutuyaku, the school began in a private house, but parents later constructed a separate school, building on a hectare of land donated by one of the parents. Teachers typically rode up from Archidona by horse every day.

6. I was never given access to the cooperative's financial accounts, and it is unclear if the leaders even maintained an accounting system consistently. Although some expenses are discussed in the *Actas*, there is little to indicate what funds were being

used for which purchases. The members I interviewed had very different perceptions as to what the cooperative's funds were spent on, spanning from "booze and
gambling" to the multiple administrative and development-oriented expenses that
are documented here.

3. The Property Debate

1. Although forest cover does not preclude gardening, as some trees are planted for
   their fruits and some crops can be planted under trees, the local staple, manioc, is
   not grown under forest cover and is very commonly planted in gardens adjacent
   to houses.

2. The analogy of a candle was inspired by Thongchai Winichakul's usage in *Siam
   Mapped*. In his use of the metaphor, power fields radiated from individuals (specifically, supreme overlords) rather than from places.

3. The construction of rural schools within what later became the cooperative's borders actually started in the early 1960s, when a priest from the Josephine Mission
   convinced some families to build one-room schoolhouses closer to people's homes
   and to send their children there. However, people did not begin to build new
   homes within view of the schools or to create collective plazas until the formation
   of the cooperative.

4. Many social scientists have elaborated on this distinction between abstract space
   (typically associated with states) and profound cultural meanings associated with
   particular places (typically associated with groups that have lived in the same place
   for generations). See, for example, Basso (1996), Escobar (2008), Feld and Basso
   (1996), Lefebvre (1991), and Scott (1998).

5. For example, FOIN pursued the case of Chambira, an indigenous community of
   approximately thirty families who were sharing less than ten hectares of land bor-
   dering extensive holdings by the mission. After FOIN applied substantial pressure on the Josephines during a civic parade and other events, the mission ceded
   seventeen hectares of land to the community (FOIN n.d., 11). Thus, many who
   were active in FOIN saw the formation of FOCIN as an attempt by the mission to
   reduce FOIN's influence in Napo Province. Starting in 1978, missionaries spoke
   highly of FOCIN in their weekly mass and during their "Voice of Napo" radio
   shows, aired daily in Kichwa and Spanish. The Christian Democratic Party (De-
   mocracia Popular — Unión Demócrata Cristiana), which had long been interested
   in having greater influence in the indigenous movement, also supported the new
   organization (FOIN n.d., 9–10).

6. When I first walked through the area that had previously been cleared for ranching in Lupinu, I was amazed at how much it looked like an old-growth forest. (My
   perceptions of such forests were shaped during my time as a graduate student in
   forestry at the University of Washington, where we visited temperate old-growth
   forests). Large trees were mixed with medium-size and smaller trees, which is the
   opposite of what one would expect if the area had been clear-cut and then aban-

doned (in that case, trees are typically all about the same size). My guide explained to me that Kichwa did not cut down all of the trees when they planted pasture grasses. Doing so was considered to be more work than was necessary, and it robbed the cattle of needed shade.

4. Conservation and Environmental Subjects

1. Shiguango ran a strong campaign and was predicted to win by all polls, but ultimately lost in a last-minute upset.

2. The Mamallactas translate the phrase "Izu Mangallpa Urcu" as "the mountain of the land of the jaguar." The new name was an attempt to use a Kichwa term for the Galeras Mountains that border the eastern edge of the cooperative, although most cooperative members claim not to be familiar with that name and simply refer to the range and the region surrounding it as "Galeras" (Rogers 1996, 116n24). The new name refers to one of the frequently related stories surrounding Cuillur and Duceru (or Luceru), the sons of an incestuous relationship between the moon and his sister. The brothers decided to do away with the great jaguar of the world, which was particularly menacing to Kichwa of the Archidona region. They dug a cave in Mount Galeras and fixed it up inside. Then they brought the jaguar there, convinced him to go inside, and moved a large boulder in front of the entrance, trapping him in the cave. The jaguar became very angry but has remained trapped inside, and when he roars, people can hear the reverberations from far away (Rogers 1996, 86).

3. It also resonates with the goals of larger indigenous organizations. A number of documents from FOIN, CONFENIAE, CONAIE, and COICA "reveal the emergence of a dialogue at various levels concerning the importance of recognizing communally operated projects as central to indigenous identity" (Hutchins 2010, 22).

4. Like many of the early human rights and environmental NGOs, GTZ arrived in Ecuador as a result of the 1987 earthquake. When the US military failed to construct more than a few kilometers of the new Hollín-Loreto Road (meant to provide an alternative way of accessing oil fields in the northeastern part of the country), the Ecuadorian government requested assistance from the Kreditanstalt für Wiederaufrau (German Reconstruction Bank), which was impressed by the region's "extraordinary faunal, floral, hydrological, and cultural richness" and agreed to construct the road on the condition that its representatives would be able to remain in the region, working for development that would both "conserve and take advantage of" the region's resources "in a sustainable manner" (Ministerio del Ambiente 2000, 3). In 1991 a bilateral agreement for the protection of the Great Sumaco tropical forest was signed between the German and Ecuadorian governments, and the former contracted a German consulting firm (AHT) and its Ecuadorian associate to conduct studies between 1992 and 1993 on the feasibility of conserving the Sumaco area (Knoblauch 2001). Based on these studies, the consultants recommended that the status of the area be switched from that of a "Forest

and Vegetation Preserve" (as it was named in 1987 after the earthquake) to that of a "National Park," which denotes a higher level of conservation. The consultants also recommended expanding the area under protected status from 59,148 hectares to 190,562 hectares. All of these suggestions were implemented by the Ecuadorian government in 1994 (Garces and Wray 1997; Knoblauch 2001), and as a further demonstration of the official commitment to conserving the region, the Instituto Ecuatoriano Foresal y de Areas Naturales y Vida Silvestre (Ecuadorian Institute for Forests, Natural Areas, and Wildlife) designated the region just to the west of the national park the "Antisana Ecological Reserve," adding an additional 120,000 hectares of protected lands to the region. Antisana also served as a biological corridor between the Sumaco National Park and the Cayembe-Coca Ecological Reserve (a 403,000-hectare reserve to the northwest, declared an ecological reserve in 1970), which meant that it was intended to facilitate movement of wildlife between the two protected areas (so that members of small populations of animals could more easily find mates and so that wildlife could seek alternative food sources when necessary).

5. The original Spanish wording is: "Una relación armónica entre el ser humano y la naturaleza a través del mantenimiento de la integridad de las áreas naturales y su material genético y el mejoramiento de la calidad de vida de su población."

6. Although the quoted passage refers to four hectares per member, the probable meaning is per person, because the estimate is based on the total population (41,888.55 hectares divided among 10,000 people equals roughly four hectares per person). According to the same report, the average age in 2007 in Rukullakta was only 22.37 years old, so counting the large number of children as "members" is deceptive.

7. "Fair trade" is a product certification program intended to improve the working conditions and wages earned by workers, typically in developing countries. It also is intended to assure purchasers of the products that certain environmental sustainability criteria are being met by producers.

5. Everyday Forms of Territory Formation

1. It seems that this person had never officially registered to be a member, which meant that he was not required to pay annual dues or attend meetings. However, he was still allowed to live in Rukullakta's territory because his father was a founding member of the cooperative. This was a common practice, and it contributed to leaders' desires to establish a new organization in 2006 (the Kichwa People of Rukullakta), in which all adults residing in the territory (including women) were strongly encouraged to become members.

2. As explained in the introduction, Peter Miller and Nikolas Rose (1990) coined the term "government at a distance," adapting the notion of "action at a distance" from Bruno Latour (1987, 219), and they have subsequently used the term in multiple publications (N. Rose 1996, 1999; N. Rose and Miller 2008). They argue

that political programs to increase national efficiency or democracy are translated by multiple, otherwise autonomous, agents, into ways of seeking to exercise authority over persons, places, and activities in distant locales. The movement is thus from what Latour calls "centres of calculation" (1987, chapter 6) into a diversity of locales across a territory, creating alignments of diverse forces and creating the possibility for that center to practice "action at a distance." In my use of "government through distance," I show how the territorial government is dependent on citizens. Thus, by remaining in distant corners of the territory rather than gathering in Rukullakta's assembly hall, citizens govern their leaders through distance.

3. This is a different dynamic than what exists in other Amazonian groups, in which shamans do not act unless hired (see, for example, Buchillet 2004).

4. Lynn Meisch notes that indigenous people in Ecuador "place a far greater emphasis on competence and hard work than they do on physical beauty" (2002, 56). Although her work has been among highland Kichwa, the ways in which points were assigned to the four contest components in Purutuyaku seem to support this claim for lowland Kichwa as well. However, since "competence" in acting out the ways in which women contribute to their families turned on the gracefulness of the performance (rather than on how hard contestants worked on these tasks in their daily lives), perceptions of attractiveness probably played a role in final scores. For a more in-depth description and analysis of both highland and Amazonian pageants in Ecuador, see Rogers (1999).

5. For more on the provisions in the Ecuadorian Constitution and elections law as they relate to women, see Valdivieso Vega (2004).

6. A July 20, 2011, review of websites that mentioned Rukullakta revealed that all referred to Rukullakta as a community or village. This included the websites for Amazon Watch and Latinamerica Press/Noticias Aliadas, and the website Indigenous Peoples Issues and Resources.

7. Ivanhoe Energy, "Ecuador — Pungarayacu: Overview," http://www.ivanhoeenergy.com/index.php?page=ecuador_-_pungarayacu_overview.

Archival Material

Actas de la Cooperativa Agropecuaria San Pedro de Rucu-Llacta, Ltda. Unpublished meeting minutes, 1970–2007, housed in the administrative offices of the Pueblo Kichwa de Rukullakta.

Alvarado, Carlos. N.d. "Historia de la Cooperativa San Pedro de Rucullacta." Unpublished essay shared with the author on March 15, 2000.

"Cuaderno de trabajos." N.d. Unpublished archival material, housed in the administrative offices of the Pueblo Kichwa de Rukullakta.

Desarollo y Autogestión. 1998–99. "Historia, población y tenencia de tierra en los subcentros de la Cooperativa San Pedro de Rukullakta." Unpublished report on community histories, demographics, and land tenure for Rukullakta's subcenters. Housed in the administrative offices of the Pueblo Kichwa de Rukullakta.

FOIN. N.d. "La lucha de los Napo Runas." Unpublished essay, probably written in 1989, housed in the CONAKINO offices in Tena, Ecuador.

"Plan de manejo, Pueblo Kichwa de Rukullakta." 2008. Unpublished archival material, housed in the administrative offices of the Pueblo Kichwa de Rukullakta.

"Plan de trabajos, San Pedro de Rucu-Llacta." 1981. Unpublished archival material, housed in the administrative offices of the Pueblo Kichwa de Rukullakta.

Published Works

Abrams, Philip. 1988. "Notes on the Difficulty of Studying the State." *Journal of Historical Sociology* 1 (1): 58–89.

Agrawal, Arun. 2001. "Common Property Institutions and Sustainable Governance of Resources." *World Development* 29 (10): 1649–72.

———. 2005. *Environmentality: Technologies of Government and the Making of Subjects.* Durham: Duke University Press.

Alexander, Catherine. 2004. "Value, Relations, and Changing Bodies: Privatization and Property Rights in Kazakhstan." In *Property in Question: Value Transformation in the Global Economy,* edited by Caroline Humphrey and Katherine Verdery, 251–74. New York: Berg.

Alvarado, Carlos. 1994. *Historia de una cultura . . . a la que se quiere matar.* Quito: CIESPAL.

Anderson, Benedict. 1983. *Imagined Communities: Reflections on the Origin and Spread of Nationalism.* London: Verso.

Appadurai, Arjun. 1996. *Modernity at Large: Cultural Dimensions of Globalization.* Minneapolis: University of Minnesota Press.

Baland, Jean-Marie, and Jean-Philippe Platteau. 1996. *Halting Degradation of Natural Resources: Is There a Role for Rural Communities?* Oxford: Clarendon Press of Oxford University Press.

Basso, Keith. 1996. *Wisdom Sits in Places: Landscape and Language among the Western Apache.* Albuquerque: University of New Mexico Press.

Bebbington, Anthony, et al. 1992. *Actores de una decada ganada: Tribus, comunidades y campesinos en la modernidad.* Quito: COMUNIDEC and Abya Yala.

Becker, C. Dustin, and Rosario León. 2000. "Indigenous Forest Management in the Bolivian Amazon: Lessons from the Yuracaré People." In *People and Forests: Communities, Institutions, and Governance,* edited by Clark C. Gibson, Margaret McKean, and Elinor Ostrom, 163–91. Cambridge: MIT Press.

Becker, Marc. 2008. *Indians and Leftists in the Making of Ecuador's Modern Indigenous Movements.* Durham: Duke University Press.

———. 2011. *Pachakutik: Indigenous Movements and Electoral Politics in Ecuador.* Lanham, MD: Roman and Littlefield.

Bennett, Drew, and Dusty Diller. 2009. *The Children of Jumandi.* http://www.imdb.com/title/tt1913154/.

Bennett, Drew, and Rodrigo Sierra. N.d. "Multi-Scaled Dimensions of Indigenous Land Tenure in the Amazon." Unpublished manuscript.

Biersack, Aletta. 2006. "Reimagining Political Ecology: Culture/Power/History/Nature." In *Reimagining Political Ecology,* edited by Aletta Biersack and James B. Greenberg, 3–40. Durham: Duke University Press.

Blackburn, Carole. 2009. "Differentiating Indigenous Citizenship: Seeking Multiplicity in Rights, Identity, and Sovereignty in Canada." *American Ethnologist* 36 (1): 66–78.

Blaikie, Piers, and Harold Brookfield. 1987. *Land Degradation and Society.* London: Methuen.

Bremner, Jason, and Flora Lu. 2006. "Common Property among Indigenous Peoples of the Ecuadorian Amazon." *Conservation and Society* 4 (4): 499–521.

Brosius, J. Peter. 1997. "Endangered Forest, Endangered People: Environmentalist Representations of Indigenous Knowledge." *Human Ecology* 25 (1): 47–69.

Brosius, J. Peter, Anna Lowenhaupt Tsing, and Charles Zerner. 1998. "Representing Communities: Histories and Politics of Community-Based Natural Resource Management." *Society and Natural Resources* 11 (2): 157–68.

Brown, Michael. 1993. "Facing the State, Facing the World: Amazonia's Native Leaders and the New Politics of Identity." *L'Homme* 33 (126): 307–26.

Brysk, Allison. 2000. *From Tribal Village to Global Village: Indian Rights and International Relations in Latin America.* Stanford: Stanford University Press.

Buchillet, Dominique. 2004. "Sorcery Beliefs, Transmission of Shamanic Knowledge, and Therapeutic Practice among the Desana of the Upper Río Negro Region, Brazil." In *In Darkness and Secrecy: The Anthropology of Assault Sorcery and Witchcraft in Amazonia,* edited by Neil Whitehead and Robin Wright, 109–31. Durham: Duke University Press.

Burchell, Graham. 1996. "Liberal Government and Techniques of the Self." In *Foucault and Political Reason: Liberalism, Neo-Liberalism and Rationalities of Government,* edited by Andrew Barry, Thomas Osborne, and Nikolas Rose, 19–36. Chicago: University of Chicago Press.

Carrier, James G., and Daniel Miller. 1998. *Virtualism: A New Political Economy.* Oxford: Berg.

Cattelino, Jessica R. 2008. *High Stakes: Florida Seminole Gaming and Sovereignty.* Durham: Duke University Press.

Chapin, Mac. 2004. "A Challenge to Conservationists." *World Watch,* November–December, 17–31.

Clark, A. Kim, and Marc Becker. 2007. "Indigenous Peoples and State Formation in Modern Ecuador." In *Highland Indians and the State in Modern Ecuador,* edited by A. Kim Clark and Marc Becker, 1–21. Pittsburgh: University of Pittsburgh Press.

COICA. 2011. "Noticias, 20 de abril de 2011." http://www.coica.org.ec/sp/noticias/dnoticias.php?id=158.

Collins, Jennifer N. 2000. "A Sense of Possibilities: Ecuador's Indigenous Movement Takes Center Stage." *NACLA Report on the Americas* 33 (5): 40–46, 48–49.

Colloredo-Mansfeld, Rudi. 2002. "'Don't Be Lazy, Don't Lie, Don't Steal': Community Justice in the Neoliberal Andes." *American Ethnologist* 29 (3): 637–62.

———. 2009. *Fighting Like a Community: Andean Civil Society in an Era of Indian Uprisings.* Chicago: University of Chicago Press.

CONAIE. 1989. *Las nacionalidades indígenas en el Ecuador: Nuestro proceso organizativo.* Quito: TINCUI-CONAIE/Abya-Yala.

Conklin, Beth A. 1997. "Body Paint, Feathers, and VCRs: Aesthetics and Authenticity in Amazonian Activism." *American Ethnologist* 24 (4): 711–37.

———. 2002. "Shamans versus Pirates in the Amazonian Treasure Chest." *American Anthropologist* 104 (4): 1050–61.

———. 2010. "For Love or Money? Indigenous Materialism and Humanitarian Agendas." In *Editing Eden: A Reconsideration of Identity, Politics, and Place in Amazonia,* edited by Frank Hutchins and Patrick C. Wilson, 127–50. Lincoln: University of Nebraska Press.

Conklin, Beth A., and Laura R. Graham. 1995. "The Shifting Middle Ground: Amazonian Indians and Eco-Politics." *American Anthropologist* 97 (4): 695–710.

Coronil, Fernando. 1997. *The Magical State: Nature, Money, and Modernity in Venezuela*. Chicago: University of Chicago Press.

Corrigan, Philip, and Derek Sayer. 1985. *The Great Arch: English State Formation as Cultural Revolution*. Cambridge, MA: Blackwell.

Crapanzano, Vincent. 2004. *Imaginative Horizons: An Essay in Literary-Philosophical Anthropology*. Chicago: University of Chicago Press.

Cruikshank, Barbara. 1993. "The Will to Empower: Technologies of Citizenship and the War on Poverty." *Socialist Review* 23 (4): 29–55.

———. 1999. *The Will to Empower: Democratic Citizens and Other Subjects*. Ithaca: Cornell University Press.

Dean, Mitchell. 1996. "Putting the Technological into Government." *History of the Human Sciences* 9 (3): 47–68.

———. 1999. *Governmentality: Power and Rule in Modern Society*. London: Sage.

Dunn, Elizabeth C. 2004. *Privatizing Poland: Baby Food, Big Business, and the Remaking of Labor*. Ithaca: Cornell University Press.

Erazo, Juliet. 2003. "Constructing Autonomy: Indigenous Organizations, Governance, and Land Use in the Ecuadorian Amazon, 1964–2001." PhD diss., University of Michigan.

———. 2007. "Same State, Different Histories, Diverse Strategies: The Case of the Ecuadorian Amazon." In *Highland Indians and the State in Modern Ecuador*, edited by A. Kim Clark and Marc Becker, 179–95. Pittsburgh: University of Pittsburgh Press.

———. 2008. *Construyendo la autonomía: Organizaciones indígenas, gobierno y uso de la tierra en la region Amazónica del Ecuador, 1964–2001*. Quito: Abya Yala.

———. 2010. "Constructing Indigenous Subjectivities: Economic Collectivism and Identity in the Ecuadorian Amazon." *Development and Change* 41 (6): 1017–39.

———. 2011. "Landscape Ideologies, Indigenous Governance, and Land Use Change in the Ecuadorian Amazon, 1960–1992." *Human Ecology* 39 (4): 421–39.

Escobar, Arturo. 1995. *Encountering Development: The Making and Unmaking of the Third World*. Princeton: Princeton University Press.

———. 2008. *Territories of Difference: Place, Movements, Life*, Redes. Durham: Duke University Press.

Feld, Steven, and Keith H. Basso, eds. 1996. *Senses of Place*. Santa Fe, NM: School of American Research Press.

Foucault, Michel. 1982. "The Subject and Power," translated by Leslie Sawyer. *Critical Inquiry* 8 (4): 777–95.

———. 1991. "Governmentality," translated by Rosi Braidotti and Colin Gordon. In *The Foucault Effect: Studies in Governmentality*, edited by Graham Burchell, Colin Gordon, and Peter Miller, 87–104. Chicago: University of Chicago Press.

Garcés, Alicia, and Natalia Wray. 1997. "Estudio socio económico, antropológico y de género de las comunidades de Huahua Sumaco, 10 de Agosto, y Huamaní." Quito: Instituto Ecuatoriano Forestal y de Areas Naturales y Vida Silvestre and the Gesellshaft für Technische Zusammenarbeit.

García, Maria Elena. 2005. *Making Indigenous Citizens: Identity, Development and Multicultural Activism in Peru*. Stanford: Stanford University Press.

García-Hierro, Pedro, and Alexandre Surrallés. 2005. Introduction to *The Land Within: Indigenous Territory and the Perception of Environment*, edited by Alexandre Surrallés and Pedro García-Hierro, 8–20. Copenhagen: International Work Group on Indigenous Affairs.

Goldtooth, Tom B. K. 2011. "Why REDD/REDD+ Is NOT a Solution." In *No REDD! A Reader*, edited by Joanna Cabello and Tamra Gilbertson, 11–24. Carbon Trade Watch. http://www.wrm.org.uy/publications/REDDreaderEN.pdf.

Gow, David, and Joanne Rappaport. 2002. "The Indigenous Public Voice: The Multiple Idioms of Modernity in Native Cauca." In *Indigenous Movements, Self-Representation, and the State in Latin America*, edited by Kay B. Warren and Jean E. Jackson, 47–80. Austin: University of Texas Press.

Gow, Peter. 1995. "Land, People, and Paper in Western Amazonia." In *The Anthropology of Landscape: Perspectives on Place and Space*, edited by Eric Hirsch and Michael O'Hanlon, 43–62. Oxford: Oxford University Press.

Griffiths, Nicholas. 1996. *The Cross and the Serpent: Religion Repression and Resurgence in Colonial Peru*. Norman: University of Oklahoma Press.

Gustafson, Bret. 2009. *New Languages of the State: Indigenous Resurgence and the Politics of Knowledge in Bolivia*. Durham: Duke University Press.

Hale, Charles. 2006. *Más Que un Indio = More Than an Indian: Racial Ambivalence and Neoliberal Multiculturalism in Guatemala*. Santa Fe, NM: School of American Research Press.

Hathaway, Michael. 2010. "Global Environmental Encounters in Southwest China: Fleeting Intersections and 'Transnational Work.'" *Journal of Asian Studies* 69 (2): 427–51.

Hicks, James F. 1990. *Ecuador's Amazon Region: Development Issues and Options*. Washington: World Bank.

Hiraoka, Mario, and Shozo Yamamoto. 1980. "Agricultural Development in the Upper Amazon of Ecuador." *Geographical Review* 70 (4): 423–45.

Hudelson, John Edwin. 1981. "The Expansion and Development of Quichua Transitional Culture in the Upper Amazon Basin." PhD diss., Columbia University.

Humphrey, Caroline, and Katherine Verdery. 2004. "Introduction: Raising Questions about Property." In *Property in Question: Value Transformation in the Global Economy*, edited by Caroline Humphrey and Katherine Verdery, 1–25. New York: Berg.

Hutchins, Frank. 2007. "Footprints in the Forest: Ecotourism and Altered Meanings in Ecuador's Upper Amazon." *Journal of Latin American and Caribbean Anthropology* 12 (1): 75–103.

———. 2010. "Indigenous Capitalisms: Ecotourism, Cultural Reproduction, and the Logic of Capital in Ecuador's Upper Amazon." In *Editing Eden: A Reconsideration of Identity, Politics, and Place in Amazonia*, edited by Frank Hutchins and Patrick C. Wilson, 3–37. Lincoln: University of Nebraska Press.

Hutchins, Frank, and Patrick C. Wilson. 2010. Introduction to *Editing Eden:*

A Reconsideration of Identity, Politics, and Place in Amazonia, edited by Frank Hutchins and Patrick C. Wilson, xi–xxxi. Lincoln: University of Nebraska Press.

Ingold, Tim. 2000. *The Perception of the Environment: Essays on Livelihood, Dwelling and Skill*. New York: Routledge.

Inter-American Development Bank. 2011. "Empowering Indigenous People in the Amazon to Address Climate Change." May 23. http://www.iadb.org/en/news /webstories/2011-05-23/indigenous-people-climate-change,9374.html.

Joseph, Gilbert M., and Daniel Nugent, eds. 1994a. *Everyday Forms of State Formation: Revolution and the Negotiation of Rule in Modern Mexico*. Durham: Duke University Press.

———. 1994b. "Popular Culture and State Formation in Revolutionary Mexico." In *Everyday Forms of State Formation: Revolution and the Negotiation of Rule in Modern Mexico*, edited by Gilbert M. Joseph and Daniel Nugent, 3–23. Durham: Duke University Press.

Jouanen, José, S. J. 1977. *Los Jesuitas y el Oriente Ecuatoriano: 1868–1898*. Guayaquil: Editorial Arquidiocesana.

Kauanui, J. Kēhaulani. 2008. *Hawaiian Blood: Colonialism and the Politics of Sovereignty and Indigeneity*. Durham: Duke University Press.

Knoblauch, Hans. 2001. "Informe de avance del Proyecto Gran Sumaco, marzo/1998– febrero/2001." In *Plan operativo anual: Marzo 2001–febrero 2002*, edited by Sergio Larrea, 2–12. Mayuna, Ecuador: Proyecto Gran Sumaco.

Kymlicka, Will, and Wayne Norman. 1994. "Return of the Citizen: A Survey of Recent Work on Citizenship Theory." *Ethics* 104 (2): 352–81.

Larrea, Sergio, ed. 2001. *Plan operativo anual: Marzo 2001–febrero 2002*. Mayuna, Ecuador: Proyecto Gran Sumaco.

Latour, Bruno. 1987. *Science in Action: How to Follow Scientists and Engineers through Society*. Cambridge: Harvard University Press.

Lauer, Matthew. 2006. "State-Led Democratic Politics and Emerging Forms of Indigenous Leadership among the Ye'kwana of the Upper Orinoco." *Journal of Latin American Anthropology* 11 (1): 51–86.

Lefebvre, Henri. 1991. *The Production of Space*. Translated by Donald Nicholson-Smith. Cambridge, MA: Blackwell.

Lewis, Tammy L. 2000. "Transnational Conservation Movement Organizations: Shaping the Protected Area Systems of Less Developed Countries." *Mobilization: An International Journal* 5 (1): 103–21.

Li, Tania. 2005. "Beyond 'the State' and Failed Schemes." *American Anthropologist* 107 (3): 383–94.

———. 2007. *The Will to Improve: Governmentality, Development, and the Practice of Politics*. Durham: Duke University Press.

Little, Paul E. 2001. *Amazonia: Territorial Struggles on Perennial Frontiers*. Baltimore: Johns Hopkins University Press.

López San Vicente, Lorenzo. 1894. *La misión del Napo*. Quito: Imprenta de la Universidad Central.

Lu, Flora E. 2001. "The Common Property Regime of the Huaorani Indians of Ecuador: Implications and Challenges to Conservation." *Human Ecology* 29 (4): 425–47.

Lyons, Scott Richard. 2010. *X-Marks: Native Signatures of Assent*. Minneapolis: University of Minnesota Press.

Macdonald, Theodore, Jr. 1979. "Processes of Change in Amazonian Ecuador: Quijos Quichua Indians Become Cattlemen." PhD diss., University of Illinois at Urbana-Champaign.

———. 1981. "Indigenous Responses to an Expanding Frontier: Jungle Quichua Economic Conversion to Cattle Ranching." In *Cultural Transformations and Ethnicity in Modern Ecuador*, edited by Norman E. Whitten Jr., 356–83. Urbana: University of Illinois Press.

———. 1999. *Ethnicity and Culture amidst New "Neighbors": The Runa of Ecuador's Amazon Region*. Boston: Allyn and Bacon.

———. 2010. "Amazonian Indigenous Views on the State: A Place for Corporate Social Responsibility?" *Suffolk Transnational Law Review* 33 (3). http://www.law.suffolk.edu/highlights/stuorgs/transnat/upload/Macdonald_final.pdf.

Meisch, Lynn. 2002. *Andean Entrepreneurs: Otavalo Merchants and Musicians in the Global Arena*. Austin: University of Texas Press.

Meyer, Chris. 2010. "Ecuadorian Indigenous Community Takes Conservation into Own Hands." October 29. http://blogs.edf.org/climatetalks/2010/10/29/ecuadorian-indigenous-community-takes-forest-conservation-into-own-hands/.

Miller, Peter and Nikolas Rose. 1990. "Governing Economic Life." *Economy and Society* 19 (1): 1–31.

Milton, Kay. 1996. *Environmentalism and Cultural Theory: Exploring the Role of Anthropology in Environmental Discourse*. New York: Routledge.

Ministerio del Ambiente. 2000. *Solicitud para la declaratoria de reserva de biosfera Sumaco por parte de la UNESCO*. Quito: Ministerio del Ambiente.

Moore, Donald. 2005. *Suffering for Territory: Race, Place, and Power in Zimbabwe*. Durham: Duke University Press.

Muratorio, Blanca. 1991. *The Life and Times of Grandfather Alonso: Culture and History in the Upper Amazon*. New Brunswick, NJ: Rutgers University Press.

Nadasdy, Paul. 2004. *Hunters and Bureaucrats: Power, Knowledge, and Aboriginal-State Relations in the Southwest Yukon*. Seattle: University of Washington Press.

Nash, June. 2001. *Mayan Visions: The Quest for Autonomy in an Age of Globalization*. London: Routledge.

Neumann, Roderick. 2002. *Imposing Wilderness: Struggles over Livelihood and Nature Preservation in Africa*. Berkeley: University of California Press.

Oberem, Udo. 1980. *Los Quijos: Historia de la transculturación de un grupo indígena en el Oriente Ecuatoriano*. Otavalo, Ecuador: Instituto Otavaleño de Antropología.

Offen, Karl H. 2003. "The Territorial Turn: Making Black Territories in Pacific Colombia." *Journal of Latin American Geography* 2 (1): 43–73.

Ong, Aihwa. 1996. "Cultural Citizenship as Subject-Making: Immigrants Negotiate

Racial and Cultural Boundaries in the United States." *Current Anthropology* 37 (5): 737–62.

———. 1999. *Flexible Citizenship: The Cultural Logics of Transnationality*. Durham: Duke University Press.

———. 2003. *Buddha Is Hiding: Refugees, Citizenship, the New America*. Berkeley: University of California Press.

———. 2006. *Neoliberalism as Exception: Mutations in Citizenship and Sovereignty*. Durham: Duke University Press.

Ostrom, Elinor. 1990. *Governing the Commons: The Evolution of Institutions for Collective Action*. Cambridge: Cambridge University Press.

Pallares, Amalia. 2002. *From Peasant Struggles to Indian Resistance: The Ecuadorian Andes in the Late Twentieth Century*. Norman: University of Oklahoma Press.

Peet, Richard, and Michael Watts, eds. 1996. *Liberation Ecologies: Environment, Development, Social Movements*. London: Routledge.

Peluso, Nancy Lee. 1994. *Rich Forests, Poor People: Resource Control and Resistance in Java*. Berkeley: University of California Press.

Peluso, Nancy Lee, and Cristian Lund. 2011. "New Frontiers of Land Control: Introduction." *Journal of Peasant Studies* 38 (4): 667–81.

Perreault, Thomas A. 2000. "Shifting Ground: Agrarian Change, Political Mobilization, and Identity Construction among Quichua of the Alto Napo, Ecuadorian Amazon." PhD diss., University of Colorado.

———. 2003. "'A People with Our Own Identity': Toward a Cultural Politics of Development in Ecuadorian Amazonia." *Environment and Planning D: Society and Space* 21 (5): 583–606.

Posey, Darrell A., and William L. Balée, eds. 1989. *Resource Management in Amazonia: Indigenous and Folk Strategies*. New York: New York Botanical Garden.

Postero, Nancy. 2007. *Now We Are Citizens: Indigenous Politics in Postmulticultural Bolivia*. Stanford: Stanford University Press.

Postero, Nancy Grey, and Leon Zamosc. 2004. "Indigenous Movements and the Indian Question in Latin America." In *The Struggle for Indigenous Rights in Latin America*, edited by Nancy Grey Postero and Leon Zamosc, 1–31. Brighton, UK: Sussex Academic.

Povinelli, Elizabeth A. 2002. *The Cunning of Recognition: Indigenous Alterities and the Making of Australian Multiculturalism*. Durham: Duke University Press.

———. 2006. *The Empire of Love: Toward a Theory of Intimacy, Genealogy, and Carnality*. Durham: Duke University Press.

———. 2011. *Economies of Abandonment: Social Belonging and Endurance in Late Liberalism*. Durham: Duke University Press.

Raffles, Hugh. 1999. "'Local Theory': Nature and the Making of an Amazonian Place." *Cultural Anthropology* 14 (3): 323–60.

———. 2002. *In Amazonia: A Natural History*. Princeton: Princeton University Press.

Rappaport, Joanne. 2005a. "Geography and Historical Understanding among the Nasa." In *The Land Within: Indigenous Territory and the Perception of Environment*, edited by Alexandre Surrallés and Pedro García-Hierro, 158–69. Copenhagen: International Work Group on Indigenous Affairs.

———. 2005b. *Intercultural Utopias: Public Intellectuals, Cultural Experimentation, and Ethnic Pluralism in Colombia*. Durham: Duke University Press.

Redford, Kent. 1990. "The Ecologically Noble Savage." *Orion Nature Quarterly* 9 (3): 26–29.

Reeve, Mary-Elizabeth. 1985. "Identity as Process: The Meaning of Runapura for Quichua Speakers of the Curaray River, Eastern Ecuador." PhD diss., University of Illinois at Urbana-Champaign.

Rogers, Mark. 1995. "Images of Power and the Power of Images: Identity and Place in Ecuadorian Shamanism." PhD diss., University of Chicago.

———. 1996. "Beyond Authenticity: Conservation, Tourism, and the Politics of Representation in the Ecuadorian Amazon." *Identities* 3 (1–2): 73–125.

———. 1999. "Spectacular Bodies: Folklorization and the Politics of Identity in Ecuadorian Beauty Pageants." *Journal of Latin American Anthropology* 3 (2): 54–85.

Rosaldo, Renato. 1994. "Cultural Citizenship in San Jose, California." *PoLAR* 17 (2): 57–63.

Rose, Carol. 1994. *Property and Persuasion: Essays on the History, Theory, and Rhetoric of Ownership*. Boulder, CO: Westview.

Rose, Nikolas. 1996. "Governing 'Advanced' Liberal Democracies." In *Foucault and Political Reason: Liberalism, Neo-Liberalism and Rationalities of Government*, edited by Andrew Barry, Thomas Osborne, and Nikolas Rose, 37–64. Chicago: University of Chicago Press.

———. 1999. *Powers of Freedom: Reframing Political Thought*. New York: Cambridge University Press.

Rose, Nikolas, and Peter Miller. 2008. *Governing the Present: Administering Economic, Social and Personal Life*. Malden, MA: Polity.

Rubenstein, Steven. 2002. *Alejandro Tsakimp: A Shuar Healer in the Margins of History*. Lincoln: University of Nebraska Press.

———. 2007. "Circulation, Accumulation, and the Power of Shuar Shrunken Heads." *Cultural Anthropology* 22 (3): 357–99.

Saavedra, Luis Ángel. 2011. "Consultation or prior consent?" *Latinamerica Press*, June 17. http://lapress.org/articles.asp?art=6402.

Salazar, Ernesto. 1989. *Pioneros de la selva*. Quito: Museos del Banco Central.

Salomon, Frank. 1983. "Shamanism and Politics in Late-Colonial Ecuador." *American Ethnologist* 10 (3): 413–28.

Santos Granero, Fernando. 2000. "The Sisyphus Síndrome, or the Struggle for Conviviality in Native Amazonia." In *The Anthropology of Love and Anger*, edited by Joanna Overing and Alan Passes, 268–87. London: Routledge.

———. 2005. "Writing History into the Landscape: Yanesha Notions of Space and

Territoriality." In *The Land Within: Indigenous Territory and the Perception of Environment*, edited by Alexandre Surrallés and Pedro García-Hierro, 170–98. Copenhagen: International Work Group on Indigenous Affairs.

Sawyer, Suzana. 2004. *Crude Chronicles: Indigenous Politics, Multinational Oil, and Neoliberalism in Ecuador*. Durham: Duke University Press.

Schama, Simon. 1995. *Landscape and Memory*. New York: Vintage.

Scott, James C. 1998. *Seeing Like a State: How Certain Schemes to Improve the Human Condition Have Failed*. New Haven: Yale University Press.

Sheahan, John. 1987. *Patterns of Development in Latin America: Poverty, Repression, and Economic Strategy*. Princeton: Princeton University Press.

Simpson, Audra. 2000. "Paths toward a Mohawk Nation: Narratives of Citizenship and Nationhood in Kahnawake." In *Political Theory and the Rights of Indigenous Peoples*, edited by Duncan Ivison, Paul Patton, and Will Sanders, 113–36. New York: Cambridge University Press.

Smith, Richard Chase. 2005. "Can David and Goliath Have a Happy Marriage? The Machiguenga People and the Camisea Gas Project in the Peruvian Amazon." In *Communities and Conservation: Histories and Politics of Community-Based Natural Resource Management*, edited by J. Peter Brosius, Anna Lowenhaupt Tsing, and Charles Zerner, 231–56. Lanham, MD: Altamira.

Stahler-Sholk, Richard. 2005. "Time of the Snails: Autonomy and Resistance in Chiapas." *NACLA Report on the Americas* 38 (5): 34–38.

———. 2010. "The Zapatista Social Movement: Innovation and Sustainability." *Alternatives* 35 (3): 269–90.

Starn, Orin. 1999. *Nightwatch: The Politics of Protest in the Andes*. Durham: Duke University Press.

Taylor, Anne Christine. 1994. "El Oriente ecuatoriano en el siglo XIX: 'El otro litoral.'" In *Historia y región en el Ecuador: 1830–1930*, edited by Juan Maiguashca, 17–67. Quito: Corporación Editora Nacional/FLACSO-Sede Ecuador/CERLAC.

Tengan, Ty P. Kāwika. 2008. *Native Men Remade: Gender and Nation in Contemporary Hawai'i*. Durham: Duke University Press.

Teuton, Sean. 2008. "The Callout: Writing American Indian Politics." In *Reasoning Together: The Native Critics Collective*, edited by Craig S. Womack, Daniel Heath Justice, and Christopher B. Teuton, 105–25. Norman: University of Oklahoma Press.

UN-REDD Programme. 2009. "About REDD+." http://www.un-redd.org/About REDD/tabid/582/Default.aspx.

Uquillas, Jorge. 1984. "Colonization and Spontaneous Settlement in the Ecuadoran Amazon." In *Frontier Expansion in Amazonia*, edited by Marianne Schmink and Charles H. Wood, 261–84. Gainesville: University of Florida Press.

Uzendoski, Michael. 2004. "The Horizontal Archipelago: The Quijos/Upper Napo Regional System." *Ethnohistory* 51 (2): 317–57.

———. 2005. *The Napo Runa of Amazonian Ecuador*. Urbana: University of Illinois Press.

————. 2010. "Fractal Subjectivities: An Amazonian-Inspired Critique of Globalization Theory." In *Editing Eden: A Reconsideration of Identity, Politics, and Place in Amazonia*, edited by Frank Hutchins and Patrick C. Wilson, 38–69. Lincoln: University of Nebraska Press.

Valdivieso Vega, Cecilia. 2004. "Questionnaire to Governments on Implementation of the Beijing Platform for Action (1995) and the Outcome of the Twenty-Third Special Session of the General Assembly (2000)." Quito: National Council for Women. http://www.un.org/womenwatch/daw/Review/responses/ECUADOR -English.pdf.

Van Cott, Donna Lee. 2001. "Explaining Ethnic Autonomy Regimes in Latin America." *Studies in Comparative International Development* 35 (4): 30–58.

Van der Werf, Guido, et al. 2009. "CO_2 Emissions from Forest Loss." *Nature Geoscience* 2 (11): 737–38.

Varea, Anamaria, et al. 1997. "Ecologismo ecuatorial." Quito: Centro de Educación Popular/Abya-Yala.

Veber, Hanne. 2007. "Memories, Identity, and Indigenous/National Subjectivity in Eastern Peru." *Diálogos Latinoamericanos* 12 (1): 80–102.

Verdery, Katherine. 1994. "The Elasticity of Land: Problems of Property Restitution in Transylvania." *Slavic Review* 53 (4): 1071–109.

————. 2003. *The Vanishing Hectare: Property and Value in Postsocialist Transylvania.* Ithaca: Cornell University Press.

————. 2004. "The Obligations of Ownership: Restoring Rights to Land in Postsocialist Transylvania." In *Property in Question: Value Transformation in the Global Economy*, edited by Caroline Humphrey and Katherine Verdery, 139–59. New York: Berg.

Viatori, Maximilian. 2007. "Zápara Leaders and Identity Construction in Ecuador: The Complexities of Indigenous Self-Representation." *Journal of Latin American and Caribbean Anthropology* 12 (1): 104–33.

Vickers, William. 1989. "Traditional Concepts of Power among the Siona-Secoya and the Advent of the Nation-State." *Latin American Anthropology Review* 1 (2): 55–60.

Wade, Robert. 1988 [1994]. *Village Republics: Economic Conditions for Collective Action in South India.* Oakland, CA: ICS.

Warren, Kay B. 1998. *Indigenous Movements and Their Critics: Pan-Maya Activism in Guatemala.* Princeton: Princeton University Press.

Warren, Kay B., and Jean E. Jackson. 2002. "Introduction: Studying Indigenous Activism in Latin America." In *Indigenous Movements, Self-Representation, and the State in Latin America*, edited by Kay B. Warren and Jean E. Jackson, 1–46. Austin: University of Texas Press.

West, Paige. 2006. *Conservation Is Our Government Now: The Politics of Ecology in Papua New Guinea.* Durham: Duke University Press.

White, Ben, et al. 2012. "The New Enclosures: Critical Perspectives on Corporate Land Deals." *Journal of Peasant Studies* 39 (3–4): 619–47.

Whitehead, Neil, and Robin Wright. 2004. Introduction to *In Darkness and Secrecy:*

The Anthropology of Assault Sorcery and Witchcraft in Amazonia, edited by Neil Whitehead and Robin Wright, 1–20. Durham: Duke University Press.

Whitten, Norman E., Jr. 1976. *Sacha Runa: Ethnicity and Adaptation of Ecuadorian Jungle Quichua*. Urbana: University of Illinois Press.

————. 1985. *Sicuanga Runa: The Other Side of Development in Amazonian Ecuador*. Urbana: University of Illinois Press.

Whitten, Norman E., Jr., and Dorothea Scott Whitten. 2008. *Puyo Runa: Imagery and Power in Modern Amazonia*. Urbana: University of Illinois Press.

Wilson, Patrick. 2010. "Indigenous Leadership and the Shifting Politics of Development in Ecuador's Amazon." In *Editing Eden: A Reconsideration of Identity, Politics, and Place in Amazonia*, edited by Frank Hutchins and Patrick C. Wilson, 218–45. Lincoln: University of Nebraska Press.

Winichakul, Thongchai. 1997. *Siam Mapped: A History of the Geo-Body of a Nation*. Honolulu: University of Hawai'i Press.

Wray, Natalia. 1996. "Economía indígena e integración al mercado: El caso de los Quichua del Alto Napo Ecuador." In *Amazonía: economía indígena y mercado*, edited by Richard Chase Smith and Natalia Wray, 61–82. Quito: COICA and Oxfam America.

Wright, Robin. 2004. "The Wicked and the Wise Men: Witches and Prophets in the History of the Northwest Amazon." In *In Darkness and Secrecy: The Anthropology of Assault Sorcery and Witchcraft in Amazonia*, edited by Neil Whitehead and Robin Wright, 82–108. Durham: Duke University Press.

Yashar, Deborah. 1998. "Contesting Citizenship: Indigenous Movements and Democracy in Latin America." *Comparative Politics* 31 (1): 23–42.

Young, Iris Marion. 1995. "Polity and Group Difference: A Critique of the Ideal of Universal Citizenship." In *Theorizing Citizenship*, edited by Ronald Beiner, 175–208. Albany: State University of New York Press.

Zamosc, Leon. 1994. "Agrarian Protest and the Indian Movement in the Ecuadorian Highlands." *Latin American Research Review* 29 (3): 37–68.

Zibechi, Raúl. 2004. "The Impact of Zapatismo in Latin America." *Antipode* 36 (2): 392–99.

Page numbers in italics refer to illustrations and maps; those followed by "n" indicate endnotes.

CONAKINO (Confederación de la Nacionalidad Kichwa de Napo y Orellana), 186

Confederación de la Nacionalidad Kichwa de Napo y Orellana (CONAKINO), 186

Confederación de Nacionalidades Indígenas de la Amazonía Ecuatoriana. *See* CONFENIAE

Confederación de Nacionalidades Indígenas del Ecuador (CONAIE), 149–50, 196

CONFENIAE (Confederación de Nacionalidades Indígenas de la Amazonía Ecuatoriana): biannual congresses, 142–44; diverse causes and, 196; formation of, 142; IMU dispute and, 149–50; REDD program and COICA vs., 164–65, 167; statement by (August 2009), 201–2

conflict management: indigenous sovereignty and, 4; organizational legitimization and, 175; property regimes and, 123, 125–27; Seminoles and, 15; sorcery accusations, territorial citizenship, and, 177–83

Conklin, Beth, 154, 168, 206n5

conservation and environmentalists: biological and cultural diversity and, 153–55; earthquake and road-building plan, attention from, 144–46; expectations and assumptions from, 18, 135; Food Security Project and, 135–38; Great Sumaco Project and biosphere reserve status, 155–58, *156*, 189, 211n4; human-natural-spiritual relationships, beliefs about, 134; impacts on indigenous views, scholarship on, 138–40; IMU plan as wake-up call, 147–51; indigenous sustainability professionals, creation of, 140; leadership and, 138, 146–47, 152–53, 168–69; logging concerns, 146–47; Mushullakta ecotourism plan, 151–52, 160; property regimes and, 127–29; Purutuyaku wildlife reproduction project, 160; REDD/REDD+ carbon trading program, 162, 164–67, 201–2; regional indigenous organizations and, 141–44; Rukullakta land management plan, 158–60; Socio Bosque Program, 128, 160–62, *163*, 168–69, 197–98; Western vs. Kichwa thinking and, 133–35, 144, 161; wilderness protection, 133–34, 160, 161

conservative perspective on property, 100, 108–13

consultation, community, 189–93

Convention on Indigenous and Tribal Peoples (ILO 169), 4, 201, 203

Cooperative, San Pedro of Rukullakta: accounting and work records, 68, 69, 209n6; change to Pueblo Kichwa de Rukullakta, xxi–xxii, 186–89; civic association takeover attempt, defense against, 171–74; debt meeting, 89–90; decline in collective work and meeting attendance, 64, 81–82; delineation project, 67; development projects, leaders associated with, 64–66; enforcement, issue of, 86; financial difficulties, 83–87; first president, question of, 22–23; health and education policies, 76–80; Inter-American Foundation funding, 88–89; legacies of 1970s age of collectivism, 67, 93–94; May 1st Pre-Association, accusations of deceit from, 116–18; *mingas* (collective work days) and work system, 66, 67–70; as model, xxv, 77–78, 138; outsider presence, complaints about, 76; political structure and, 65–66; semidirected project, 72–74, 76, 82–83, 91; size of, 74, 84–85; spending decisions and expenses, 75–76, 86–87; state withdrawal of support, 82–83, 89; subcenter organizations, shift toward, 90–94; Venezuelan consolidation of state power compared to, 65, 81; written history, desire for, xxiii–xxiv. *See also* subcenters; territory formation, everyday

cooperative leadership. *See* leaders

cooperative organizing: community building for, 44–49; community center proposal and subcenters compromise, 51–54, *54*, *55*; early efforts, 39–44; land holding issues and grand vision for empower-

IERAC (Instituto Ecuatoriano de Reforma Agraria y Colonización): Alvarado's visit to, 40; civic association takeover attempt and, 171; community property plans and, 54; complaints about presence of officials from, 76; IMU dispute and, 150; Josephine Mission land expansion attempt and, 48; May 1st Pre-Association and, 116–18; replaced by INCRAE, 82–83; topographers from, 110
illiteracy, 45–46, 208n10
ILO 169 (International Labour Organization Convention on Indigenous and Tribal Peoples), 4, 201, 203
imagined community, 45, 47
Imbate, 61
IMU (Fundación Izu Mangallpa Urcu), 147–51, 211n2
INCRAE (Instituto Nacional de Colonización de la Región Amazónica Ecuatoriana), 82–83, 171–72
India, community-based forest councils in, 139, 167
inequality as obstacle to community, 47–48
informed consent, 189–93
INREDH (Fundación Regional de Asesoría en Derechos Humanos), 192–93
Instituto Ecuatoriano de Reforma Agraria y Colonización. *SEE IERAC*
Instituto Ecuatoriano Forestal y de Areas Naturales y Vida Silvestre, 155, 212n4
Instituto Nacional de Colonización, 38
Instituto Nacional de Colonización de la Región Amazónica Ecuatoriana (INCRAE), 82–83, 171–72
Inter-American Development Bank, 165, 167
Inter-American Foundation, 88–89
intereses personales, 189
International Indigenous Peoples Forum on Climate Change, 164, 165
International Labour Organization Convention on Indigenous and Tribal Peoples (ILO 169), 4, 201, 203
International Solidarity Institute, 42–43
"intimate" government, 2, 206n1

Istandi subcenter/community, 70, *71*
Ita Kipilina subcenter/community, *115, 163,* 172–73
Ivanhoe Energy Ecuador, 18–19, 188, 189–93, 197–98, 203

jails, 86
Jatun Sacha research station, 148
jealousy, 94, 179
Joseph, Gilbert, 177
Josephine missionaries: arrival of, 35; CEDOC and, 41, 43; changes around Archidona due to, 37–38; FOIN vs. FOCIN and, 116; intermittent engagement with, 35–36; land expansion attempt, 48; market economy and, 37; schools of, 53–54, 208n10, 209n5, 210n3
Juan Shiguango Medical Dispensary, 47, 77
Jumandy, 32, 61–63, *62*, 96, 173

kinship groups: community building beyond, 45; *compadrazgo* (ritual kinship), 58, 65; extension of vision beyond, 28, 57–58; *muntún* (patrilineal group), 58; mutual obligation ties in, 50; patrilineal property control, 36; property regimes and, 98, 111–13; smaller organizations based on, 28–29; territorial government vs., 17–18
Kluane, 139
knowledge: environment-specific, 15, 136; *samay* (spiritual knowledge or power), 179
Kreditanstalt für Wiederaufrau (German Reconstruction Bank), 211n4

land claims. *See* property regimes
land management plan, Rukullakta, 158–60
land purchases: of indigenous lands by others, 40, 41, 47, 48, 209n5; by Rukullakta, 84–85, 91, 97
land reform: Agrarian Reform and Colonization Law (1964), 27, 38–39; cooperative formation as, 49; history of, 38–39
landscape, property regimes inscribed on. *See* property regimes

lished at, 208n10, 209n5; shamanism dispute, 181–82; wildlife reproduction conservation project, 160

Raffles, Hugh, 16
Reategui, Juan, 167
REDD/REDD+ (Reducing Emissions from Forest Destruction and Degradation), 162, 164–67, 201–2
reducciones, 32
Reducing Emissions from Forest Destruction and Degradation (REDD/REDD+), 162, 164–67, 201–2
relationship networks. *See* kinship groups
resources, autonomy without, xix–xx, 63, 162
revolts against Spanish, 32, 61
rights: increasing international attention to rights of indigenous people, 4; indigenous rights organizations, 5; obligations and responsibilities vs., 9–13. See also *specific rights organizations*
Rodríguez-Lara, Guillermo, 72
Rogers, Mark, 147–48, 179–80, 205–7
Rose, Nikolas, 206n3, 212n2
rubber trade, 34–35
Rukullakta and Upper Napo region: description of, xxi; General Rodríguez-Lara visit to, 72; history, early 20th century, 35–38; history, pre-20th century, 30–35. See also *specific topics, such as* leadership
Rukullakta Cooperative. *See* Cooperative, San Pedro of Rukullakta
Rukullakta subcenter/community, 55, 73, 126

Salomon, Frank, 183
samay (spiritual knowledge or power), 179
San Pedro of Rukullakta Cooperative. *See* Cooperative, San Pedro of Rukullakta
schools and education: cooperative policies and construction projects, 79–80; dates of schools established, 209n5; Josephine missionaries and, 53–54, 208n10, 209n5, 210n3; secondary, 119
Scott, James, 52, 168, 210n4

secret ballots, 192–93
seguro campesino (peasants' health insurance program), 76–78, 86–87
semidirected project, 72–74, 76, 82–83, 91
Seminoles of Florida, 15
shamans: Council of Amautas, 187; forest conservation and, 160; Jumandy's rebellion (1578) and, 32, 61; land claims by, 47–48, 105; land disputes and, 98; motivations for hiring, 179; sorcery accusations and conflict resolution and, 179–83; *yachaj* vs. *samay*, 179
Shiguango, Fausto, 161, 188
Shiguango, Francisco, 111–12
Shiguango, Jaime, 140, 211n1
Shiguango, José, xvii–xviii, 10–11, 187
Shiguango, José Francisco "Bartolo," 68, 76, 77
Shiguango, Juan: community building and, 49; early efforts to organize, 43; first Cooperative president, question of, 22–23; land offered for community center, 51–52; *seguro campesino* chapter and, 77; vision for cooperative, 41
Shiguango, Maria Inés, 67
Shiguango, Medardo, 26
Shiguango, Sisawa, *185*
Shuar, xix, 84
Shuar Federation, 41, 142, 207n7
Shushufindi, 73
siempre colaboran, 189
Sierra, Rodrigo, 85, 101, 158
Simpson, Audra, 3
sinchi yachaj (wise or powerful person), 136
slave trade, 34–35
Socio Bosque Program, 128, 160–62, *163*, 168–69, 197–98
soils, 157
Sólo unidos venceremos! slogan, xviii, 126
sorcery, 78, 79, 94, 177–83, 187
sovereignty, indigenous, xix–xxvi, 2–4, 10, 14, 17, 135, 199. *See also* citizenship, territorial
Soviet bloc, former, 17–18, 99, 117
Spanish colonial history, 30–33, 61, 111–12
Special Law for the Oriente (1894), 35